Studies in Celtic History VII

FROM KINGS TO WARLORDS

STUDIES IN CELTIC HISTORY

ISSN 0261–9865

General editors
Dauvit Broun
Máire Ní Mhaonaigh
Huw Pryce

'Studies in Celtic History' aims to provide a forum for new research into all aspects of the history of Celtic-speaking peoples throughout the whole of the medieval period. The term 'history' is understood broadly: any study, regardless of discipline, which advances our knowledge and understanding of the history of Celtic-speaking peoples will be considered. Studies of primary sources, and of new methods of exploiting such sources, are encouraged.

Founded by Professor David Dumville in 1979, the series is now relaunched under new editorship. Proposals or queries may be sent directly to the editors at the addresses given below; all submissions will receive prompt and informed consideration before being sent to expert readers.

Dr Dauvit Broun, Department of History (Scottish), University of Glasgow, 9 University Gardens, Glasgow G12 8QH

Dr Máire Ní Mhaonaigh, St John's College, Cambridge CB2 1TP

Dr Huw Pryce, School of History and Welsh History, University of Wales, Bangor, Bangor, Gwynedd LL57 2DG

For titles already published in this series
see the end of this volume

FROM KINGS TO WARLORDS

The Changing Political Structure of Gaelic Ireland in the Later Middle Ages

KATHARINE SIMMS

THE BOYDELL PRESS

First published 1987
The Boydell Press, Woodbridge
Reprinted in paperback 2000

Transferred to digital printing

ISBN 978-0-85115-784-9

The Boydell Press is an imprint of Boydell & Brewer Ltd
PO Box 9, Woodbridge, Suffolk IP12 3DF, UK
and of Boydell & Brewer Inc.
668 Mt Hope Avenue, Rochester, NY 14620, USA
website: www.boydellandbrewer.com

A CiP catalogue record for this book is available
from the British Library

This publication is printed on acid-free paper

CONTENTS

GENERAL EDITOR'S FOREWORD

THE seventh volume of *Studies in Celtic History* returns us to mediaeval Ireland, but this time to the closing centuries of the Irish middle ages. Gaelic Ireland in the thirteenth to fifteenth centuries in particular was for long a neglected field of scholarly historical endeavour. But in the 1960s, and especially the 1970s, young historians with a good knowledge of the Irish language began to be attracted to the subject. Dr Katharine Simms, the writer of this book, is a distinguished representative of that small group: she is already known for a series of important papers dealing with a wide range of issues concerning the history and literature of later mediaeval Ireland. In the present volume she investigates the changing perceptions of Irish kingship in the late middle ages: from succession and inauguration to deposition and death, all aspects of the Irish king's public life are here studied in some detail – politics, ritual, diplomacy, overlordship, administration, taxation, and military activity each receives its share of profitable attention. For the first time, the history of mediaeval Irish kingship now has chronological depth: we can see changes in nomenclature, in institutions, and in political context. She has drawn imaginatively and extensively upon the native vernacular literature, especially the classical bardic poetry, with exciting results. One can only hope that this will be but the first of many such works from Dr Simms's hand.

David Dumville
Girton College, Cambridge

PREFACE

The hardback version of this book was originally completed in 1983, though not actually published till 1987. It began as an expanded and rewritten version of the introductory section to my Ph.D. thesis (Trinity College Dublin, 1976) on 'Gaelic lordships in Ulster in the later middle ages'. I had realised through trial and error that a political narrative on its own would be almost meaningless unless the structure and organisation of Gaelic society, its customs and presuppositions, were fully understood. A real problem is posed for the conventionally-trained mediaevalist who grapples for the first time with a western European culture operating outside feudal custom. Consequently the opening chapters of my thesis discussed Gaelic lordship as an institution, and its development from pre-Norman kingship, using evidence from every part of Ireland, though admittedly with a preponderance of material from Ulster and the north of Ireland generally, while the period surveyed ranged from the end of the early Christian period to the late sixteenth century.

Besides the more familiar sources – annals, genealogies, Anglo-Norman and ecclesiastical administrative documents, and sixteenth- and seventeenth-century state papers and memoirs – my research led me into the realms of bardic poetry, one of the most under-used sources for the history of later mediaeval and early modern Ireland. Not only did the poems provide many insights into the conceptual framework shaping the thoughts and aspirations of poet and patron, but once I had become familiar with the underlying concepts, the poetry itself became more understandable, because the technical terms which the bards use, such as *eineach, comairce, oireacht, tighearnus*, or *aos grádha* (on all of which see the Glossarial Index at the back of this volume) need more than a brief dictionary definition to make sense to the modern reader, and I found myself devoting the better part of a chapter to each.

In the interests of economy, this paperback edition is a straight-forward reprint of the 1987 hardback volume, and in many ways, little has changed in the meantime. I still believe in the interpretations it contains, and while many articles on particular aspects of Gaelic Ireland in the later middle ages have appeared since its publication, there have been no further books. Bardic poetry has received more attention as a historical source since those days, especially from early modern historians; I have written a short survey of their debate on the topic in *Progress in Medieval Irish Studies*, edited by K. McCone and K. Simms (Maynooth 1996). I have since published much of the substance of the political narrative chapters from my thesis in the Geography Publications' History and Society volumes for Donegal, Derry/Londonderry, and forthcoming ones on Tyrone and Armagh. An expansion of the views I expressed in Chapter VIII below will be found in my contribution to *A Military History of Ireland*, edited by T. Bartlett and K. Jeffery (Cambridge 1996). I look forward to a considerable deepening of our knowledge of the matters discussed in Chapters III and IV with the imminent publication of two monographs arising from theses I had the pleasure of supervising, one on inauguration sites and ceremonies by Dr Elizabeth Fitzpatrick and the other on kingship in early Ireland and the traditional rules governing regnal succession by Dr Bart Jaski.

The debts of gratitude I mentioned in the preface to the 1987 edition, to Kenneth Nicholls of University College Cork, and Gearóid MacNiocaill, of National University of Ireland, Galway, to my thesis supervisor, James Lydon and to my husband, Kim McCone, still stand.

Katharine Simms,
Department of Medieval History,
Trinity College,
Dublin
November 1999

I

THE HISTORICAL SOURCES

A prime cause for the neglect of the mediaeval chieftains hitherto shown by Irish historians is the intractability of the sources for this subject. Quite simply, the native Irish chiefs did not keep administrative records of the chancery and exchequer type, and although they acquired copies of charters and indentures from time to time, concerning grants of land, and treaties with the English, little care seems to have been taken to preserve them. For instance, in 1449 Muircheartach Ruadh Ó Néill Buidhe promised the Duke of York 'for to be my loordis trwe man ... and to bere my lord accordyng to the endentures there of made by my lordis progenitours and his aunceters of old tyme yf they may be founde and yf they mey no*gh*t be founde, thenne to appointe of the newe with my lorde'.[1] This cavalier attitude to the written word arose for two reasons. Legitimate ownership and legitimate authority in this society was not traced to a recorded contract, but was founded on physical force and to a lesser extent on immemorial tradition, a view repeatedly expressed in bardic poetry:

> Thou shalt seek no other charter except thy own reliance on thy gallantry; to charge against the sharp spears that pierce thee is thy true charter to thy land.[2]

> A good charter on the land of his forefathers is the evil he suffered from childhood's years, shedding his blood on its behalf, till he displayed the fame of his exploits.[3]

> Thy nobility is thy charter; Art's Isle was held by thy ten forebears.[4]

In the rest of Europe mediaeval kings recruited their civil servants from the ranks of the clergy, who wrote in Latin and inherited many administrative practices from the Roman empire. Ireland too was supplied with clerical latinists, but it supported in addition a secular learned class whose education laid heavy emphasis on oral tradition, who wrote in Irish only, and whose profession had experienced little or no influence from imperial Rome. In their eyes a recorded contract was less valid than a myth or a

[1] *Registrum Iohannis Mey*, edd. Quigley & Roberts, p. 156.
[2] *Aithdioghluim Dána*, ed. McKenna, II.73.
[3] *The Bardic Poems of Tadhg Dall Ó hUiginn*, ed. Knott, II.158.
[4] *Aithdioghluim Dána*, ed. McKenna, II.58.

genealogy, and a recent historical claim was often restated in mythical or genealogical terms. A series of treaties concluded during the fifteenth and early sixteenth centuries dealt with the claims of Ó Néill and Ó Domhnaill to the allegiance of lesser chiefs on their common frontier, and their relationship to each other,[5] and in 1543 when Conn Bacach Ó Néill, earl of Tyrone, and Maghnus Ó Domhnaill, lord of Tír Conaill, brought their disputes to be adjudicated by Sir Anthony St Leger, Ó Domhnaill did come armed with written documents in which former O'Neills had renounced their ownership of the peninsula of Inis Eoghain, but for the rest St Leger complained that 'Both the Earl and O'Donnell have produced no other titles or legal proof than certain old parchments or bills, confirmed by no seal, signature or other testimony but such as are composed by vain poets ... blinded by affection for their lords'.[6]

Texts of the kind to which Sir Anthony referred are the prose and verse statements of the 'rights' of kings. A few of these can be dated on linguistic grounds to the Old Irish period, but the earliest comprehensive collection is contained in the late eleventh-century Book of Rights.[7] From that period onwards, separate statements of rights for the kings of individual territories continued to be handed down from generation to generation. Subsequent recensions were modified to allow for historical developments which had since taken place, but the fiction of immemorial and immutable tradition was preserved. Many of these tracts are now available only in early eighteenth-century manuscripts, late recensions further complicated by corrupt transmission and misguided antiquarianism.[8] They are difficult texts to handle, but it would be a serious mistake to dismiss them unread. In the first place they were widely accepted by partisans in their own day as an ideological statement, a platonic ideal to which the rights and territorial authority of the existing king corresponded but imperfectly. 'The Quartering Rights of the Uí Dhomhnaill' was a prose tract, extant in the sixteenth century, which claimed that Ó Domhnaill was entitled to billet his mercenary soldiers on every chief in Ulster except the household of the Great Ó Néill. However, *Ceart Uí Néill*, another prose tract, claimed that it was Ó Néill who had billeting-rights over all the Ulster chiefs including Ó Domhnaill.[9] Both versions had some historical justification in terms of the eleventh and twelfth centuries; neither had contemporary validity, but the existence of such claims had relevance to the continuing state of hostility between Ó Néill and Ó Domhnaill in the sixteenth century. From another point of view, if the tracts themselves are subjected to detailed analysis, it becomes possible to distinguish petrified fragments of earlier information

[5] AU 1442, 1452, 1456, 1488, 1514; AConn 1512.7, 1514.13, 1542.14 and 19.
[6] Mathews, *The O'Neills of Ulster*, III.60; *State Papers, Henry VIII, Ireland 1538–46*, p. 478(–9).
[7] *Lebor na Cert*, ed. Dillon; see Byrne, *Irish Kings*, pp. 174, 315.
[8] Some examples are discussed in my article ' "Gabh umad a Fheidhlimidh" '.
[9] 'Quartering Rights', ed. O'Keeffe; 'Ceart Uí Néill', ed. Dillon.

from the later additions and modifications. In *Ceart Uí Néill* the section on Ó Domhnaill by its allusions to the extinct families of Ó Maolghaoithe and Ó Taircheirt and by its omission of all reference to the Clann Suibhne shows that it could not have been compiled later than the twelfth or thirteenth century, while that on the Uí Raighilligh can be placed firmly in the sixteenth century on the basis of the coin-names which it contains.[10] A single text can thus provide clues to the course of political change over a number of centuries.

However, the staple diet for a historian dealing with the Irish chieftains must be the annalistic compilations. They have the great attraction of being edited with parallel English translations and with indices of personal and place-names. For the most part the manuscripts date from the fifteenth, sixteenth, and seventeenth centuries and, for entries dealing with the post-Norman period, the question of their sources and process of transmission is simple enough. They have abbreviated and sometimes reworded entries from earlier books of annals compiled during the twelfth and thirteenth centuries in a monastic environment and from the fourteenth century onwards in the secular schools of hereditary bardic historians.[11] Some non-contemporary literary material has been inserted, as for instance in the Annals of the Four Masters under the years 1213 and 1258; and the selection and omission of entries displayed by different compilations can reflect a political bias – in favour of the Ó Domhnaill family in the Annals of the Four Masters, in favour of the Uí Néill in the Annals of Ulster. Another obvious problem concerns the geographical coverage provided by the books of annals. Each has a regional interest; there are no native Irish compilations dealing with Leinster, and none centred on Munster after the year 1320.

Nevertheless, these are relatively minor drawbacks. Paradoxically, the real danger of the annalistic compilations lies in the fact that they seem so easy to use. A single item of information – a battle, the death of a famous man, the burning of an abbey – can be retrieved simply by looking up the date, the name of the place, or the surname of the chief participants. Moreover, the annalists themselves present their information as the record of a series of isolated incidents, giving neither causes, results, nor moral judgments, and failing to weave the events of successive years into a single narrative. This leads local historians into the trap of, for instance, looking up the name of an abbey in the indices, and listing the entries which they find as all the information available in annalistic texts about that foundation. The result is a sterile series of abbots' obits, punctuated by an occasional burning.[12] Yet a deeper reading of the same annals would reveal how many of the abbots named belonged to the local ruling dynasties and how many had connexions with the hereditary learned families, whether the burning of the abbey could be related to a local

[10] Dolley & Mac Niocaill, 'Some coin-names'.

[11] Mac Niocaill, *The Medieval Irish Annals*; O'Dwyer, 'The Annals of Connacht and Loch Cé'.

[12] For example, Frost, *The History*, pp. 125–6.

feud, and so forth. The brief and unconnected statements of such annals provide only the raw materials from which the modern reader must deduce for himself a continuous narrative by combining each entry with evidence from external sources where possible, but above all by comparing each statement with other annalistic entries and records of what happened in the same place before and after the event in question or of what happened at the same time in other places, and thus gradually building up a context for events, a chain of cause and effect.

The absence of a narrative context and the almost complete silence of the annalists on the subject of the motives and long-term objectives of the principal characters mean that outsiders, dipping into these annalistic texts for the first time, bear away an impression of confusion and mindless violence.[13] It would be idle to deny that the Irish chiefs in the later middle ages lived in a society where cattle-raiding had the same honourable status accorded to duelling in the eighteenth century, but their forays were far from motiveless. For the purpose of elucidating the chieftains' aspirations, their self-image, and the degree to which their political and religious preconceptions were influenced by developments in the outside world, the surviving corpus of bardic poetry is an important source. Unlike the constantly revised tracts on royal rights and the excerpted annalistic compilations, bardic poems are strictly contemporary with the chieftains whom they eulogise and are directly addressed to them. Because of their demanding metrical structure, and because they were normally of financial value only to the patron addressed, they constitute a class of document relatively free from forgery. Yet, of all the possible historical sources, bardic poetry has been the one hitherto most scrupulously avoided by historians.[14]

The difficulties involved in making full use of these poems are both practical and conceptual. On the practical side, the total number of such compositions now extant has not yet been ascertained and there is no comprehensive guide indicating where the scattered manuscripts containing them may be found. As a result of preliminary work on such a survey, I have concluded that the surviving corpus of poems is somewhat in excess of two thousand and that of this number about 41.5% have been published with an English translation, and a further 23% have been edited without translation. A higher survival-rate for poems from the end of the bardic period has meant that only half the total, let us say a thousand poems, can be dated to a period earlier than 1566. Nevertheless, these figures imply that a substantial body of some four hundred poems is already available in English translation for the use of mediaeval historians, though often tucked away as single items in journals devoted to Celtic studies, local history, or ecclesiastical interests.

The language used in these compositions is Classical, or Early Modern, Irish, a linguistic period for which no comprehensive modern grammar

[13] For example, Thornley, *England under the Yorkists*, p. 259.

[14] The potential value of bardic poetry as a historical source is touched on by Watt, *The Church in Medieval Ireland*, pp. 212–14.

has yet been produced although it originated as an artificial literary standard governed by rigid rules with even its vocabulary being carefully controlled. Apparently its very predictability has operated to its disadvantage, causing linguists to neglect it as uninteresting with the result that historians are inevitably handicapped by the absence of a grammatical handbook. In the hands of an expert, the extremely complex metrical system of this verse can be of immense assistance towards detecting corruptions in a manuscript-text and thus restoring the author's original intention. Again, few historians are equipped for this work. Somewhat between a quarter and a third of all the poems is preserved in approximately contemporary vellum and paper manuscripts of the fourteenth, fifteenth, and sixteenth centuries, but the majority of texts can be found only in later anthologies of the seventeenth, eighteenth, and nineteenth centuries.[15] Restoring the true wording of an early thirteenth-century poem from a late eighteenth-century manuscript can be a delicate task indeed.[16]

Beside these practical difficulties, modern readers often have problems also with the subject-matter of bardic odes. These are principally eulogies and elegies, with some warnings of impending satire or apologies arising out of personal differences between the bard and his patron. Contrary to popular preconceptions, very few can be described as inauguration-odes or incitements to war. Within each poem, most of the space is given up to certain stock motifs, repeatedly used in many periods and for many patrons – praise of the patron's personal appearance, his hospitality, piety and justice, his prowess in war, the fertility of the land during his reign, and so on. Familiarity with the bardic style allows one to lay less emphasis on these sections of the poem and thus to focus with greater precision on the five or six stanzas containing an individual message. Thus winnowed, the purport of these poems can be very interesting indeed. They were composed to endorse and publicise the views of the patron himself, who paid heavily for this service. Poems from different areas and periods reveal varying attitudes towards the Anglo-Irish colony: hostility, apathy, or even on occasion positive friendship.[17] One king is praised for the peacefulness of his reign, another for his constant warfare; one is said to be universally feared, another universally loved. Some of these variations depend not only on the individual patron's character but on the changing concepts of kingship and law from one century to another, on a prevailing climate of opinion. It is also possible to treat these poems as mines of factual information. Many contain a *caithréim*, or list of a patron's military victories, giving place-names and usually one or two added details – the burning of a castle or the name of an important prisoner. They also address the patron as 'son of *x*' and 'grandson of *y*' supplying not only his father and paternal grandfather's names but also

[15] The manuscript-tradition is discussed by Ó Cuív, *The Irish Bardic Duanaire*.

[16] See Bergin, *Irish Bardic Poetry*, p. 169.

[17] For example, *Aithdioghluim Dána*, ed. McKenna, no. 27; *The Book of O'Hara*, ed. McKenna, pp. 42, 54, 98.

his mother's name and those of her parents, often ending the poem with a complimentary verse to his wife. They are thus of use in reconstructing the pattern of dynastic intermarriage, giving far more details than the patrilinear genealogical compilations.

The genealogical manuscripts themselves cannot be treated simply as preserving factual records. The great twelfth-century compilations were written in an ecclesiastical environment. The changed monastic ideal typified by the Cistercian reform meant that the tradition of native secular learning in Irish monasteries was cut short, and no similar writings survive from the thirteenth century.[18] The genealogical collections of the later middle ages were compiled by hereditary secular historians, the earliest being that in the mid-fourteenth-century Ó Cianáin manuscript (Dublin, National Library of Ireland, MSS. G.2–3) which is closely related to material in the later Books of Uí Mhaine, Ballymote, and Lecan. The pedigrees of contemporary chieftains, as given in these manuscripts, can be followed back for three or four generations with some confidence and are corroborated by the evidence of annalistic texts; but when the genealogists deal with the generations which flourished about the year 1200 there are often signs of uncertainty – a blank space on the page,[19] the repetition of the same names with suspicious regularity,[20] insertion of too many or too few generations. The compilers

[18] That is, no genealogical *manuscripts* from this period are extant. There is evidence for some localised genealogical research in the late thirteenth century, apparently in the secular bardic schools. The genealogies of the chiefs of Bréifne, which were more or less ignored in the twelfth-century manuscripts (see *Corpus Genealogiarum Hiberniae*, I, ed. O'Brien, p. 175), are set out in detail in a long poem whose closing verses seem to claim part-authorship for a certain Giolla Bearaigh, *saoi leighis*, or 'sage in leechcraft'. The manuscript (Dublin, Royal Irish Academy, MS. 471, fos 1–5), is signed by the fourteenth-century scribe Ádhamh Ó Cianáin. It is almost illegible, but one of the clearer passages deals with the pedigree of Brian Breaghach MagShamhradháin (*ob.* 1298). A poem in the Book of Magauran (ed. McKenna, pp. 210, 370) states that the hereditary historian MacFirbhisigh had traced Brian Breaghach's ancestry. At least three other late thirteenth-century pedigrees survive in later manuscripts, that of Éinrí Crosach MacGiollafhinnéin (*ob.* 1285) in the Book of Ballymote, p. 85b36, Brian na gCoileach Aifrinn MagMathghamhna (*ob.* 1311) in Dublin, National Library of Ireland, MS. G.2, fo 25(26)v, 1r(margin), and Eachmharcach Ó hAnnluain (*fl.* 1266–1290) in the Book of Lecan, fo 79re10. The territories of all these chiefs were located along the southern borders of Ulster, and this may be a clue to the locality of the school of historians whose work is involved.

[19] In the Book of Ballymote, p. 85b9, an original gap in the O'Donnell pedigree has been filled in by a later scribe.

[20] 'm. Uidhir m. Searraigh m. Oirghiallaigh m. Uidhir m. Searraigh m. Oirghiallaigh' (Maguire pedigree, Book of Lecan, fo 78r); 'm. Eachadha m. Mathghamhna m. Neill m. Maghnusa m. Mathghamhna m. Neill' (MacMahon pedigree, *ibid.*, fo 79r); 'm. Aedha m. Donnchaidh m. Domhnaill m. Neill m. Donnchaidh m. Domhnaill' (O Rourke pedigree, Book of Ballymote, p. 92); all the above repetitions can be referred to the period 1150–1250, and the

of the Books of Ballymote and Lecan, or of their common exemplar, had access to the twelfth-century ecclesiastical Book of Leinster.[21] From this and other early material they could trace the royal dynasties back from the twelfth century to Adam, and if not truthfully, at least along lines which were generally agreed and hallowed by repetition. Ordinary folk-memory could bring them from the mid-fourteenth century back to the mid-thirteenth, but it looks as if the gap between the latter period and the monastic collections was difficult to span, as if a time of neglect had intervened before schools of secular historians undertook the task abandoned by monastic genealogists; later compilers, faced with this gap, had on occasion resorted to invention.

Beside these inaccuracies in detail, genealogists were capable of transferring a pedigree wholesale from one royal dynasty to another, in response to the political needs of the day. For instance, a pedigree in the Book of Ballymote traces the late thirteenth-century Éinrí Crosach Mac Giollafhinnéin, a sub-chief of Fermanagh, back to Maolruanaidh Ó Maoldoraidh, king of Tír Conaill (?*ob.* 1027). This claim can be associated with the political alliance between the Mac Giollafhinnéin chiefs and the rulers of Tír Conaill in the thirteenth century. On the other hand, a much later genealogy for the same family links it to the Mac Carthaigh kings of Munster, presumably in emulation of Miler Magrath, also from Fermanagh, who after he became Protestant archbishop of Cashel in 1571 had his own pedigree traced to the Munster Dál gCais.[22] In short, the work of the native genealogists may often hold greater interest as a political manifesto than as a reliable record of any chieftain's descent, and a comparison of the variant readings in compilations of different date can be a thought-provoking exercise.

Closely related to the genealogies are the historical tracts recounting the glories of one chiefly family or another. For the post-Norman period the most ambitious text in this class is *Caithréim Thoirdhealbhaigh*, dealing with the civil wars among the O'Briens in the late thirteenth and early fourteenth centuries. Since its original compilation appears to date from the mid-fourteenth century, within the lifetime of some of the participants, its narrative is plausible enough in spite of some inaccuracies in detail,[23] and its political stance has considerable interest. The same may well be true of the undated *Cath Fhochairte Brighite*, dealing with

---

latter two involve an excessive number of generations occurring between two ascertainable dates.

[21] *The Book of Leinster*, edd. Best *et al.*, I.xiii.

[22] Book of Ballymote, p. 85b36; AConn 1231.8; AFM 1234; 'Geinealaighe Fearmanach', ed. Ua Cadhla, p. 140; 'The O Clery Book of Genealogies', ed. Pender, p. 152.

[23] See Orpen, *Ireland under the Normans*, IV.67–8; McNamara, 'The *Caithréim Thoirdhealbhaigh* manuscripts', p. 125; cf. Nic Ghiollamhaith, 'Dynastic warfare'.

the Bruce-invasion of the early fourteenth century, which survives only in a nineteenth-century paper manuscript.[24] However, other tracts – such as *Craobhsgaoileadh Chlainne Suibhne*,[25] *Leabhar Eoghanach*,[26] and *Seanchas na mBúrcach*[27] — were compiled as late as the sixteenth century and, when dealing with events in the twelfth, thirteenth, and fourteenth centuries, show gross distortions of time-scale as well as the introduction of international folk-motifs. Any of their statements which are unsupported by evidence from other sources have to be regarded with extreme suspicion.

In all, then, the use of Irish-language sources for the history of the chieftains of the later middle ages entails a constant battle of wits with the members of the secular learned classes who compiled those sources and inflated or garbled the facts to suit their own purposes. For this reason the fragments of relevant material to be gleaned from the Anglo-Norman administrative records have particular value. They provide more precise and more authentic dating than the annalistic texts and, if not a completely impartial record, at least an alternative version of many battles and conflicts. However, as the Dublin administration was not directly responsible for areas under Irish rule, its records do not supply a continuous narrative but merely reflect sporadic incursions by hostile Irish neighbours; and their lack of genealogical detail often makes it difficult to identify an Irish leader with any certainty in relation to the rest of his family. Sometimes, indeed, their phonetic rendering of an Irish place- or personal name is distorted beyond hope of recognition. Moreover, the area effectively administered by the central government shrank in the later middle ages to the four counties in the immediate neighbourhood of Dublin, and references to areas farther afield became rarer and rarer. Some supplementary material may be obtained from the muniments of the great Anglo-Irish families, the collection of the Ormond deeds being an outstanding example,[28] but the only organisation whose records consistently covered the whole country was the Church.

Here the disadvantages concern the subject-matter. Apart from the important registers of the archbishops of Armagh,[29] few local ecclesiastical records survive from the middle ages and nationwide coverage comes only through the papal archives. At that administrative level much information can be gleaned about the hereditary clerical families whose

[24] 'An Irish account of Bruce's invasion', ed. Ua Muirgheasa; see Frame, 'The Bruces in Ireland', pp. 16–18. However, recent research by one of my students, Mr John Duffy, strongly suggests that this tract is a forgery.

[25] *Leabhar Chlainne Suibhne*, ed. Walsh, pp. 2–75.

[26] *Leabhar Cloinne Aodha Buidhe*, ed. Ó Donnchadha, pp. 1–40.

[27] 'Senchus na mBúrcach', ed. Ó Raghallaigh.

[28] *Calendar*, ed. Curtis.

[29] These are at present on permanent loan to the Public Record Office of Northern Ireland; transcripts are kept in the Library of Trinity College, Dublin, and in the Public Library, Cathedral Hill, Armagh. Primate Mey's register has been published in full (see above, n. 1). Calendars of some of the others are listed by Gwynn, *The Medieval Province of Armagh*, p. ix.

members filled ecclesiastical benefices in Ireland and litigated briskly about their right to do so,[30] but the Irish chiefs are usually mentioned in connexion only with dispensations to marry or gross violations of the Church's immunities.

When one attempts to trace the process of change within Gaelic society, two further groups of material become relevant, although neither is contemporary with the later middle ages. In the first place there are the scanty and obscure Old Irish law-tracts, accompanied by a vast corpus of glosses and commentaries on the original texts. The tracts themselves date largely from the seventh and eighth centuries and have no historical validity, as descriptions of social custom, for a later period. The glosses and commentaries accumulated gradually between the ninth century and the sixteenth; they require much further study to show how far they confine their attention to explaining the archaic texts and how far they reflect the changed usages of their own day. Until then, the law-tracts must remain 'very unreliable guides' to the customs and institutions of Irish society after the eighth century.[31]

At the other end of our period, abundant description and commentary on Irish social customs can be gleaned from the state-papers, political memoirs, and propagandist writings of the Tudor reconquest. This evidence is rich in detail and has all the advantages of quantity, clarity, and contemporary observation. However, the English administrators were normally ignorant of the language and cultural background of the society which they were describing, many of their reports were deliberately distorted for political purposes,[32] and Irish society in the sixteenth century was undergoing further changes, showing greater instability and violence as a result of the pressures imposed by the reconquest itself.[33] These reservations must be borne in mind when using the Old Irish law-tracts as a starting-point, and the Tudor state-papers as an ending, to a study of the developments taking place in this society during the high middle ages.

The essential challenge in writing the history of Gaelic Ireland is to utilise threads of evidence from many disparate sources and to weave from them a coherent pattern and a continuous narrative. With patience and scepticism it becomes possible to distil a few guarded certainties from a mass of flamboyant uncertainties. The remainder, instead of being discarded totally, can serve as evidence for ideals, aspirations, and attitudes of mind. Where the source-material is exiguous, it would be criminal to allow any of it to go to waste.

[30] For example, Ó Doibhlin, *Domhnach Mór*, chapter 3.
[31] Binchy, 'The linguistic and historical value', pp. 210–12, 220, 225–7.
[32] See Quinn, *The Elizabethans and the Irish*.
[33] Nicholls, *Gaelic and Gaelicised Ireland*, pp. 4–5.

II

THE POLITICAL BACKGROUND – 'GAELIC' AND 'ANGLO-NORMAN' IRELAND

Society in Ireland changed and developed with the passage of time, just as it did in the rest of Europe. This should be an unnecessary truism, but nineteenth-century writers such as P. W. Joyce[1] described the customs of 'Celtic Ireland' as if they were static and timeless, enshrined in the Old Irish law-tracts and their glosses and commentaries, and surviving unaltered from the sixth century to the sixteenth. A more discriminating use of historical sources gradually emancipated later scholars from this preconception, but the successive stages of development noted were at first attributed wholly to outside intervention. The viking-invaders were praised for the introduction of towns, coinage, and international trade, and blamed for the secularisation of the Irish Church, the weakening of familial ties, and the increasing emphasis on militarism in Irish society.[2] Any further changes occurring after the Anglo-Norman invasion of the twelfth century were assumed to have been brought about by that event. More recently, however, the emphasis has shifted towards an appreciation of this society as a growing organism, containing within itself the possiblility of evolution.

Similarly, Irish attitudes to kingship and authority were seen to have changed in the post-viking period, most notably in 1002, when the Munsterman Brian Bóroimhe broke a six-hundred-year-old tradition by supplanting the Uí Néill dynasty in the 'kingship of Tara'.[3] In the early middle ages the primary political unit had been the *tuath*, an area covering about a quarter or a fifth of a modern county. Although a number of these districts could be loosely bound together into group-kingdoms and provincial overkingdoms, the only territory ruled directly by an overlord was his own *tuath*; he could exercise control over the other subject-areas only through the obedience of his vassals, the local kings.[4]

[1] Author of *A Social History*. MacNeill (*Celtic Ireland*, p. 154, and *Phases* p. 295) criticises writers like Joyce and G. H. Orpen for 'ignoring time and change' but falls into the same trap on many occasions, citing (for example) the evidence of Caesar's 'Gallic War' on the subject of law-enforcement in twelfth-century Ireland (*ibid.*, pp. 313–16).

[2] Binchy, 'The passing'; Hughes, 'Introduction', pp. 26–8.

[3] Ó Corráin, *Ireland before the Normans*, p. 125.

[4] Binchy, 'The passing', pp. 123–4.

Kingship itself was vestigially sacral in character, with a strong pagan inheritance. The assumption of power was seen as a marriage with the local goddess of sovereignty, resulting in the fertility of people, cattle, and crops under the right king's rule.[5] The administration of a local king, or *rí tuaithe*, was minimal, and his judicial and legislative powers very limited.[6] However, in the post-viking period the title of *rí* or 'king' is reserved for the ruler of a *tír*, a larger territory approximating in size to the modern county, while the *tuath* has become a mere subdivision within this new unit, controlled by a *taoiseach* or *dux*, a vassal-chieftain.[7] Kings on this larger scale employed a wider variety and a greater number of royal officials, took a more direct role in legislating and enforcing punishment for crime, and justified their authority by the theocratic arguments then in vogue in the rest of Europe, rather than by the ultimately pagan tradition of their forefathers.[8]

The beginnings of this movement towards a Continental model of kingship have been traced back to the eighth, and even the seventh, century.[9] Its subsequent progress was signposted by the 'ordaining' of provincial kings at the hands of leading ecclesiastics,[10] by the destruction during the tenth, eleventh, and twelfth centuries of the sacred trees which grew at traditional inauguration-sites,[11] and by the long reign of Donnchadh son of Brian Bóroimhe after an incident in which his hand had been cut off, despite the earlier insistence that a true king should be *dianim*, 'without blemish'.[12] Twelfth-century Irish kings employed chancellors and issued charters,[13] acquired houses in the Norse sea-ports or in monastic 'cities',[14] presided over reforming synods of the Church – gatherings which might also issue regulations on secular matters[15] – and claimed territorial ownership of the kingdoms which they ruled.[16] The high kings in this later period did not content themselves with direct control of their own locality and the personal submission of neighbouring kings. In a number of cases they either appointed a royal governor to enforce their rule among their vassals[17] or actually replaced a local dynast

[5] Binchy, *Celtic and Anglo-Saxon Kingship*, pp. 8–12.

[6] *Ibid.*, pp. 18–21.

[7] Todd, *Cogadh Gaedhel*, p. 48; of Ó Corráin, *Ireland before the Normans*, pp. 29–32.

[8] Ó Corráin, 'Nationality' and 'Foreign connections'.

[9] Byrne, *The Rise*, pp. 5–7; *Irish Kings*, pp. 34–5, 159.

[10] *Ibid.*, pp. 159, 256.

[11] AFM 981/2, 1051, 1099, 1111, 1143; Lucas, 'The sacred trees', pp. 25–6.

[12] Binchy, *Celtic and Anglo-Saxon Kingship*, p. 10; AFM 1018; AI, ALC, AT, AU 1019.

[13] Below, pp. 65–6, 80.

[14] AI 1114.4, 1116.4; AU 1123.1–2; AT 1173; *Expugnatio Hibernica*, edd. Scott & Martin, p. 174; AU 1187, 1188.

[15] Below, pp. 63–4.

[16] Ó Corráin, 'Nationality', pp. 24–6; Dugdale, *Monasticon Anglicanum*, VI.2, p. 1134.

[17] Ó Corráin, 'Nationality', pp. 26–8.

with a member of their own family, a son or a brother with whom they could hope to share an identity of interests.[18]

When, in the years immediately preceding the Norman invasion, the Connacht high king, Ruaidhri Ó Conchobhair, took the kingship of Dublin, the largest urban settlement in Ireland, and presided over a near-national synod at Athboy, exacted successive submissions from all the other Irish rulers, and celebrated his country-wide authority by holding the Fair of Tailtiu,[19] it seems quite clear that he was consciously aiming at an effective monarchy for the whole island and that his initial efforts had met with success. The church of Armagh had already achieved ecclesiastical primacy over all Ireland, a primacy which received official papal recognition at the Synod of Kells in 1152. Academic unity was imposed ten years later by another synod which decreed that only scholars trained at Armagh could teach in Irish Church-schools. The fact that the chief lector at Armagh *ca* 1154–1174 had previously pursued his studies for twenty-one years in France and England links this decision to the growth of universities on the Continent during the same period; and when in 1169 Ruaidhri Ó Conchobhair permanently endowed a lectorship at Armagh, in his own name and that of his successors, for the education of Irish and Scottish students, his paternalism seems to outstrip that of contemporary European kings and anticipates the secular patronage of universities which became common in the thirteenth and fourteenth centuries.[20]

These tentative steps towards national unity and effective royal government were permanently halted by the coming of the Anglo-Normans, and it would be absurd to minimise the extent of the change of direction of Irish history thereafter. However, their advent was not in itself an unprecedented bolt from the blue. The search for a new kind of kingship had brought with it a new kind of warfare. Whereas earlier overlords demanded only the personal submission of neighbouring rulers, and enforced their compliance by cattle-raiding, Ruaidhri Ó Conchobhair and his immediate predecessors reduced the territorial power of their opponents, compelling them to share their kingdom with a local rival, or even confiscated their lands altogether, as in 1169 when Ruaidhri took West Meath from the Ó Maoilsheachlainn family and kept it for himself.[21] Campaigns had become violent and protracted, and armies were expected to travel far from their home territories, in fact throughout the length and breadth of Ireland. For such extraordinary military service a king's own vassals now received wages, or *tuarastal*,[22] but in addition the high kings imported mercenary soldiers from abroad, Norsemen from the Hebrides, like Mac Scelling who served Muircheartach Mac Lochlainn in 1154,[23] or

18 Ussher, 'Veterum Epistolarum Hibernicarum Sylloge', pp. 518–19; AI 1075.4, 1113.7; AU 1126.7; AFM 1143, 1144.

19 AFM, AT, AU, 1166, 1167, 1168. See Binchy, 'The Fair', pp. 126–7.

20 AU 1162, 1174; Rashdall, *The Universities*, I.82–4.

21 AFM 1169.

22 See below, pp. 101–3.

23 AFM 1154.

Anglo-Normans, like Arnulf de Montgomery, the son-in-law of Muircheartach Ó Briain.[24]

Ruaidhri Ó Conchobhair's annexation of Dublin in 1166, while presaging the eventual development of an urban capital for a unified kingdom of Ireland, had the immediate effect of seriously diminishing the power of Diarmait Mac Murchadha, king of Leinster. His very natural opposition resulted in his defeat and expulsion. When he returned with Norman allies in 1167, their initial role was that of hired mercenaries fighting under Mac Murchadha's command. A radical departure from the past only came with the death of Diarmait in 1171, when his new son-in-law, Richard de Clare, earl of Pembroke, claimed the right to succeed him in the kingship of Leinster, at first offering to fulfil the obligations of a vassal-king to Ruaidhri Ó Conchobhair.[25] Thereafter, his success in defeating the high king and establishing his rule in Leinster provoked his own liege-lord, Henry II, to come over to Ireland with an army in order to forestall the development of an independent Norman kingdom on his western frontier. The Irish kings submitted to Henry in the hope that he would restrain the barons from further aggression against his newly acquired subjects, and the lordship of Ireland became thenceforward attached to the English Crown.

During the first fifty years of Norman activity in Ireland, Leinster, Meath and Louth, much of Munster, and the eastern coast of Ulster were conquered, subinfeudated, and planted with peasant-colonists from England and Wales. In those parts of Ireland which remained under Gaelic rule, all the achievements of the long drive towards centralisation and theocratic kingship were gradually dismantled. In purely geographical terms, politics once more became localised. When the first Anglo-Norman justiciar, Hugh de Lacy, took control of Meath 'from the Shannon to the sea', the effect was to split Gaelic Ireland into two halves. He and his successors made it impossible thereafter for any king of the north of Ireland to lead his troops down to Munster or for any Munster king to invade Derry and Inishowen, as had happened during the early twelfth-century wars between 'high kings with opposition'. Now it was the English king and his justiciar who enjoyed the freedom of movement and military strength necessary to play the part of high king in Irish society. Already Henry II had become, as it were, high king of Ireland when he received the submissions of the Irish rulers in 1171/2 and was granted a tribute from all Ireland by the Treaty of Windsor in 1175.[26] His son, King John, fulfilled the role of a high king even more realistically during his second expedition to Ireland in 1210. On that occasion he is said to have received the submission of more than twenty Irish kings, including the Uí Bhriain, Ó Conchobhair, and Ó Néill, and these provincial overkings seem to have brought their forces to join John's hosting against the rebel

[24] Curtis, 'Murchertach O Brien', p. 120.
[25] Orpen, *Ireland under the Normans*, I.227.
[26] *Ibid.*, I.259, 261–2, 264–7, 349–50.

earl of Ulster, Hugh de Lacy the younger.[27] King John mediated in the Uí Bhriain succession-dispute, and exacted hostages from Ó Conchobhair of Connacht. However, the statement in the Annals of Inisfallen that Ó Néill, though coming to pay his respects to the English king, refused to yield him hostages,[28] is one of several indications that while the English had destroyed the high kingship, considerable power remained as yet with the provincial kings in areas which were not actually colonised. In the first half of the thirteenth century Ó Conchobhair and Ó Briain still issued charters in regal style, Ó Conchobhair indeed employing a chancellor and using the title *Dei gratia rex Connactie*,[29] while Ó Néill demonstrated his practical power on a number of occasions by entering the province of Connacht on hosting and installing a candidate of his choice in the kingship there.[30]

As the thirteenth century went on, however, the process of conquest continued. This second stage of expansion was not the work of fresh invasions from England. Rather it represented an internal migration led by the descendants of the first conquerors, de Burghs, FitzGeralds, de Lacys, and Butlers. Much land in the western half of Ireland passed into the ownership of the Anglo-Norman aristocracy, and some towns were established, but the countryside was not colonised by English and Welsh peasantry on the scale which had given such reality and durability to the earlier settlement of the east coast. Not only do the barons seem to have relied heavily on Irish tenants for the cultivation of their manors in the west, but large tracts of territory were left in the hands of the Irish kings and chiefs to rule as they pleased provided that they rendered tributes and service to their Anglo-Norman overlords.[31]

Just as the high kingship had passed to the Plantagenets and their justiciars, so now the role of the provincial kings was taken up by the FitzGeralds in Desmond and Sligo, de Clare in Thomond, de Burgh in Connacht and Ulster. These lords received hostages and tribute from their Irish vassal-kings, deposed them at will and inaugurated the candidates of their choice, summoned them to join their overlord's hosting with all their forces in time of war, and punished them for rebellion with heavy fines.[32] The provincial dynasts, Ó Néill, Ó Conchobhair, and Ó Briain, found their hereditary pretensions to authority undermined in two ways. Their own former vassals were no longer treated as subject in the first

27 *Ibid.*, II.268; AI, ALC 1210.

28 AI 1210.2

29 D'Arbois de Jubainville, 'Chartes', pp. 81–6; Orpen, 'Some Irish Cistercian documents', p. 306.

30 AConn 1225.5 and 25, 1226.12, 1230.8; ALC 1200, 1201, 1224.

31 Orpen, *Ireland under the Normans*, IV.258–61; 'The earldom of Ulster', pt IV; 'The Normans in Tirowen and Tirconnell'; Knox, 'Occupation'; Frame, 'Power', pp. 8–9.

32 Orpen, *Ireland under the Normans*, III.138, 142–3, 145, 175–7, 186–9, 284; IV.66–75, 81–6, 107–126, 134, 140–1, 148; Simms, ' "The King's Friend" ', p. 233, n. 2.

instance to them, but all were given an equal footing as fellow-tenants of the Anglo-Norman overlord, a development particularly well documented in the case of Ó Néill of Tír Eoghain and his sub-chieftains.[33] This could have the effect of confining the direct rule of such a dynast to his home-district so that he was reduced to being a *rí tuaithe* in all but name. Moreover, the Anglo-Norman lords were inclined to encourage the claims of more than one candidate for kingship at a time so that an Irish ruler might have to share even his reduced territory with a rival.[34]

Not only were the descendants of the twelfth-century Irish rulers no longer overkings, but the Irish Church, over whose synods their ancestors had presided, was now absorbed into the English political structure. In spite of disagreements leading to the murder of Thomas Becket and the interdict of the realm under King John, the appointment of bishops and abbots in England had remained under royal control, and this control extended to every part of Ireland occupied by the Anglo-Normans. The primatial see of Armagh lay in an area not actually colonised, and for much of the thirteenth century its archbishops maintained some degree of independence, but in 1285 the activities of Primate Nicholas Mac Maoil Íosa led Edward I's advisers to recommend 'that no Irishman should ever be an archbishop or bishop(?), because they always preach against the king and always provide their churches with Irishmen'.[35] With one exception the see of Armagh was filled thereafter by English or Anglo-Irish prelates until the appointment of the Italian Octavian del Palacio in 1479. Before this development of racial exclusivism, Henry II in his role as 'high king' had presided over a national synod of the Irish Church at Cashel in 1171/2 and had been welcomed by the native clergy as an ally in their plans for ecclesiastical reform.[36] In effect, the reforming churchmen abandoned their former reliance on the local Irish kings; and the rapid identification of the interests of the Church with those of the invaders may be one cause underlying the curious hints of a pagan revival in the early thirteenth century, centring round the prophesied messiah 'Aodh Eanghach', who was expected to drive out the foreigners, restore the high kingship, rebuild the walls of Tara, and even bring back the druids.[37]

Any real recrudescence of paganism was checked in the mid-thirteenth century by the preaching of the Dominican and Franciscan friars,[38] but the reign of the future Aodh Eanghach remained a common theme in bardic poetry for the rest of the middle ages. Gone was the theocratic ideology which derived the king's authority from God through the mediation of the Church. The whole movement towards centralisation,

[33] Simms, 'The O Hanlons', p. 80; Orpen, 'The earldom of Ulster', pt IV, p. 141.

[34] Orpen, *Ireland under the Normans*, IV.72–4, 85; 'The earldom of Ulster', pt IV, pp. 136, 141.

[35] *CDI 1285–92*, p. 10. See Gwynn, 'Nicholas Mac Maol Íosa', p. 397.

[36] Sheehy, *Pontificia Hibernica*, I.20.

[37] See below, pp. 26–7.

[38] Sheehy, *Pontificia Hibernica*, II.251–2; Watt, *The Church in Medieval Ireland*, pp. 76–7.

unity, and increased legislative and executive powers for the king from the seventh century to the twelfth had been greatly influenced by the Irish Church. As a Latin-speaking organisation, ultimately under the authority of Rome, it had been the channel through which Continental ideas reached Ireland. It looked to a strong secular authority to supply social stability and peace, and its clerics served as chancellors and notaries in the more sophisticated administrations of the twelfth-century kings. In the post-Norman period, when control of the Church rested largely with the English king and the Continental monastic orders, Irish rulers had to turn elsewhere to find a theoretical justification for their authority – to the secular learned classes of bards, brehons, and historians, and to the immemorial tradition expressed in the secular inauguration-rites.

For a brief period even these customary rites may have fallen into abeyance. Around the year 1300, when the English conquest of Ireland had reached its fullest geographical extent, and in theory at least every Irish leader was vassal to an Anglo-Norman lord, there are annal-entries which suggest that the formal installation of an Irish chief might be performed by his Norman overlord, who presumably curtailed or omitted the traditional ceremonies. In 1310 the inauguration of Feidhlimidh Ó Conchobhair is described as an antiquarian revival 'in the manner remembered by the old men and recorded in the old books'.[39] The same implication of deliberate revival seems to attend the Leinstermen's elevation of Domhnall son of Art Mac Murchadha to an obsolete provincial kingship in 1328.[40] In both these cases and to a large extent in the Ó Briain saga, *Caithréim Thoirdhealbhaigh*,[41] the new provincial kings are not said to have seized power, but to have had it thrust upon them by their leading vassals, in order that they might cement an alliance of local chieftains against their enemies, both Anglo-Norman and Irish.

To accept that the powers of overkingship and the traditional inauguration-rites had been more or less suppressed at the height of Anglo-Norman rule and that they were subsequently revived is an important step, because it implies that such continuity as the fourteenth- and fifteenth-century Irish leaders show with their twelfth-century predecessors is in great measure the outcome of deliberate choice. Certain traditions were maintained because they served a contemporary political purpose, while others were discarded as no longer functional. For instance, the open-air inauguration-ceremonies of the later mediaeval chieftains apparently fulfilled a contemporary need, because they were imitated by the hibernicised Anglo-Norman families, such as the Mayo Burkes.[42] On the other hand, the office of *reachtaire*, or 'mayor of the palace', does not appear in the annalistic texts after 1301, and in the

[39] AConn 1293.3, 1310.7; AU 1291 (see Orpen, 'The earldom of Ulster', pt IV, p. 134).

[40] *Chartularies*, ed. Gilbert, II.365–6. On the ending of the Leinster provincial kingship, see *The Book of Leinster*, edd. Best *et al.*, I.184.

[41] Edd. O'Grady & Flower, I.5, 31; II.6, 32.

[42] *Beatha Aodha Ruaidh*, ed. Walsh, I.114.

fifteenth century the title of *rí* ('king') was discontinued.[43]

The selective revival of certain traditions connected with the kingship of earlier times is epitomised in the topographical poem *Triallam timcheall na Fódla* by Seaán Mór Ó Dubhagáin (*ob.* 1372). In it the author sets out to list the ruling families of each territory in Ireland as they flourished in the twelfth century, noting from time to time where these have been supplanted in his own day by another Irish dynasty but passing over the Norman conquests in silence.[44] This same Ó Dubhagáin or his pupil, Ádhamh Ó Cianáin, was responsible for compiling the genealogies of the mid-fourteenth-century Irish kings[45] and thus providing the earliest known comprehensive updating of the ecclesiastical twelfth-century genealogical collections. His patron, Uilliam Ó Ceallaigh, was the first layman to entertain a general gathering of the hereditary learned classes of Ireland in 1351, at a time when the professional poets had feared that their art was falling into disrepute and being subjected to criticism and attacks from the Church.[46] Thereafter the evidence of poems and manuscripts shows that this upsurge of interest in Gaelic history, genealogies and literature was maintained at a high level down to the early seventeenth century. The illuminations which decorate these manuscripts show a conscious antiquarianism, seen also in certain artefacts such as the leather satchel of the Book of Armagh, made in the fifteenth century, and the carving on the Trinity harp.[47]

As the description of Feidhlimidh Ó Conchobhair's inauguration reminds us, this cultural revival was merely a symptom of a political recovery experienced by those areas of Ireland which were under Gaelic rule during the fourteenth and fifteenth centuries. Already at the end of the thirteenth century the roll of the Irish parliament held in 1297 shows the Anglo-Norman colony to be under some strain. There was an inevitable tension between the English king's government at Dublin, which under Edward I pressed increasingly towards centralised administration of justice and collection of taxes and refused to sanction the existence of private wars, and on the other hand the great barons who ruled the frontiers of the colony and controlled the Irish chiefs. The barons were forced to maintain private armies and to implement a local war and peace at their own discretion; central government was therefore faced with the dilemma of either provoking the rebellion of these marcher lords by bureaucratic interference or else of abdicating responsibility for considerable areas of the colony by delegating authority. Commonly, the latter solution was preferred as being the cheaper, since Edward I was

43 See below, p. 39.

44 *Topographical Poems*, ed. Carney. Ó Dubhagáin's original plan to describe all Ireland was left unfinished, and the work completed by Giolla na Naomh Ó hUidhrín; see *ibid.*, p. viii.

45 Ní Shéaghdha, *Catalogue*, I.13, 17.

46 Knott, 'Filidh Éireann go haointeach'; Ó Cuív, 'An appeal'; Chart, *The Register of John Swayne*, p. 11.

47 Cone, *Treasures*, pp. 193, 196, 217–19; Stalley, 'The long middle ages', p. 97.

constantly abstracting large sums from the Irish exchequer to finance his campaigns in Scotland and Wales.[48] As the fourteenth century wore on, this inherent weakness in the Anglo-Irish central government was accentuated by the decay of the colony itself. The cycle of inclement weather experienced by all northern Europe in the early fourteenth century[49] was of a nature to affect the cereal-growing regions of Leinster and East Munster more adversely than the largely pastoral uplands and west coast which were occupied by the Gaelic Irish. The devastation spread by the invading Scots under Edward Bruce in the years 1315–18 had its counterpart in other years as a result of violence on a smaller scale, raids by the Gaelic Irish, or feuds among the barons themselves. Peasant-colonists began to abandon their holdings, migrating either to the towns or back to England.[50] Their decline in numbers was then accelrated by the Black Death (1348/9) which, contemporaries alleged, affected the Anglo-Irish, clustered in their towns and villages and particularly in the sea-ports, far more severely than the scattered Gaelic population.[51]

While these were reasons for weakness in the colony, military reorganisation had given the areas under Irish rule an added strength. The twelfth-century overkings, besides paying wages to their vassals for campaigns which required them to travel far from their home territory, had also employed limited numbers of native and foreign mercenaries. Diarmait Mac Murchadha had not been the only Irish king to hire detachments of Norman troops to use in wars against his neighbours in the early years of the invasion. However, the fighting which accompanied the extension of the Norman conquest saw the proliferation of mercenaries, both the native-born kerne and, from the second half of the thirteenth century onwards, imported Scottish galloglass also. They were employed not merely by the dynastic successors of the provincial kings, but by sub-chieftains and ambitious nobles who had no formal title to authority.[52] Their immediate effect was to make the Irish armies more formidable. Where once the chieftains had hired Norman auxiliaries, there was a trend in the late thirteenth and early fourteenth centuries for government-officials to hire Irish troops.[53] Irish leaders won some notable victories – as at Dysert O Dea (1318), Uriel (1346), and Downpatrick (1374) – which were associated with the reoccupation of formerly colonised lands.[54]

Nevertheless, territorial expansion was not to be the dominant feature

[48] Lydon, *The Lordship*, pp. 120–41.

[49] Titow, 'Evidence of weather'.

[50] Lydon, *The Lordship*, pp. 206–7.

[51] Otway-Ruthven, *A History*, pp. 267–70.

[52] For example, AConn 1305.3, 1307.10, 1310.5, 1316.2, 1367.5 and 7.

[53] Simms, 'The O Hanlons', p. 86; *CJRI 1305–7* p. 293; Dublin, National Library of Ireland, MS. 760, pp. 290–1.

[54] Gilbert, *Chartularies*, II.283, 358, 389; AConn 1346.6, 1374.7, 1375.5 (see Otway-Ruthven, *A History*, p. 305, n. 61); Curtis, *A History*, pp. 244, 272, 288, 295.

of the Gaelic resurgence. The lowlands and the east coast, areas which had been thickly planted in the first fifty years after the Norman invasion, remained in the hands of the Anglo-Irish aristocracy, though not always within the sphere of the Dublin government. The descendants of Anglo-Irish families also continued to hold North Kerry and a large part of Connacht. In the rest of the West and North, and in the wooded and hilly districts of Leinster and Meath, the Irish chiefs had in great measure broken free from their vassalage to the barons, and it became possible to rebuild once more centralised overkingships such as had flourished in the twelfth century. The task was not to prove an easy one. The fact that relatively minor sub-chiefs could command armies of hired mercenaries tended to perpetuate that equality of status, among all local Gaelic Irish rulers, originally fostered by the Anglo-Norman overlords. Thus it came about that much of the hardest fighting in the Gaelic resurgence was not directed against the English settlements at all, but took place between the Irish themselves as the major chiefs sought to impose their authority on their neighbours. Most, though not all, of these paramount chiefs were descended directly or collaterally from the provincial kings of the twelfth century, and thus had everything to gain by constant reference back to the rights exercised by their ancestors in former times. In another sense they were replacing the more recent overlordship of the Anglo-Normans, and some of the dues which they claimed were based on this inheritance. Ó Néill imitated the de Burgh earls of Ulster by billeting a standing army, 'the Bonaght of Ulster', on his vassal-chiefs.[55] O'Donnell claimed the burgage-rents and cockets of Sligo, a town founded by the FitzGeralds.[56] At the same time, the nature of the authority wielded by the paramount chiefs of the fifteenth and sixteenth centuries was evolving away from the earlier pattern of kingship. A leader whose military strength was based on a professional army rather than on a hosting of his own free subjects had little need to consult the wishes of those subjects, except of the half-dozen or so chief vassals who, like himself, controlled hired troops. Increasingly, elections to kingship became a formality, as succession was decided by primogeniture or main force.[57] Sixteenth-century observers held that war could be declared, or taxation arbitrarily extended, at the will of the ruler.[58] In 1583 Nicholas Malby, the English president of Connacht, remarked that 'if any principal lord or chief of his country be ill dealt withal by his own freeholders . . . the said lords were wont for the supressing of such to entertain Scots and kerne and galloglass'.[59] It is symptomatic of the changed relationship between the chief and his subjects that the terminology for kingship fell into disuse and was

[55] Empey & Simms, 'The Ordinances', pp. 180, 183; Brewer & Bullen, *Calendar of the Carew Manuscripts*, I.288; 'Ceart Uí Néill', ed. Dillon, pp. 4–9.

[56] 'Agreement', ed. M. Carney, pp. 288 and 290 n. 5.

[57] See below, pp. 48–9.

[58] See below, pp. 75, 127–8.

[59] See Hayes-McCoy, *Scots Mercenary Forces*, pp. 44–5.

replaced by words denoting lordship and ownership in the chiefs' titles and inauguration-rites.[60]

The new emphasis on lordship and landownership brought the position of the Gaelic Irish chiefs closer to that of their neighbours, the Anglo-Irish barons. Since by the later fifteenth century many of the latter were independent of the Dublin government and based their authority on their hired kerne and galloglass, the two aristocracies were fast becoming indistinguishable. Culturally this situation was reflected on the one hand by Anglo-Irish patronage for the native poets, brehons, and historians, and on the other hand by the translation of many French and English works of romance or devotion into Irish. Politically the tendency towards assimilation culminated in the Deputyships of the earls of Kildare, whose extensive power derived in great measure from their personal lordship over many Irish and Anglo-Irish leaders living beyond the bureaucratic control of the Dublin government.[61] The Great Earl of Kildare may not have succeeded in making himself literally 'king of Ireland', but he had certainly acquired powers comparable to those wielded by Ruaidhri Ó Conchobhair on the eve of the Norman invasion. It was not a style of authority which appealed to the less hibernicised colonists in the Dublin area, however, and their complaints induced the Tudor monarchs to destroy the house of Kildare and embark on the reconquest of Ireland. For a second time the long-drawn process of development from over-lordship to centralised government had been aborted before unity was achieved.

[60] See below, pp. 31,39.

[61] Bryan, *Gerald FitzGerald*, pp. x, 134, 235–41; Ellis, 'Tudor policy', pp. 248–50.

III

INAUGURATION-CEREMONIES, TITLES, AND THE MEANING OF KINGSHIP

There are no contemporary accounts of the rites used to confer kingship before the twelfth century, but some hints occur in literary and allegorical form in the Old and Middle Irish sagas, dealing chiefly though not exclusively with the high kingship of Tara. These indicate that Ireland once had sacral kings of a type widely known in other primitive societies and that many of the symbols and conventions associated with this institution were vividly remembered as late as the twelfth century, though not always fully understood.[1] The fundamental theory underlying such literary references is that right order in society can only flourish under the rule of the right king. The peaceful succession of property from father to son, the due fulfilment of contracts, security from outside attack, fertility in man and beast, increase of crops, clement weather, absence of disease, are all secured if the land herself, or the local goddess of sovereignty, is 'married' to a true king. The truth of the ruler is demonstrated by the absence of any physical blemish or character-defect – such as inhospitality, injustice, or cowardice – and by his royal ancestry. A true king can become false in the course of his reign by incurring a bodily defect, or by committing mean, unjust, or cowardly acts. The prosperity of the land and the fabric of society itself will suffer under such a false king until he is replaced by a 'true' ruler.[2]

Until recently, scholars who found it easy to accept that the assumption of kingship in Ireland took the form of a symbolic mating with the goddess of sovereignty, were nevertheless inclined to balk at that often quoted passage in the *Topographia Hiberniae* written by Giraldus Cambrensis between the years 1185 and 1188:[3]

There is in the northern and farther part of Ulster, namely in Kenelcunill [Tír Conaill], a certain people which is accustomed to consecrate its king with a rite altogether outlandish and abominable. When the whole people of that land has

[1] Loomis, *Celtic Myth*, pp. 215–22, 296–301; Ó Máille, 'Medb Chruachna'; Thurneysen, 'Zur Göttin *Medb*'; O'Rahilly, 'On the origin'; Mac Cana, 'Aspects'; Draak, 'Kingship'.

[2] McCone, 'Fírinne agus Torthúlacht'.

[3] Giraldus Cambrensis, *Topographia Hibernie*, III.25 (ed. O'Meara, pp. 93–4; transl. O'Meara, pp. 109–10). See O'Rahilly, 'On the origin', p. 18, n. 6.

been gathered together in one place, a white mare is brought forward into the middle of the assembly. He who is to be inaugurated, not as a chief, but as a beast, not as a king, but as an outlaw, embraces the animal before all, professing himself to be a beast also. The mare is then killed immediately, cut up in pieces and boiled in water. A bath is prepared for the man afterwards in the same water. He sits in the bath surrounded by all his people, and all, he and they, eat of the meat of the mare which is brought to them. He quaffs and drinks of the broth in which he is bathed, not in any cup, or using his hand, but just dipping his mouth into it round about him. When this unrighteous rite has been carried out, his kingship and dominion have been conferred.

It is now generally agreed that so many parallels to this account can be found in the ritual of other Indo-European peoples that it is out of the question to accuse Giraldus of fabrication.[4] However, his is not an eye-witness account: was his description derived from a literary or oral tradition about a long discontinued rite, or are we to accept that such a ceremony was performed in Tír Conaill in the twelfth century? Two conclusions at least seem indisputable. Giraldus's informants accepted that there were marked regional variations in the manner in which kingship was conferred in twelfth-century Ireland, and they could envisage a pagan survival of this kind in a remote area.

Such scraps of information as can be collected from other sources associate horses to a greater or lesser degree with royal inaugurations in the northern half of Ireland, but not with the installation of the kings of Leinster, the area with which Giraldus himself was most familiar. The second Irish Life of Maedóc of Ferns is a late mediaeval recension, but largely based on a twelfth-century core.[5] It claims an active role, with concomitant privileges, for the coarbs or successors of St Maedóc at the monastic sites of Ferns and Drumlane in the inauguration of the kings of Leinster and Bréifne respectively. The coarb's rights in Leinster were[6]

the suit of the king of Leinster the day he is made king, except his silk shirt and his one spear, and one of his shoes full of silver; and the successor of Aed son of Sétna [Maedóc] to go three times round about him. And if he or his successor shall place the wand (of office) in the hand of the king, he will be preeminent in strength and valour.

The circuit round the king and the handing over of a rod of office are also mentioned for the more northerly kingdom of Bréifne. Here the only difference is the presence of the king's riding-horse:[7]

The horse and the robes of the king of Bréifne on his coronation day to be given to the family of Maedóc, or else ten horses [*or* 'marks'?] or twenty kine. Maedóc's *Brec* [a house-shaped shrine] to be carried round the king, to pledge him thereby

[4] Schröder, 'Ein altirischer Krönungsritus'; Puhvel, 'Aspects of equine functionality'; Byrne, *Irish Kings*, pp. 17–18.

[5] Doherty, 'The Historical Value'.

[6] Plummer, *Bethada*, II.249.

[7] *Ibid.*, II.196–7.

to do right between man and man, whether weak or powerful ... twelve coarbs of Maedóc to go round him in procession ... and let O'Duffey give the wand (of office) to the king of Bréifne in honour of Maedóc. And this wand must be cut from the hazel of Maedóc in Sescenn Uairbeoil in Leinster, which place is (now) called Disert Maedócc (Maedóc's hermitage).

In the Life of Colmán son of Luachán, apparently composed shortly after the unearthing of this saint's relics in 1122, in the reign of Murchadh Ó Maoilsheachlainn, king of Meath, a strange inauguration-rite for the kings of Tara includes the use of a horsewhip:[8]

Colman, however, said to [Maelumae son of Forannán] '... it shall be a successor of thine who proclaims the King of Tara till Doom ...' (viz. 'The kingship and headship of Ireland to thee, O king!' 'Uodergc(?) upon thee,' saith the King as he makes a cast at him, 'hast thou brought Conall Guthbinn with thee?' And thus it should be done, the king to be at the foot of the Pillar-stone of the Hostages above, and the man of the Hui Forannan upon the flag-stone below, an open horsewhip in his hand so as to save himself as best he can from the cast, provided that he do not step forth from the flag-stone). 'The king who shall slay [*or* "wound"] a descendant of thine shall decay or die an early death, unless his steed and his dress be given to him for it.'

In a tract on the inauguration of the kings of Connacht, at least parts of which seem based on a twelfth- or thirteenth-century original,[9] the king's horse plays a slightly larger role in the proceedings:[10]

It is Ó Maol Chonaire [the *ollamh* of history] who is entitled to give the rod of kingship into his hand at his inauguration, and none of the nobles of Connacht has a right to be with him on the mound save Ó Maol Chonaire who inaugurates him and Ó Connachtáin who keeps the gate of the mound. His horse and his raiment to the coarb of Dá Chonna, and he shall mount that horse from Ó Conchubhair's back.

The picture here presented of the Ó Conchobhair king stooping, or on all fours, with an ecclesiastic standing on his back, brings us closer to Giraldus's king, 'professing himself to be a beast also'. Its possible significance is underlined by a mid-thirteenth-century elegy for the chiefs Maghnus and Eachmharcach Ó Catháin, in which the poet recollects playing at inaugurations with Eachmharcach when they were both children:[11]

We used to give the chieftainship, in our sports
To him, when high-spirited youths,
We and the king on a mound which he disgraced not,
Going thrice around it [*or* "around him"].

8 Meyer, *Betha Colmáin*, p. 73.
9 Simms, ' "Gabh umad a Fheidhlimidh" ', pp. 140–1.
10 Dillon, 'The inauguration', p. 197.
11 'Fearghal Og Mac an Bhaird's poem on the Battle of Dun' [*Leacht carad i gcath Bhriain*], qq. 13–16 (ed. O'Donovan, p. 409).

Until he would take me on his back
I used to continue to shed tears after him,
At all times I was the rider,
Our horse was [always] Eachmarcach.

His stipend (*a thuarastal*) to me was always coming to us
Just as if we were his *oireacht*.[12]
He had for me as much as for two.
Far are we for ever again from our gambols!

I used to go with a poem on his manly form,
As if it were [the poem] of my ollamhship;
He gave much for my poem to me,
Although that which I made was not a poem!

No doubt the second verse here quoted could allude merely to a pair of children playing pickaback, but the other quatrains in this passage show the mimic king being inaugurated, receiving the homage of his vassals and a ceremonial praise-poem from his *ollamh* so that both the context and the parallel with the Connacht inauguration-tract suggest a half-way house between Giraldus's account and the expurgated ceremonies found elsewhere, in which the king mimed the role of a horse, however briefly, with his chief poet standing or sitting on his back.

It will be seen that there was some competition for the role of inaugurator between the secular learned class, namely the *ollamhain* who installed Ó Conchobhair and Ó Catháin, and the ecclesiastics, or hereditary tenants of Church-lands, who are said to inaugurate the kings of Bréifne and Tara. In the case of Leinster, a blessing awaits the king *if* he should be inaugurated by Maedóc's successor, but this is not stated to be the invariable practice. The anxiety of churchmen to play a key-role in twelfth-century inaugurations is matched by a growth in specifically christian and even clerical maxims in Middle Irish texts purporting to give advice to kings. In the Old Irish period the earliest of such tracts, *Audacht Morainn* (*ca* A.D. 700), is notable for its lack of christian allusions. Peace, prosperity, and fertility of cattle and crops are brought about not through God's providence but through the ruler's truth: 'For he whom the living do not glorify with blessings is not a true ruler'.[13] In the ninth-century *Tecosca Cormaic*, prosperity marks God's favour towards the righteous king: 'for it is through the truth of a ruler that God gives all that'.[14] However, it is left to the Middle Irish poems in the Book of

[12] O'Donovan's text has *oighrighacht*, 'heirs', at this point, one of a number of slips which identifies his source as Dublin, Trinity College, MS. 1291, by the eighteenth-century scribe Aodh Ó Dálaigh. Ó Dálaigh's exemplar however was the late seventeenth-century manuscript, Dublin, Trinity College, MS. 1381, and both this and another late seventeenth-century version, London, British Library, MS. Add. 40766, read *oireacht* in this quatrain. On the term itself, see below, pp. 64–5, 67–70.

[13] *Audacht Morainn* (Redaction B), § 59 (ed. Kelly, p. 19).

[14] *Tecosca Cormaic*, § 1, line 46 (ed. & transl. Meyer, *The Instructions*, pp. 4–5).

Leinster to make narrowly ecclesiastical suggestions as to how the king should earn God's blessing:[15]

> Leave the churches untaxed ... Do not plot treachery, do not sue the clergy; if you be a just prince all will be well during your time.
>
> Purchase the goodly mast, and heat from the sun; purchase corn and milk, as every famous king has done.

It is noticeable that the poem here quoted, *Cert cech ríg co réil*, and its companion, *Diambad messe bad ri réil*, lay great stress on the exaction of hostages by the king to make his power fully effective; they advise him to exercise this power in ruthless taxation of all laymen, high or low, and in enforcing law and order: 'though it were your son who opposed you he should not be spared by you';[16] 'a hard fetter on the foot, and a strong gallows nearby(?), a filthy pit, ooze, a prison with its back to a ditch ... it is these that cause peace during a gracious king's reign'.[17]

This combination of piety and severity is faithfully mirrored in the Connacht annalist's obituary for his king, Cathal Croibhdhearg Ó Conchobhair (*ob.* 1224):[18]

> the king most feared and dreaded on every hand in Ireland; the king who carried out most plunderings and burning against Galls and Gaels who opposed him; the king who was the fiercest and harshest towards his enemies that ever lived; the king who most blinded, killed and mutilated rebellious and disaffected subjects; the king who best established peace and tranquillity of all the kings of Ireland; the king who built most monasteries and houses for religious communities; the king who most comforted clerks and poor men with food and fire on the floor of his own habitation; the king whom of all the kings of Ireland God made most perfect in every good quality; the king on whom God most bestowed fruit and increase and crops.

Identical qualities are singled out for praise in a bardic ode to the same Cathal, *Táinic an Croibhdhearg go Cruachain.*[19] The annalists also praise Cathal Croibhdhearg for his marital chastity and for the introduction of parochial tithes during his reign. This is not just a king who reflects and sustains the natural order by a kind of sympathetic magic, as in pagan times, nor even a king who does the will of God, but one who obeys God's will as interpreted by the Church-hierarchy. It is surely significant that the poem *Cert cech ríg co réil* is anachronistically represented as addressed by Fothad na Canóine to Aed Oirdnide (*ob.* 819), a Cenél nEogain high king whose nickname, 'the ordained', suggests that he had

[15] 'Cert cech ríg co réil', qq. 15–16 (ed. O'Donoghue, p. 263).
[16] 'Advice to a Prince' [*Diambad messe bad ri réil*], q. 5 (ed. O'Donoghue, p. 51).
[17] 'Cert cech ríg co réil', qq. 43, 44 (ed. O'Donoghue, p. 271).
[18] AConn 1224.2.
[19] 'A poem by Gilbride Macnamee' [*Tainic an Croibhdherg go Crúachain*], qq. 31–6 (ed. Quiggin, p. 174).

been anointed at the hands of an ecclesiastic, perhaps in imitation of the carolingian kings and even of the Emperor Charlemagne himself.[20] Such ritual innovations were merely the outward sign of an intended change in the king's role. Instead of simply representing his people in their external relations, both human and divine, the ecclesiastical politicians wished to see their ruler actively guiding the internal affairs of his kingdom, upholding the moral order by a system of rewards and punishments, acting – in short – as the 'secular arm of the Church'. The Continental origins of such a theocratic theory of kingship, and its direct link with the physical presence of the Irish kings at the reforming synods of their Church in the twelfth century, are made crystal-clear in a letter from Lanfranc, archbishop of Canterbury, to the high king Toirdhealbhach Ó Briain, written in 1074:[21]

> God grants no greater mercy to a land than when he raises to the government of souls and bodies those who love peace and justice, and most especially when he entrusts the kingdoms of this world to the rule of good kings. For hence comes peace, strife is calmed and (to include everything in brief) observance of the Christian religion is made firm ... Being mindful, therefore, of the divine judgement at which you must render account to God of the kingdom he has entrusted to you, command the bishops and religious to come together in unity, show your own presence with your nobles to this holy assembly and strive to rid your kingdom of all these evil customs.

The relations between the high kings Brian Bóroimhe and the church of Armagh,[22] and Muircheartach Mac Lochlainn and the head of the Columban *familia*,[23] demonstrate the interdependence of Church and king in the process of innovation and the centralisation of power taking place in Ireland from the tenth century to the twelfth. This link, however, was broken when the Irish Church turned to Henry II at the time of the Norman invasion, and in the minds of the laity older pagan traditions of kingship died hard.

In 1224, the year when Cathal Croibhdhearg died, a bardic poem to celebrate the succession of his son Aodh – *Congaibh róm t'aghaidh, a Aodh* – associates the fertility of the land under his rule not with his justice but with his royal blood, with the legitimacy of his claim to the kingship of Connacht. The aristocratic names of the high kings and provincial kings from whom he is descended are contrasted with the ancestors of the Norman usurpers, 'William', 'Henry', and 'Hubock' (little Hubert). Aodh is the prophesied king of Ireland, foretold in the vision of St Bearchán.[24] In point of fact, the text of prophetic verses attributed to Bearchán has been preserved in late manuscripts, and one

[20] Byrne, *Irish Kings*, pp. 159, 256, 262.
[21] Watt, *The Church in Medieval Ireland*, pp. 5–7.
[22] Gwynn, 'Brian in Armagh', pp. 41–50.
[23] AU 1161, 1162, 1164, 1166.
[24] 'Con*n*uimh rom taigh*idh* a Aodh' (Dublin, Royal Irish Academy, MS. 490, p. 162) – qq. 15, 16, 20.

section does indeed allude to an 'Aodh Eanghach' from Cruachan who will win many victories and inflict slaughter on both the Irish and the foreigners.[25] Giraldus Cambrensis, in his *Expugnatio Hibernica*, refers to a prophecy of Bearchán that 'almost all the English will be dislodged from Ireland by a king who will come from the lonely mountains of Patrick, and on the night of Our Lord's day will overrun a castle in the wooded region of Uí Fhaeláin'.[26] Some such popular expectation of a messianic king called Aodh, who would deliver his country from the Norman invaders, apparently lies behind a cryptic entry in the Annals of Ulster and of Loch Cé under the year 1214: 'in this year, moreover, appeared the false Aedh, who was called "the Aider" ' (*in Cabhortach*).

It is of considerable interest, however, that the poem *Congaibh róm t'aghaidh a Aodh* distinguishes carefully between the prophecies attributed to saints and other more sinister prognostications ascribed here to fortune-tellers and soothsaying women. The author implores Aodh Ó Conchobhair to pay no heed to these, but to remain at one with the King of Heaven. The allegation that there were some overtly pagan prophecies about 'Aodh Eanghach' in circulation seems to be borne out by references in later bardic odes to the foretellings of 'Flann File', although no written text of these survives. From these allusions it can be deduced that Flann the Poet promised that a messiah bearing the name of Aodh (*an tAodh ainm*) would be proclaimed by Nature herself, bursting forth in superabundant fertility. Druids and prophetesses would identify him by signs in the sky. The Lia Fáil would cry out under his feet. He would rebuild the walls of Tara, expel the foreigners from Ireland, and celebrate three *aonaigh*,[27] presumably a garbled reference to the legendary 'three noble meetings' of the men of Ireland, the *Mórdháil Uisnigh, Aonach Tailltin*, and *Feis Teamhra*.[28] One of the later odes containing such allusions is careful to deprecate the paganism of the original prophecy: 'it is not the Lia Fáil which prophesies our shepherd but God, for He alone is our true prophet'.[29]

This disclaimer comes in a fourteenth-century poem. In the early thirteenth century it seems that there were still some remnants of actual paganism in Irish society. Giraldus Cambrensis gives a credible report of islanders off the coast of Connacht who had 'heard nothing of Christ and knew nothing about him'.[30] More strikingly, Maol Pádraig Ó Scannail, a reforming Dominican friar and bishop of Raphoe, complained to the

25 'The Prophecy of Berchán' [*Airis bic, a mheic bhic bháin*], qq. 72–80 (ed. Anderson).

26 II.34 (edd. Scott & Martin, p. 233).

27 Quiggin, 'O'Conor's house at Cloonfree' [*An tú arís, a ráith Teamhrach*?], qq. 1, 8, 14, 37–41; McKenna, *Aithdioghluim Dána*, no. 4 [*An deimhin anos teacht don tairrngire*?], qq. 1, 2, 14; no. 20 [*Lá i dTeamhraigh ag Toirrdhealbhach*], q. 2.

28 Binchy, 'The Fair', p. 113.

29 McKenna, *Aithdioghluim Dána*, no. 4, q. 14.

30 *Topographia Hibernie*, III.26 (ed. O'Meara, p. 95).

pope in 1256 that some laymen in his diocese worshipped idols and infected various of the faithful in those parts with their errors.[31] The diocese of Raphoe was coextensive with the kingdom of Tír Conaill, named by Giraldus Cambrensis as the scene of the extremely primitive inauguration-rite quoted at the beginning of this chapter. In 1258, during the episcopacy of Ó Scannail, Gofraidh Ó Domhnaill, the king of Tír Conaill, died and was succeeded by his younger brother, Domhnall Óg. A bardic poem addressed to Domhnall Óg states that he was made king in the church at Raphoe,[32] that is, in the cathedral, under the eye of the bishop.

On the face of it, this seems a deliberate attempt to break away from the traditional inauguration-site and the customs associated with it. The O'Donnell family originally came from the area around Kilmacrenan, and later records indicate that this was where their kings were normally inaugurated,[33] at a Columban monastic site situated on comparatively flat land, out of which the great Rock of Doon juts up unexpectedly, in its general configuration looking not unlike the Rock of Cashel. Beside it is a prestigious holy well, apparently the same as that called *Tobar Eithne* in the sixteenth century, whose waters ran blood whenever an Ó Domhnaill was about to die a violent death.[34] In this case 'Eithne' is explained as being Colmcille's mother, but in the saga-literature the name Eithne occurs more than once as that of a more or less thinly disguised sovereignty-goddess.[35] In the early nineteenth century a powerful fairy was thought to live at the foot of the Rock itself.[36] Interestingly, oral tradition is divided as to whether the Uí Dhomhnaill were in fact inaugurated in the open air on this rock, or in the church-building nearby.[37] The Life of Aodh Ruadh Ó Dhomhnaill, written in the early seventeenth century by Lughaidh Ó Cléirigh, states that Ó Domhnaill was inaugurated in the church by the erenagh, or hereditary administrator of the church-lands, Ó Firghil:[38]

> and he performed the ceremony of naming him in the legal way that was the custom of his nation hitherto, and he called him Ó Domhnaill. The clergy of the church proceeded to supplicate the Lord on his behalf, and to sing psalms and hymns in honour of Christ and [St] Colum of whom we spoke, for the success of his sovereignty, as was usual with them.

In the case of Aodh Ruadh, this liturgical form of inauguration may not

31 *Pontificia Hibernica*, ed. Sheehy, II.251–2.
32 'Ceathrar is fhéile fuair Flann', in *The Poems of Giolla Brighde Mac Con Midhe*, ed. Williams, no. ix, q. 36.
33 AU 1129.4; Armstrong, 'The shrine', p. 391; AFM 1461, 1505, 1592, 1603.
34 *Betha Colaim Chille*, edd. O'Kelleher & Schoepperle, p. 111.
35 Mac Cana, 'Aspects', pt 1, pp. 86–8.
36 Ponsonby, 'Tour', p. 286.
37 Archdall, *Monasticon* (edd. Moran *et al.*), I.201.
38 *Beatha Aodha Ruaidh*, ed. Walsh, I.41.

have been exceptional. Dom Philip O'Sullevan Beare[39] indicates that it was common practice to combine the conferring of chieftainship with the celebration of mass in the late sixteenth century, a time when the influence of the Counter-Reformation was at its height. On the other hand, the Church-inauguration of an Ó Domhnaill in 1258 has no recorded parallel and the decision to locate the ceremony in the diocesan cathedral was to be abandoned by later generations. The hymns sung in 1592 to Christ and St Columba for the success of the king's sovereignty are described as customary, and it is possible that, when the Uí Dhomhnaill returned to their traditional inauguration-site of Kilmacrenan, they returned to the church rather than to the Rock, and continued to use an expurgated inauguration-rite in which the ecclesiastical elements introduced under Bishop Ó Scannail's influence were maintained from the mid-thirteenth century to the late sixteenth. At any rate, the scanty evidence available to us indicates a historical break in the thirteenth century, followed by a revival of the older tradition in a modified form.

Just such a break in the thirteenth century, followed by a modified revival, is suggested by evidence relating to the Uí Chonchobhair of Connacht. In 1293 Aodh son of Eoghan Ó Conchobhair was 'made king by the Justiciar and by the King of England's men'.[40] During his subsequent reign certain rival O'Conors are said from time to time to have 'assumed the kingship', taken hostages of the country, or received submissions.[41] None of these phrases necessarily excludes a ceremonial inauguration, but in 1310 there is in the annalist's statement an implication that the full rites had not been performed for a considerable period:[42]

Fedlimid mac Aeda meic Eogain was proclaimed in a style as royal, as lordly and as public as any of his race from the time of Brian son of Eochu Muigmedoin till that day. And when Fedlimid mac Aeda meic Eogain had married the province of Connacht his foster-father [Mac Diarmata] waited upon him during the night in the manner remembered by the old men and recorded in the old books.

The prominent role here assigned to Mac Diarmada occurs again in annal-entries for the years 1461 and 1488, when the Mac Diarmada of the day is said to inaugurate Ó Conchobhair as chief by putting on his shoe.[43] A prose tract on the 'Rights of Mac Diarmada', which in its present form cannot antedate the mid-fourteenth century, states categorically that 'no king is entitled to be inaugurated king of Connaught except the king who is inaugurated by Mac Diarmada',[44] a claim which is repeated in a fifteenth-century bardic poem.[45] On the other hand, a Middle Irish poem on the

[39] O'Donovan, *The Genealogies*, p. 439.
[40] AConn 1293.3.
[41] AConn 1293.4, 1296.2, 1309.2.
[42] AConn 1310.7.
[43] AConn and ADF 1461; AFM 1488.
[44] Ní Shéaghdha, 'The Rights', p. 164.
[45] 'Dá mhac rugadh do rígh Connacht', in *Aithdioghluim Dána*, ed. McKenna, no. 31, qq. 17–18.

rights of MacDiarmada, attributed to the twelfth-century(?) Aodh OllbharrÓ Carthaigh,[45a] makes no mention of Mac Diarmada's role as inaugurator, and in the prose tract on the making of the kings of Connacht[45b] the function of conferring kingship clearly belongs to Ó Maoilchonaire, the *ollamh* of history, while Mac Diarmada is merely listed among the by-standers. In other words, it was only after *ca* 1300 that the leading part in the ceremony of inauguration passed from the king of Connacht's hereditary *ollamh* to his chief vassal, whose support was of key political importance to the Uí Chonchobhair during the later middle ages.

A similar modification of the traditional rite to adapt it to political reality is said to have taken place in the fourteenth or fifteenth century in the customary installation of the head of the Mac Suibhne family. The early sixteenth-century tract *Craobhsgaoileadh Chlainne Suibhne* tells of a succession-struggle after the death of Toirdhealbhach Caoch Mac Suibhne in 1399:[46]

It was the successors of Columcille who used to inaugurate MacSuibhne in Iona as long as they remained in Scotland, but after their coming to Ireland ... they used to give the task of inauguration to Ó Firghil [erenagh of Kilmacrenan] ... but on this occasion Toirrdhealbhach [Ruadh] conceded whatever he asked to Ó Domhnaill for his making him chieftain in preference to these kinsmen of his.

The historical accuracy of this account is less important that the mere fact that an early sixteenth-century historian in Tír Conaill could envisage the role of king-maker being removed from the hands of a hereditary churchman and transferred for political reasons to a secular chief. Leaders of the Mic Shuibhne continued thereafter to be instituted at Kilmacrenan by their overlord, Ó Domhnaill.[47] In the same way Ó Catháin, who in the early thirteenth century was probably inaugurated by his own *ollamh* of poetry,[47a] by the end of the sixteenth century was regularly installed by his overlord, Ó Néill.[48]

With this trend in the later middle ages towards inauguration by a secular chief, whether a leading vassal or an overlord, there came a change of emphasis in the ritual by which power was conferred. In most of the earlier descriptions key-importance was attached to the action of handing over the 'rod of kingship' (*slat na ríghe*), and the stipulation in the case of the king of Bréifne that this rod should be 'cut from the hazel of Maedóc in Sescenn Uairbeoil' suggests a connexion between these rods and the sacred trees which grew at traditional inauguration-sites until the twelfth century.[49]

[45a] Cited below, p. 133, n. 33.
[45b] Cited above, p. 23.
[46] Walsh, *Leabhar Chlainne Suibhne*, p. 51.
[47] *Ibid.*; AFM 1461; O'Grady *et al.*, *Catalogue*, I.386.
[47a] See above, pp. 23–4.
[48] *CSPI 1606–8*, pp. 155–6.
[49] Above, pp. 22–3; AFM 981, 982, 1051, 1099, 1111, 1143; Lucas, 'The sacred trees', pp. 25–6.

In the fifteenth and sixteenth centuries, although the practice of handing over a rod was continued, it was no longer called 'the rod of kingship'. An elegy composed in 1580 refers to Mac Suibhne as receiving *in slait tigiornais*, 'the rod of lordship', from Ó Domhnaill.[50] More significantly, two fifteenth-century bardic odes speak of *an tslat sheilbhe*, 'the rod of possession'.[51] In other contexts the *slat seilbhe* or *craobh seilbhe* was a twig handed to the new owner of an estate as livery of seisin, the symbolic transference of legal ownership.[52] It was precisely as formal evidence of seisin that this part of the inauguration-rite was cited in the Dublin Court of Chancery in 1592:[53]

MacCartie delivered [O Donovan] a Rod wherefore he entered to all the Lordshipp and Lands, and was seised without interruption these eight years past, as was and is for him lawful.

Seen in this narrow light, the ceremony of handing over the rod created not a king, but a landlord.

The threefold circuit round the king seems also to have lost something of its mystical or quasi-religious content and to have become more straightforwardly political. In the Life of Maedóc, clerics carry the saint's shrine in a circle round the king of Bréifne, and this ceremony is explicitly associated with the *Deiseal*, the traditional right-handed turn which brought luck and blessings.[54] In the thirteenth-century poem on Uí Chatháin, the future poet goes three times around the play-king.[55] The poets, to whom some remnants of the druidic function remained, were, like the churchmen, traditionally empowered to bestow a blessing. However, there is a tract on the inauguration of Ó Dubhda inserted into the Great Book of Lecan 'in a beautiful hand very nearly as ancient as the original',[56] thus dating to the late fifteenth or early sixteenth century. Here it is Ó Caomháin, a principal vassal, who walks three times round the new chief after his inauguration, and the order in which the associated privileges are listed makes it seem probable that Ó Caomháin was introduced into this function at a late stage, between the king and his *ollamh* of history, Mac Firbhisigh – that the sub-chief has displaced the chronicler:[57]

[the privilege of] first drinking [at the banquet] was given to Ó Caomháin by Ó Dubhda, and Ó Caomháin was not to drink until he first presented [the drink] to

[50] O'Grady *et al.*, *Catalogue*, I.386.

[51] 'Máirg danab oighrecht Éire' (q. 27) in the Book of O Conor Don, fo 129v; 'Do briseadh riaghail ríogh Sacsann' (q. 12) in *Aithdioghluim Dána*, ed. McKenna, no. 38.

[52] Plummer, *Vitae Sanctorum Hiberniae*, I.civ; O'Donovan, *The Tribes and Customs*, pp. 8–9; McKenna, *Philip Bocht*, p. 21, line 4.

[53] O'Donovan, *The Genealogies*, p. 440.

[54] Ferguson, 'On the ceremonial turn'.

[55] Above, p. 23.

[56] O'Donovan, *The Genealogies*, p. 440.

[57] *Ibid.*; Mac Cana, 'An archaism', p. 181.

the poet, that is, to MacFirbis; also the weapons, battle-dress and steed of Ó Dubhda after his nomination [were given] to Ó Caomháin, and the weapons and battle-dress of Ó Caomháin to MacFirbis.

A similar process may have occurred in the case of the shoe-ceremony. When Mac Diarmada placed a shoe on Ó Conchobhair's foot in the fifteenth century, or when Ó Catháin threw a shoe over Ó Néill's head in the sixteenth century,[58] the principal result was to demonstrate that the new chief had the full support of his most powerful vassal. However, in the case of Ó Néill's inauguration, the traditional privilege of throwing a shoe over the chief's head was also claimed by a less powerful family, Uí Ágáin,[59] whose importance derived from long association with the inauguration-site itself. In the eleventh and twelfth centuries they had the office of hereditary seneschal (*reachtaire*) at what was presumably then a royal residence at Tulach Óg.[60] Until the early seventeenth century they continued to occupy the hill of inauguration and at least a thousand acres of the surrounding land.[61] Their claim to throw the shoe may therefore stem from an earlier period than that of Ó Catháin, whose temporal power was the clearest argument for his holding the privilege. The rite of the single shoe has itself been seen as originating in pagan times, with analogies throughout the Indo-European world and beyond.[62]

The cumulative effect of such minor changes in the rite is to demonstrate that, although the concept of inauguration as a marriage with the goddess of sovereignty continued to be set forth by the bardic poets in a surprisingly detailed and articulate form well into the seventeenth century,[63] it had long since become a mere poetic conceit. The symbolism of marriage loses its force when the ceremony is no longer performed by a member of a priestly or druidic caste. Instead, during the fifteenth and sixteenth centuries a new reverence was attached not to the vestigial rites of sacral kingship but to the chieftain's surname. Until A.D. 1300 annalistic texts invariably use the words *ríoghadh*, 'an enkinging', and *oirdneadh*, 'an ordination', to denote the conferring of royal authority, but after 1400 one meets phrases like *gairm anma*, 'the proclamation of the name', *ord an anma*, 'the ritual of the name'.[64] The details of

[58] Above, p. 29; *CSPI 1606–8*, pp. 155–6; Hayes-McCoy, 'The making', p. 91.
[59] Perrott, *The Chronicle of Ireland* (ed. Wood), p. 106.
[60] AU 1056.7, 1103.4; AFM 1122. On the term *reachtaire* see below, pp. 79–82.
[61] Hill, *An Historical Account*, p. 288 and n. 124; Hayes-McCoy, *Ulster*, plate V; O'Donovan, *The Genealogies*, p. 432 and n. a.
[62] Killeen, 'Fear an Énais'; Mac Cana, 'The *topos*', pp. 165–6.
[63] As in the poem 'Malairt chrotha ar chrích Luighne' (*The Book of O'Hara*, ed. McKenna, no. xxv).
[64] AFM 1445; O'Donovan, *The Genealogies*, p. 443; *Beatha Aodha Ruaidh*, ed. Walsh, I.40. See also McC 1437.6; AConn 1461.23. The fourteenth century was a period of transition when inauguration was expressed by the verb of proclamation combined with the title rather than the surname, viz *an ghairm*

such a ritual are found in the passage inserted in the Great Book of Lecan:[65]

it is not lawful ever to nominate the O Dubhda until O Caomhain and MacFirbis [first] pronounce the name, and until MacFirbis brings the body of the rod over the head of O Dubhda; and after O Caomhain and MacFirbis every clergyman and comharba of a church and every bishop, and every chief of a district, pronounces the name.

The traditional elements found here, the rod of kingship and the active participation of an *ollamh*, even the open-air inauguration-site, were apparently not essential. In special circumstances the mere calling aloud of the candidate's surname by an authorised person in the presence of witnesses could constitute a valid installation. In Ó Cléirigh's Life of Aodh Ruadh Ó Domhnaill, Ó Néill and Ó Domhnaill disagree during a banquet as to which of two rival candidates should be confirmed in the MagUidhir chieftaincy:[66]

O Domhnaill takes the cup from the butler's hand and looked around ... and did not see Cúchonnacht Óg in the house ... he ordered him to be called to him immediately ... when Cúchonnacht was seated, he then drank the cup and raised it in his hand for a space over him, and called him by the title of Maguidhir [*dogara an anmain as Maguidhir*] in presence of the chief men of the province generally.

This simple action is subsequently called an inauguration (*oirdneadh*).

Dom Philip O'Sullevan Beare, a younger contemporary of Ó Cléirigh, tells us that a new chief was created Ó Súilleabháin or Ó Raighilligh, etc., by a certain fixed form of words, recited by the inaugurator. He was named by his surname, then proclaimed by the bystanders, and after this ceremony it was no longer the custom to address him by his own baptismal name, the surname in itself serving as a formal title like marquis, earl, viscount, or baron.[67] Annal-entries, and miscellaneous documents of the fifteenth and sixteenth centuries, fully bear out Dom Philip's account. In 1402 Aughuistín Magraidhin noted that 'Maol Mórdha O Raighilligh was made "Ó Raighilligh" '(*O Raighilli do dheanamh do Mael Mora h. Raigilli*),[68] and this formula is found in

---

ríogh – see AI 1310.2; AConn 1315.2; ALC 1315; AU 1359.

65 O'Donovan, *The Genealogies*, pp. 441–2.

66 *Beatha Aodha Ruaidh*, ed. Walsh, I.245–7.

67 O'Donovan, *The Genealogies*, p. 439.

68 Ann. Rawl. B.488 (ed. Ó hInnse), 1402.33. Another early occurrence of this formula comes in AU 1461, 'Mac Cathmhail do denum d'Eoghan MacCathmhail'. An isolated instance of the surname Ó Briain used as a title in the early fourteenth century occurs in McC 1306.2, but this seems a fifteenth-century re-wording of the parallel passage in AI 1306.1, where the verb is *do rígad*, the more normal expression for this earlier period.

annalistic texts with increasing frequency as a way of expressing inauguration. The same clear distinction between a man's personal surname and the surname when used as a title of authority is found in the dating clauses of mid-sixteenth-century charters: ***Murchadh Ó Briain 'na Ó Briain an tan so*** ('Murchadh Ó Briain was "Ó Briain" at this time');[69] *Conn Ó Néill dob Iarla 7 dob Ó Néill an tan sin* ('Conn Ó Néill was Earl and "Ó Néill" at that time').[70]

Dom Philip's other assertion, that chiefs were no longer called by their baptismal names after inauguration, is also supported by annalistic usage. From the earliest period in which surnames were generally used in Ireland, the ruling member of the family was often designated simply 'Ua Canannáin', 'Ua Conchobuir', 'Ua Riain', 'Ua Muireadaigh',[71] although such a man might also be called by his title of *rí* or *taoiseach* or by his baptismal name. However, in the fifteenth and sixteenth centuries chieftains are identified in annalistic texts by a curious formula giving their surnames first, followed by their christian names in parenthesis. This form was used only when the title of *rí* or *tighearna* had been omitted, as became almost invariably the case in the sixteenth century. Entries from two years picked at random from the Annals of Connacht, one from the fourteenth and one from the fifteenth century, should sufficiently illustrate the marked contrast in usage:

> [1366] ... Cathal Mag Flannchaid, chieftain of Dartry, was killed ... Cormac Donn Mag Carthaig, king of the Uí Cairpri and the Uí Echach Muman, was treacherously killed ... Conchobar Ó Conchobair, king of Ciarraige Luachra, was killed ... Seoán Mac Goisdelb, lord of Sliab Luga, died ...

> [1489] ... O Neill, Énrí son of Eogan, died. Ó Baigill, Toirrdelbach son of Niall Ruad, died. Ó Fialáin, Eogan, [died] this year ... Mac Uigilin, Seincin Ruad, was killed ... Sefraid Mac Gilla Patraic king of Ossory died ... Ó Cerbaill, Seán son of Maelruanaid, died.

The same contrast as between the fourteenth and sixteenth centuries, from the use of christian name, surname and title, to the use of surname alone, is found in the correspondence of the chieftains themselves. When writing to King Richard II in 1395, the Irish leaders subscribed themselves 'Nellanus O Nell, Princeps Hibernicorum Ultonie, Nellanus iuvenis O Neyll, Gubernator Hibernicorum Ultonie, Tatheus Makarthy, Princeps Hibernicorum Dessemonie, Berandus O Brien, Princeps Tothmonie, Maurichius MacGyngussa, Dominus de Oveach, Magnellus O Kahan, sue nacionis capitaneus',[72] and so forth. However, the sixteenth-century Seán an Diomais Ó Néill signed letters written in both Irish and Latin with the phrase *misi Ó Néill* ('I, Ó Néill'), and his successors followed his example

[69] Hardiman, 'Ancient Irish deeds', p. 57.
[70] Ronan, 'Some mediaeval documents', p. 239.
[71] These examples all come from AU 1103.
[72] Curtis, *Richard II*, pp. 68, 75, 90, 131, 132, 143.

when in their less submissive moods.[73] The significance of this employment of the surname as a title is underlined in the Act of Attainder passed against Seán Ó Néill in 1569:[74]

> The name of O Neill, in the judgements of the uncivil people of the realm, doth carry in itself so great a sovereignty as they suppose that all the lords and people of Ulster should rather live in servitude to that name than in subjection to the crown of England.

Indeed it was said of Seán's successor, Aodh Ó Néill, earl of Tyrone, that 'he has evermore had a thirsty desire to be called O Neale – a name more in price to him than to be intituled Caesar'.[75]

From 1542 onwards the English government had made repeated attempts to ban or suppress this title of 'Ó Néill' and the inauguration-ceremonies connected with it.[76] It was recognised as a mark of incipient rebellion when in 1595 Sir Henry Bagenal reported of Hugh, or Aodh Mór Ó Néill, earl of Tyrone, that 'the Traitor [is] gone to the Stone to receave that name'.[77] During the course of the Nine Years' War the revival of inauguration-rites and the assumption of the unadorned surname as a mark of authority became a hallmark of insurrection for many other chiefs in the Irish confederacy.[78] After the defeat of the Irish at Kinsale in 1602, when the Lord Deputy, Mountjoy, was ravaging Ó Néill's lands in Tír Eoghain, he visited the site of Tulach Óg and smashed the stone inauguration-chair there.[79] If we contrast this official attitude with the willingness of the Dublin Court of Chancery to accept the handing over of the 'rod of ownership' as evidence of seisin in 1592,[80] it would seem that the essential concept of sovereignty, of an authority which could challenge the rule of Queen Elizabeth, had been transferred from the rod to the 'stone' and the 'name'.

The idea that the new king should stand or sit on a stone throne, situated in the open air and sometimes at the foot of a sacred tree, is apparently of extreme antiquity, dating back to the period of a common Indo-European language and culture. Versions of this practice have been noted in India and Carinthia, as well as in Scotland and Ireland.[81] In Irish written sources, however, the emphasis is normally placed on the hill or mound of inauguration rather than on the stone itself. The *Lia Fáil* at Tara is the only inauguration-stone to be mentioned before the fifteenth

73 Hore, 'Facsimiles'; O'Donovan, 'Original letters'.
74 Hayes-McCoy, 'The making', p. 89.
75 Brewer & Bullen, *Calendar of the Carew Manuscripts*, III.107.
76 Hayes-McCoy, 'The making', pp. 89–90.
77 *CSPI 1592–6*, p. 386.
78 Brewer & Bullen, *Calendar of the Carew Manuscripts*, III.136; *Beatha Aodha Ruaidh*, ed. Walsh, I.114–18.
79 Moryson, *An Itinerary*, III.205–6.
80 Above, p. 31.
81 Auboyer,'Le caractère', p. 182; Lynch, *Cambrensis Eversus* (ed. Kelly), III.345 (cap. xxx); Martin, *A Description* (ed. Macleod), p. 273.

century. Then we hear of *Leac na Ríogh*, 'the stone of the kings', at Tulach Óg where Eoghan Ó Néill was made 'king of the province [of Ulster]' in 1432.[82] By 1602 three flat stones had been leant against the back and sides of this rock to form a stone chair.[83] Another stone, *Leac Mic Eochadha*, is named by Keating as the inauguration-site of the Uí Cheinnsealaigh,[84] and further such stones at other sites have in modern times been identified with greater or lesser reliability by the evidence of oral tradition or seventeenth-century surveys.[85]

Whatever the function of the stone throne in pagan prehistory, we may hazard a guess that it was important in the sixteenth century principally as a symbol of continuous and immemorial tradition, a prescriptive justification of the chieftain's rule independent of the new system of surrender and regrant, of the letters patent by which the English government appointed chiefs as if they merely held an authority delegated from the Crown. Similarly, the calling out of the chieftain's surname and its repetition by his assembled subjects in effect signified their consent to his leadership. It was a formalised election, and as such provided another title to power which did not derive from the permission of the English government.

In this case, however, there was a historical irony involved, for it appears that the cult of the surname as title in the later middle ages, and perhaps even the new emphasis on the proclamation of the name in the rite of inauguration, stemmed from the efforts of an earlier English bureaucracy to eliminate the title of 'king' in these contexts and to treat the Irish leaders simply as heads of their own families.

In the twelfth and thirteenth centuries government-officials had been quite happy to call local Irish rulers *reges* or *reguli*,[86] but after 1300 this ceased to be acceptable, a new attitude presumably having developed as a result of Edward I's general policy of undermining local jurisdictions and promoting the central authority of the Crown. A jury in 1305 alluded retrospectively to Cathal Croibhdhearg's son as 'a certain Irishman, by name Feylym Oconoghur, who called himself King of Connaught'.[87] Appeals to the Irish leaders for assistance during the Bruce wars addressed them as *duces Hibernicorum*.[88] Aodh Reamhar Ó Néill (*ob.* 1366), who used the title *rex Hibernicorum Ultonie*[89] and indeed was acknowledged by the Anglo-Irish chronicler Clyn to occupy the position

[82] AU 1432.

[83] Hayes-McCoy, *Ulster*, plate v.

[84] Keating, *Foras Feasa*, II.1 (edd. Comyn & Dineen, III.14).

[85] For example, Livingstone, *The Fermanagh Story*, p. 410 (and see note); Jones, 'The proclamation stone', p. 46; Frazer, 'The Clandeboy O Neills' stone inauguration chair'.

[86] For example, Giraldus Cambrensis, *Expugnatio Hibernica*, I.30 and 41; 'The Irish pipe roll', edd. Davies & Quinn, pp. 24, 36, 62; *CDI 1171–1251*, nos 1001, 1840, 2716; Gilbert, *Facsimiles*, II, plate lxxiii.

[87] *CJRI 1305–7*, p. 133.

[88] Rymer, *Foedera*, II.1, p. 245; *CCR 1313–18*, p. 218.

[89] Reeves, 'The seal'.

of *rex Ultonie*,[90] was styled merely *Odo Onell de Ulvester* and *Odo Onel de Ultonia* by the English and Irish chanceries.[91] Regularly, during the first half of the fourteenth century, men who were elsewhere described as kings were referred to in official documents by their christian name and surname, sometimes followed by the bald addition 'Irishman' (*hibernicus*).[92]

The term 'chieftain', in French *cheueteyn*, in Latin *capitaneus*, was originally used to describe the heads of the great Anglo-Irish kindreds. Under the year 1287 Friar Clyn writes of Gerald fitzMaurice FitzGerald as *capitaneus Geraldinorum*. In the same entry he refers to the extended kin-group of the FitzGeralds as a 'nation' (*natio*).[93] In 1310 complaint was made in parliament that unruly members of such noble kindreds frequently robbed merchants with impunity, protected by their powerful connexions, and it was decreed that every *cheif de graunt lygnage* should make himself responsible for the punishment of malefactors among his own kinsmen. In 1324 the Anglo-Irish magnates were forced by ecclesiastical sanctions into a solemn undertaking by indenture to arrest law-breakers of their own kindred and surname. The names of those making this promise include the earls of Ulster, Kildare, and Louth, and most of the leading barons of the day, who are referred to in the proceedings of the next year's parliament as *chescune Cheueuteigne de graunt lyneage*.[94]

In this way statute-law sanctioned the jurisdiction of certain magnates over men who were otherwise supposed to be free subjects of the English king. This authority was delegated from the Crown and not intended to rival it, since such malefactors, if arrested in 'the land of peace', were to be handed over to the courts of Common Law. However, it is striking that this power was to be held on a personal rather than on a territorial basis and to extend over not only kinsmen, but retainers and adherents also.

The first evidence which we have of an Irish leader being expressly included in such an arrangement comes in 1350, when the Justiciar Thomas de Rokeby personally supervised the election, by eleven named kinsmen and followers, of Walter Harold as *capitaneus progeniei des Harolds*, followed by that of Seaán Ó Broin as *capitaneus de O Bryns* and Matthew Archbold as *capitaneus de Archbolds*. Each was made to swear that if his kinsmen or adherents robbed the King's lieges they would capture the offender and deliver him to the King's prison on receiving due notice.[95] Next year it was ordained by a great council held at Kilkenny that every *cheueteyn de lynage* who failed to hand over trespassers among his kinsmen, adherents or retainers, should himself be

[90] Clyn's Annals (ed. Butler), *s.a.* 1344.
[91] *CPR 1350–4*, p. 148; *CCH*, p. 62, no. 100.
[92] For example, *CJRI 1305–7*, pp. 133, 502; *CCR 1333–7*, p. 250; *CPR 1348–50*, p. 55.
[93] Clyn's Annals (ed. Butler). See Lydon, 'The middle nation', pp. 3–4.
[94] *Statutes and Ordinances*, ed. Berry, pp. 264–6, 306–8, 312.
[95] Curtis, 'The clan system', pp. 116–17.

imprisoned.[96] In view of Rokeby's agreement with Seaán Ó Broin, this act may have been intended to apply to some or all of the Irish leaders, although when this decree was reenacted among the Statutes of Kilkenny in 1366 it was explicitly confined to the Anglo-Irish: *ascun chieftayne de linadge Engleis*.[97]

The administrative records of the Dublin government are very imperfectly preserved for the later middle ages, but it seems clear that the expression *sue nacionis capitaneus* was first regularly employed by the Irish chancery as a title for Gaelic rulers in the second half of the fourteenth century.[98] The earliest occurrence of this phrase which I have found comes in the Red Book of the Earls of Kildare, under the year 1358, shortly after Rokeby's justiciarship: 'Dominus Comes constituit ipsum Dongho capitaneum nacionis sue'.[99] A little over a decade later, the London chancery referred to Toirdhealbhach Maol Ó Briain as an 'Irishman, appointed by our Court of Ireland captain of his nation', and to Mac Murchadha as 'captain of his nation, claiming to be King of Leinster'.[100] It would seem that for an Irishman to call himself 'king' expressed defiance, but the style 'captain of his nation' suggested a hope that such a man could be held answerable at law for the behaviour of his kinsmen and followers towards the King's lieges.

The first documented use of the surname as title occurs in precisely the samc kind of context. In 1367 Edward III confirmed Diarmaid Mac Murchadha as chief in Leinster with the words: 'Volumus quod idem Dyermyd nomen de Makmorghyth habeat et gerat'.[101] In 1417 a reference to 'the greate O'Nele pretendinge himselfe to bee Kinge of the Irish in Ulster' demonstrates that the unadorned surname was a title acceptable to Anglo-Irish ears, whereas the claim to royalty was not.[102]

Interestingly, by the early fifteenth century the Irish themselves became conscious of a distinction between their own local 'kings' and the heads of evolving nation-states in the rest of Europe. Under the year 1418 in the Annals of Connacht it is carefully pointed out that the Hundred Years' War was being fought between the 'crowned kings' (*etir na rigaib coronta*) of England and France. If the Irish had wished to ape such great ones, there was nothing to prevent them from introducing a coronation-ceremony into their inauguration-rites. Instead, they revised their own titles, using *princeps* as the Latin equivalent of *ri* from the late fourteenth to the mid-fifteenth century,[103] and thereafter gradually

[96] *Statutes and Ordinances*, ed. Berry, p. 378.

[97] *Ibid.*, p. 448.

[98] *CCH*, p. 81, no. 8; p. 84, no. 32; p. 86, nos 21 and 22; p. 87, no. 65; p. 88, no. 82.

[99] *The Red Book*, ed. Mac Niocaill, no. 167.

[100] Curtis, *Calendar*, II.158–9.

[101] Rymer, *Foedera*, III.2, p. 830.

[102] Ellis, *Original Letters*, 2nd S., I.58.

[103] *CCH*, p. 17 no. 84, p. 25 no. 160; Curtis, *Richard II*, pp. 68, 75, 132; White, *Irish Monastic and Episcopal Deeds*, pp. 26–7; Register of Archbishop Prene, Lib. i, fos 182r, 187r, 194r; Register of Archbishop Octavian, Lib. i, fo 18v.

discarding *rí* itself in favour of the style *dominus* or *tighearna*.[104]

This change in title seems to reflect a changing perception of the nature of the authority wielded by an Irish chief. The essence of the old inauguration was a 'kingship-marriage' (*banais ríghe*) whereby the new king was wedded to the *tuath*, that is, to the territory itself and the people who occupied it. He became in this way their protector and representative, but this did not imply either that the land passed into his personal possession or that the majority of the inhabitants was related to him by blood.[105] On the other hand, the inauguration-ritual of the later middle ages, with its stress on the proclamation of the chief's surname and on the handing over of a 'rod of ownership', suggested first that such a man's authority was not based on a king-subject relationship with every inhabitant in the territory but on his position as head of the dominant kin-group or faction, and secondly that on his accession to power he inherited the whole land as demesne, the freeholders who inhabited it being regarded as his tenants. Certainly by the later sixteenth century it had become difficult to make a distinction between a small lordship and a private estate, between a lord's 'tenants' and his 'subjects'. Kenneth Nicholls has put forward the hypothesis 'that late Gaelic society was moving rapidly towards a situation in which all land-rights within a territory would be dependent on the will of its lord'.[106] In 1601 the inhabitants of Inis Eoghain informed Captain Docwra that 'all the country goods and people whatsoever was O'Dogharty's, and whatsoever fell confiscate belonged of right unto him'.[107] A few years later, however, the threat of plantation made the Ulster Irish more wary because, if it were admitted that an Irish chief held his whole lordship in demesne, all would be forfeited to the Crown in the event of his rebellion and attainder. Surveying the county of Fermanagh in 1607, Sir John Davies noted:[108]

> touching the inferior gentlemen and inhabitants, it was not certainly known to the State here whether they were only tenants-at-will to the chief lords, whereof the uncertain cutting which the lords used upon them might be an argument, or whether they were freeholders yielding of right to their chief lord certain rights and services, as many of them do allege, affirming that the Irish cutting was an usurpation and a wrong.

104 In 1410 Toirdhealbhach-an-Fhíona Ó Domhnaill is described as *dominus Conallie* (Register of Archbishop Fleming, fo 32v); his son Neachtain was called *tigerna Thíre Conaill* (ALC 1452). Conchobhar Ó Briain (*ob.* 1496) is styled *tigearna Tuathmhumhan* in an undated brehon-charter (Hardiman, 'Ancient Irish deeds', p. 27). The annalists tend to avoid the use of the word *rí* altogether in entries for the sixteenth century, with the following exceptions – AU 1510; ALC 1509, 1510; AConn 1510, 1536, 1539.

105 Binchy, *Celtic and Anglo-Saxon Kingship*, pp. 7–8, 11–12.

106 Nicholls, *Gaelic and Gaelicised Ireland*, pp. 22, 69–70; Nicholls, *Land*, pp. 5, 15–20.

107 *CSPI 1601–3*, p. 94.

108 Morley, *Ireland under Elizabeth and James I*, p. 348.

The freeholders of Cavan made a similar protest, but were eventually overruled in the interests of the plantation-scheme.[109] This anxiety to reduce free landowning subjects to the status of tenants did not originate solely with the English government, however; it was also a preoccupation of the paramount chiefs themselves. Also in the year 1607, Aodh Mór Ó Néill, earl of Tyrone, claimed that Uí Chatháin, the family of his most powerful vassal-chief, were 'but tenants at sufferance' on his demesne-land, and this attitude was shared by his ally, Rudhraighe Ó Domhnaill, earl of Tyrconnell.[110] After the Flight of the Earls, Sir Tobias Caulfield referred to the inhabitants of almost all Tír Eoghain as the 'tenants' of Ó Néill, and wanted to 'make it appear to them that His Majesty would be a better and more gracious *landlord* to them in all respects than Tyrone was or could be'.[111] The development from *ri* to *tighearna* which took place during the fifteenth and sixteenth centuries seems to have been but a half-way house on the road towards the *tighearna talmhan*, the landlord.

[109] *Ibid.*, pp. 375–6, 386–7.
[110] Canny, 'Hugh O'Neill', pp. 10 and 15.
[111] *CSPI 1608–10*, p. 534.

IV

METHODS OF CHOOSING AND DEPOSING A KING – THE *TÁNAISTE*, THE *MAC RÍOGH*

The Old Irish law-tracts tell us nothing about the method by which a candidate was selected for kingship in the eighth century.[1] A number of scholars have attempted to reconstruct the rules by analogy with the laws of inheritance to private property, by tracing the use of the terms *rígdomna* and *adbar ríg* ('royal heir') in the annals, and by examining the history of the succession to kingship in specific dynasties, but no general agreement has resulted.[2]

Non-legal texts for the early period, such as sagas and *tecosca* (tracts on the duty of kings), mention three possible routes to power: seizure of the kingship by military force, selection by the gods, and appointment by the inhabitants of the kingdom after they have taken counsel together. The seventh-century tract *Audacht Morainn* speaks disparagingly of 'the ruler of occupation with hosts from outside' as distinct from 'the true ruler',[3] but a couple of centuries later the text *Tecosca Cormaic* is less clearly condemnatory. The question 'whence is chieftaincy taken?' was answered:[4]

> By virtue of shape and race and knowledge, through wisdom and rank and liberality and honesty, by virtue of hereditary right and eloquence, by the strength of fighting and an army it is taken.

The excellences of character and appearance and the hereditary right to kingship referred to in this quotation were the qualities which caused a candidate to be chosen by gods and men. The verdict of the gods might be sought in visions or by subjecting rival claimants to one or more tests. One such ritual is described in parallel passages from *Togail Bruidne Da Derga* and *Serglige Con Culainn* and is probably derived from some earlier common source dealing with the inauguration of the kings at

[1] Binchy, *Celtic and Anglo-Saxon Kingship*, p. 25.

[2] MacNeill, *Celtic Ireland*, pp. 114–43; Hogan, 'The Irish law'; Mac Niocaill, 'The "heir designate" '; Ó Corráin, 'Irish regnal succession'; Charles-Edwards, 'The heir-apparent'.

[3] *Audacht Morainn*, ed. Kelly, p. 19.

[4] Meyer, *The Instructions*, p. 13.

Tara.[5] The men of Ireland kill a white bull, one man eats its flesh and drinks its broth and goes to sleep while four druids sing an incantation of truth over him. The future king appears to him in a vision. By contrast, in *Scéla Conchobar* the kingship of Ulster is transferred from Fergus mac Rossa to Conchobar mac Nessa by a more mundane procedure: ' "A colloquy about it!" say the Ulstermen. They took counsel in a single assembly ... and 'tis then that Conchobar was called the overking of a fifth of Ireland.'[6]

The early tract *De Shíl Chonairi Móir* is of particular interest in this context because it shows all three modes of procedure operating simultaneously. After the death of Eterscél Mór, the men of Leinster and the race of Conn Cétchathach held counsel to choose a new king of Tara. Lugaid Ríabnderg was excluded from kingship because the gods had not spoken on his behalf – the stone pillar of Fál would not screech against his chariot-axle. However, when Conaire Mór son of Eterscél heard that this council was determining the succession to his father's throne he exclaimed, "If I had men now to win the sovereignty, they would not be let deal thus". With his mother's assistance he marched on Tara at the head of a host, seized the inauguration-site and the regalia, and then passed the divine tests so that the stone of Fál cried aloud in token of the gods' approval. Hearing this, the assembled inhabitants 'give him the sovereignty and his father's territories'.[7] Evidently no hard and fast line can be drawn between divine and human election, between military seizure and voluntary submission.

In the Late Middle Irish period one further avenue to kingship is indicated in *Fled Dúin na nGéd*, a saga composed in the language of the eleventh or the early twelfth century. Here the candidate is appointed by an overking who also defines the limits of his protégé's jurisdiction. Congal Caech complains in this saga to the high king of Ireland: "My father, Scannall of the Broad Shield, died ... and I came to thee to be made king [of Ulster] as thou hadst promised me. Thou didst not perform thy promise except to a small extent, for thou didst deprive me of Cinel Conaill and Cinel Eoghain, and also of the nine cantreds of Oirghiall."[8] If we turn from literary to historical records, these signs of the overlord's role as kingmaker, though unconfirmed by the annals in earlier years, are amply supported by what we know of the 'high kings with opposition', Muircheartach Ó Briain (*ob.* 1119) and Toirdhealbhach Ó Conchobhair (*ob.* 1156). The relevant annal-entries make it clear that appointment by the high king was simply another way of seizing kingship by military force, as, for instance, in 1093, when there was[9]

> a hosting by Muirchertach Ua Briain to Connachta and the Síl Muiredaig joined his assembly, and he imprisoned the son of Cathal Ua Conchobuir, king of Síl

[5] McCone, 'Fírinne agus Torthúlacht', pp. 156–7.
[6] Stokes, 'Tidings', p. 25.
[7] L. Gwynn, 'De Šíl Chonairi Móir', pp. 133–5, 138–40.
[8] O'Donovan, *The Banquet*, p. 39; *Fled Dúin na nGéd*, ed. Lehmann, p. 11.
[9] AI 1093.2; and see 1094.2, 1095.11.

Muiredaig. Ua hEidin entered the patrimony of Ua Conchobuir Chonnacht, and Ua Briain gave the kingship of Síl Muiredaig to him.

A yet more obvious example comes in 1144:[10]

a hosting by Toirdelbach Húa Conchobair into Meath, and he divided Meath between two kings, after inflicting [such] slaughter and loss on the Meathmen that the battle he delivered on the descendants of Senchán was like the Day of Judgement.

Of course it was also possible to seize kingship without the support of a patron. In 1176, we are told, Cormac Liathánach Mac Carthaigh proclaimed himself king (*rígh do radhadh rís féin*), and during the thirteenth and fourteenth centuries many more kings are said by the annalists to have taken kingship 'by force' (*ar écin*),[11] compelling submission from their chief vassals by plunder or the threat of plunder.[12] No implied criticism of such proceedings can be detected in the narrative. On the contrary, Feidhlimidh Ó Conchobhair, who was forcibly inaugurated as king of Connacht in 1310, is said to have been 'proclaimed in a style as royal, as lordly and as public as any of his race from the time of Brian son of Eochu Muigmedoin till that day'.[13] This attitude recalls the explanation given in the tale of the encounter of Niall of the Nine Hostages with the hag at the well, who was transfigured by his embrace into a beautiful young woman: 'As thou hast seen me loathsome, bestial, horrible at first and beautiful at last, so is the sovranty; for seldom it is gained without battles and conflicts; but at last to anyone it is beautiful and goodly'.[14] The original mythology behind the two faces of sovereignty is in reality more complex,[15] and the rationalisation given in this Late Middle Irish tale may represent a change in political ethics since the days of *Audacht Morainn*; but it was to be an enduring change. Éinri Óg Ó Néill, who succeeded to the chieftaincy of Tír Eoghain in 1493 by murdering his elder brother, Conn Mór, was both usurper and fratricide but, far from glossing over the violence of his accession to the throne, the bardic poet who composed his inauguration-ode made it his central theme:[16]

I am certain, whichever of you has the best right to the land of Ireland, until he adds his might to the right he may not obtain union with her inheritance. Power is not won without peril ...

[10] AT 1144, and see 1122, 1125, 1126, 1127, 1132, 1143, 1152.
[11] McC 1176.2; AConn 1262.10, 1288.3, 1290.6, 1310.7, 1352.2.
[12] AConn 1225 (*passim*), 1296.3, 1315.7.
[13] AConn 1310.7.
[14] Stokes, 'The Death', p. 201.
[15] Coomaraswamy, 'On the loathly bride'; McCone, 'Fírinne agus Torthúlacht', pp. 138–42, 166; Mac Cana, 'Aspects', pt I, pp. 84–5.
[16] 'Mairg danab oighrecht Éire', in the Book of O Conor Don, fo 128v.

Similarly, Tadhg Mac Fithil, when writing *ca* 1532–44 a book whose whole object was to glorify the family of Mac Suibhne, recounts quite openly that three of his patron's immediate ancestors took the chieftaincy by force.[17]

As one might expect, historical records from the twelfth century onwards contain no mention of pagan oracles being consulted to determine succession; but a possible trace of this approach may be found in a legal miscellany compiled in the later middle ages which recommends that if two candidates for kingship are equal in age and qualifications, lots should be cast to decide between them.[18] However, the more normal route to power during the twelfth and thirteenth centuries was apparently a form of election, not unlike the election of the Holy Roman Emperors in Germany, nominally by the whole body of subjects, actually by a group of leading vassals. Under the year 1123, for instance, the annals in Mac Carthaigh's Book tell us that[19]

> Ó Mathghamhna, Ó Suilleabháin, Ó Caoimh, Ó Muircheartaigh and Ó Faoláin deposed Tadhg son of Muireadhach Mac Carthaig; and Cormac son of Mac Carthaigh, his own brother, took the kingship from them in his presence.

It is hardly conceivable that any man could rule south Munster in practice without the consent of such an array of sub-chieftains, but the chroniclers treat them as representing all the inhabitants of the kingdom in theory. The same source tells us that three years later Cormac Mac Carthaigh was in turn deposed by the nobles of Munster (*do maithibh Mumhun*), while the Annals of Inisfallen use the phrase 'by the Munstermen themselves' (*do Mubneciab féin*).[20] Other depositions in 1127 and 1151 are credited to 'the Leinstermen', '[the men of] Thomond',[21] while during the thirteenth century members of the Ó Conchobhair family were habitually made king 'by the men of Connacht'.[22] The precise meaning of this latter phrase is suggested under the year 1225, where the annals say that 'the whole of Connacht revolted' against the king, yet the invitation to the new rulers came separately from each of the members of the *oireacht* or territorial council of sub-chieftains.[23] As with most mediaeval societies, the leading nobility were understood to act on behalf of the population as a whole. Four times in the next hundred years annalistic texts note the ruler of some territory being deposed or killed by his own *oireacht*,[24] whose members were thus clearly in a position to veto the candidacy of anyone aspiring to kingship over them. In 1261 it is explicitly stated that the chieftains (*taísig*) of Bréifne and Conmaicne gave the kingship of Bréifne

[17] Walsh, *Leabhar Chlainne Suibhne*, pp. 50, 64, 72.
[18] Binchy, *Corpus*, IV.1289; *Ancient Laws*, edd. Hancock *et al.*, IV.372.
[19] McC 1123.2.
[20] McC 1126.5; AI 1127.2.
[21] AU 1127.5; McC 1151.1.
[22] AConn 1228.4; 1274.3 and 4; 1280.2.
[23] AConn 1225.4 and 5. See below, pp. 64–70.
[24] AConn 1262.9, 1296.2, 1306.3, 1317.10.

to Art Ó Ruairc.[25] In 1310 not only was Donnchadh Mac Carthaigh deposed by the nobles of Desmond (*do maitib Deasmuman*) who then bestowed the kingship on his kinsman Diarmait, but when the nobles restored Donnchadh to his earlier position of power they did not take the title of king (*ainm rígi*) away from Diarmait.[26] This indicates that the chief vassals could withdraw from a ruler not only the substance of power, by simple rebellion, but even the title of king, by formal deposition and the appointment of a successor. The annalist recognised their legitimate authority to do so. To be fully effective, such a deposition required general agreement. By contrast, in 1317 only the Ó Súilleabháin family rebelled 'contra Dermicium, principem Desmonie Aquilonaris et eum quantum in eis fuit deprincipauerunt'.[27]

In view of the evidence cited above from both sagas and twelfth-century annals, it is strange to find James Hogan asserting, in contradiction to Eoin MacNeill, that[28]

> I have been unable to find any evidence in support of the view that in pre-Norman times the nobility and clergy took the initiative in determining the order of succession ... it was the members of the dynasty, and not as is sometimes stated, the nobility and clergy, who made the final selection as between collaterals.

It is true that in many cases the sub-chiefs were connected by real or imaginary genealogical links with the ruling dynasty; this position is reflected in annalistic entries like that of 1151, when Diarmuid Mac Carthaigh was said to have been made king by *Sliocht Eoghain Mhóir*,[29] that is, by all the ruling families of Munster who collectively composed the Eoghanacht. Here it is possible to maintain that selection of a ruler had taken place within his 'dynasty'. On the other hand, cases where annalistic texts say that the kingship was conferred by the Munstermen, the Connachtmen, or the Leinstermen lend considerable support to MacNeill's argument for a theoretical right of appointment vested in all the freemen of a territory, though expressed in practice only by the leading nobles. Even stronger evidence that the sub-chiefs were empowered to confer kingship as leaders of the people rather than as members of the ruling dynasty is the handful of cases in which kingship was offered to an outsider who had no significant dynastic link with his prospective subjects. For example, one version of the obituary of Donnchadh Ó Cearbhaill, king of Airghialla, adds 'to whom was offered many times the kingship of Cinéal Eóghain',[30] while the Annals of Ulster assert that in 1199 'Cenél Conaill gave the kingship to Ua Eicnigh'. Indeed, Hogan himself discussed a yet more striking instance of kingship being voluntarily

[25] AConn, ALC 1261.
[26] AI 1310.2.
[27] AI 1317.10.
[28] Hogan, 'The Irish law', pp. 190, 193.
[29] McC 1151.3.
[30] McC 1167.5.

bestowed on an alien in his 'Ua Briain kingship in Telach Óc'.

It was, nevertheless, often the case in the later middle ages that the ruling family of an area had spread to the point where most of the land was held by cadet-branches of the main dynasty,[31] and thus a council of the nobility automatically became a family-affair. When there was a dispute in 1445 over the lordship of Anghaile, the two parties involved in proclaiming rival candidates for the succession were entirely composed of kin-groups among the Ó Fearghail family.[32] However, other annalistic entries concerning similar disputes at this period list a very much wider variety of participants, which might include sub-chiefs, an overlord, and neighbouring allies.[33] References to inaugurations taking place 'by will of God and men, bishops and ollams'[34] suggest that the formal consent of local church-leaders might be required on occasion, as in 1455 when Éinri son of Eoghan Ó Néill asked for confirmation of his election as chief from the Anglo-Irish archbishop of Armagh;[35] but there is no evidence in the annalistic collections that clerics were ever able materially to influence the course of a disputed succession. The advisory role of the *ollamhain*, the masters of native learning, is still more obscure; but, like the ecclesiastics, they took part in the actual ceremony of inauguration.

The Anglo-Norman barons soon became involved, after their invasion of Ireland, in the succession-disputes of the Irish kings. As allies or overlords they did not shrink from imposing their own candidates for kingship by military force,[36] but sometimes the conflicting claims of the overlord and the chief vassals seem to have been resolved by a compromise resembling the practice of *congé d'élire* in the mediaeval English Church, whereby the canonical electors, the chapters of a cathedral or an abbey, exercised their customary rights subject to the approval of the English king.[37] In 1228 Aodh son of Ruaidhri Ó Conchobhair was chosen as king by 'all the Connachtmen' at a great court of the English and Irish convened by the justiciar, Richard de Burgh.[38] In 1350 Seaán Ó Broin was elected, apparently by his own kinsmen and adherents, in the presence of the justiciar, Thomas de Rokeby.[39] Meanwhile in Connacht, Éamonn Albanach Mac Uilliam, head of the Burkes or de Burghs of Mayo, continued his family's control of the Ó Conchobhair kingship,[40] though now without royal authority for his interference. In 1342[41]

[31] See Simms, 'The medieval kingdom', pp. 132–3.
[32] AFM 1445.
[33] AConn 1461.23 and 24, 1468.17; AU 1449, 1493.
[34] AU 1430, 1432.
[35] Simms, 'The concordat', pp. 71–2.
[36] AConn 1286.2, 1291.3, 1293.3.
[37] See Cross, *The Oxford Dictionary of the Christian Church*, p. 332.
[38] AConn 1228.4.
[39] See above, p. 37.
[40] See AConn 1230.3 and 8, 1232.4, 1296.3, 1309.3, 1310.5 and 6; 1318.4; 1330.3.
[41] AConn 1342.17.

Aed son of Aed Brefnach son of Cathal Ruad O Conchobair was made king by the men of Connacht and MacWilliam Burke.

In 1350[42]

Aed son of Toirrdelbach was deposed by MacWillian Burke and the Tuatha of Connacht, and they made Aed son of Feidlim king in his stead.

During the same period Ó Néill of Tír Eoghain, who styled himself 'king of the Irish of Ulster', intervened in the regnal succession of Tír Conaill when in 1343[43]

Niall O Domnaill was deposed by Aengus O Domnaill, Domnall Dub O Baigill and O Dochurtaig, supported [*le nert*] by Aed Remor O Neill and by the Clann Suibne at large. These all made Aengus king.

In this case the sub-chiefs who cooperated with Ó Néill constituted only a section of the country's leaders, and the appointment resulted in war. However, by the fifteenth century Ó Néill on a number of occasions appointed kings in territories subject to him without contradiction,[44] and at least once received payment for the favour.[45] By the later sixteenth century this payment was claimed as Ó Néill's customary due from 'every lord and chieftain in the province of Ulster'.[46] Of Ó Catháin it was said at this period that[47]

freeholders and immediate followers ... who yielded unto O Cahan chief rent and Irish services ... took upon them ... to make choice of such an one of the name and race of O Cahan as by birth, years and worth was fittest to be made O Cahan; who being so elected by them, received his full confirmation and establishment from him that was then O Neale, as from their superior lord.

In south Munster at the same time Ó Donnabháin was chosen by a similar collaboration between his vassals and his overlord Mac Carthaig Riabhach.[48] In Tír Conaill, Ó Domhnaill began to nominate the Mac Suibhne chief of Fanad at the beginning of the fifteenth century and continued the practice thereafter, turning the initial bribe for his support into a customary payment.[49]

The importance of an overlord's influence in the later sixteenth century is well demonstrated in Lughaidh Ó Cléirigh's account of the election of MacWilliam Burke of Mayo. Here there were altogether eight contenders

42 AConn 1350.9.
43 AConn 1343.13.
44 AU 1433, 1452, 1456, 1461; ADF 1446.
45 AU 1456.
46 'Ceart Úí Néill', ed. Dillon, p. 9.
47 *CSPI 1606–8*, pp. 155–6.
48 O'Donovan, *The Genealogies*, p. 445.
49 Walsh, *Leabhar Chlainne Suibhne*, p. 50.

for the chieftaincy and only five nobles entitled to make the choice between them: three barons of Anglo-Irish origin, MacCostello, MacJordan and MacMorris, one Irish chief, Ó Máille, and the constable of the galloglass, Marcus Mac Domhnaill. By a majority these nobles favoured the eldest kinsman among the candidates, but Aodh Ruadh Ó Domhnaill, who had come with an overwhelming military force to supervise the election, appointed the choice of the minority – a younger, more vigorous man, who had been promised the title by Ó Domhnaill before the election began.[50]

This difference of opinion between electors and overlord raises the whole question as to the qualifications which entitled a man to kingship. Among members of the same royal dynasty considerable stress was laid on seniority. When Richard de Burgh presided over the Connachtmen's choice in 1228, an annalist commented[51]

> Most unfortunate was the decision they came to there, to give the kingship to the younger and expel the elder, Toirrdelbach son of Ruaidri, though he was irreproachable as regards valour, nobility and generosity.

And there are other annal-entries expressing the principle that 'it is not right to oppose a good senior kinsman'.[52] Seniority was apparently decided on two grounds, personal age and descent. In assessing his own chances of succeeding to the chieftaincy in the late sixteenth century Florence Mac Carthaigh Riabhach wrote:[53]

> Mr Daniel MacCarthy ... is ... by the custom of tanistship, to enjoy the said country before me, because his father was my father's eldest brother, and that he is elder than myself.

However, in order to divert the suspicions of the English government, Florence omitted to add that seniority was far from being an absolute criterion. A mid-sixteenth-century manuscript – London, British Library, MS. Egerton 88 – contains a tract on the principles of succession to office, whether kingship, headship of a kin, church-appointment, or the chair of a master-poet. It is a miscellany of older maxims introduced with a promise: 'By this book, if I can, in the name of God, I will bring the senior before the junior in every case, as these laws down here state. Beyond this I will make an intermixture of their laws altogether.'[54] Yet the opening phrase *Sinnsear la fine, feabta la flaith* has been justifiably glossed by the mid-seventeenth-century genealogist, Dubhaltach Mac Firbhisigh, as meaning 'to put the eldest of a kin in the headship of that kin, and to put the person who possesses most clients and power, if he is

[50] *Beatha Aodha Ruaidh*, ed. Walsh, I.114–18.
[51] AConn 1228.4.
[52] AConn 1288.3, 1398.18, 1401.10.
[53] Bird *et al.*, Calendar, III.451–2.
[54] *Ancient Laws*, edd. Hancock *et al.*, IV.372(–3), n. 1.

as noble as his elder, into the sovereignty or lordship'.[55] This particular maxim is cited in another tract[56] and presumably both citations go back to some earlier common original although it is not, as Mac Firbhisigh suggests, to be found in the present text of the *Senchus Már*. Certainly in the first half of the fifteenth century, a bardic poem addressed to Aodh Buidhe II Ó Neill (*ob.* 1444) states as a long-accepted principle of brehon law that the elder kinsman must give place to the younger if the latter is better qualified.[57] Qualifications listed by the Egerton-88 tract on succession include being the son and grandson of a king, possessing wealth, and having a greater number of clients than one's rivals.

Obituaries and eulogies of chieftains and would-be chieftains in annalistic texts and bardic poetry are another guide as to what the Irish learned classes considered necessary for a king. They often emphasise nobility of birth on the mother's side as well as the father's. Thus when Niall Óg Ó Néill died in 1403 he was called[58]

> A man whom the [learned] companies and pilgrims of Ireland thought would take the kingship of Ireland on account of the prowess of his hands and the nobility of his blood – to wit, the blood of Niall of the Nine Hostages and the daughter of the king of the Saxons.

Similarly Niall Óg's grandson was addressed as[59]

> Fruit-branch of the royal flesh and blood, smooth-browed son of Eoghan ... he springs from the noblest of the Nialls and the Aodhs ... Son of Catherine of the House of Té, noble his birth; Teamhair of Té shall be his without dispute.

Although illegitimacy does not of itself seem to have excluded a king's son from the succession, the brehon laws had held that the children of a slave, a hired woman, or a female satirist were ineligible for chieftaincy.[60] At a later period, the Ó Domnhaill genealogies for the fourteenth and fifteenth centuries demonstrate that those sons who succeeded to the kingship were born of noblewomen,[61] while the line of succession in the Ó Néill and Mág Uidhir families at the same time shows a well defined tendency towards legitimacy and primogeniture.[62] In their obituaries,

[55] Ó Raithbheartaigh, *Genealogical Tracts*, p. 30.
[56] ed. Binchy, *Corpus*, IV.1232.
[57] 'Ní haois fhoirfidheas, a Aedh', *Leabhar Cloinne Aodha Buidhe*, ed. Ó Donnchadha, p. 59.
[58] AU 1403. The 'daughter of the king of the Saxons' was Cairne, mother of Niall of the Nine Hostages.
[59] 'Díleas breath do bhreith le seilbh', in *Aithdioghluim Dána*, ed. McKenna, no. 17, qq. 34 and 39.
[60] Power, 'Classes', p. 105.
[61] *Beatha Aodha Ruaidh*, ed. Walsh, II.166–74.
[62] Ó Néill kings styled *primogenitus* of their predecessor in contemporary documents are Niall Óg (*CPR 1388–92*, p. 404), Brian Óg (*CCH*, p. 147, no. 222) and Éinrí mac Eoghain (Prene's Register, Lib. i, fo 33r). In 1316

annals frequently speak of men who deserved kingship for their personal beauty, intelligence, and hospitality.[63] Whatever the practical advantages of these qualities, such statements lend a political significance to the flattery invariably used in bardic praise-poems.[64] Conversely, when the fifteenth-century Scottish poet, Giolla Críost Brúilingeach, called Tomás MágUidhir[65]

> the stingy grudging man, the stinking-gummed half-blind oaf ... the withered leper ... the shameless misshapen monster ... the wicked incompetent feeble boor,

he was declaring his erstwhile patron unfit for kingship, as the repeated use of the term 'boor' (*daoi*) indicates.

In earlier times it had been an accepted convention that a king must be without blemish, and even a minor physical disability debarred him from the throne.[66] That this was not so strictly observed at a later period is suggested by the existence of chiefs with names like *An Cammhuinéalach* ('the wry-necked') Ó Baoighill,[67] and Conn *Bacach* ('the lame') Ó Néill.[68] The eleventh century may mark a turning point in attitudes: when Donnchadh son of Brian Bóroimhe lost his hand in a conflict in 1019 his 'mutilation' was widely recorded as one of the most startling events of that year,[69] but he continued to reign for the next forty years and more. Yet eleventh-century annals contain some of the earliest references to the practice of severe mutilation – blinding,[70] castration,[71] the amputation of more than one limb,[72] or a combination of the first two injuries[73] – with the object of rendering a rival physically incapable of ruling, as in 1272 we find Tadhg Dall Ó Conchobhair described as 'the most eligible successor to the province, till he was blinded'.[74] The tendency to mutilate

---

Seaán Ó Néill held a position of authority as *primogenitus* (Fleming's Register, fo 38r), but predeceased his father. On the Mag Uidhir family, see Simms, 'The medieval kingdom', p. 132.

63 AU 1188, 1342, 1343; AConn 1309.2, 1320.3, 1328.16, 1333.6, 1461.2.

64 See Byrne, *Irish Kings*, p. 16.

65 Jackson, *A Celtic Miscellany*, pp. 233–5; Watson, *Scottish Verse*, pp. 48–55.

66 Byrne, *The Rise*, p. 17; Binchy, *Celtic and Anglo-Saxon Kingship*, p. 10.

67 AFM 1247.

68 AFM 1559.

69 AT 1018/19; AU, ALC, AI 1019; AFM 1018.

70 AT 982, 1020, 1029, 1092, 1136, 1141, 1153, 1158, etc.; ALC 1185, 1204, 1208, etc.; AU 1496.

71 AU 1478. There is reason to suppose that this operation is often concealed beneath the annalists' euphemisms of *dalladh*, 'blinding' (AConn 1224.3, 1244.2, 1272.4), and *scathadh*, 'lopping off' (AU 1490, 1496, 1503, 1504).

72 AU 1435, 1461.

73 ALC 1118; AConn 1272.4.

74 AConn 1272.4.

rivals rather than killing them outright seems to have arisen from the rule that a murderer, especially a kin-murderer, was disqualified from kingship. Not only is this implied in the Old Irish text *Audacht Morainn*[75] and stated explicitly in the Middle Irish work *Lebor na Cert*,[76] but the principle appears to have had some practical force in post-Norman times. In 1402[77]

Cathal Ruad MacRaghnaill, chieftain of Muinntear Eolais ... was killed by the family of Maol Sheachlainn MacRaghnaill in treachery, though there was no enmity. Raghnall son of Maol Sheachlainn took the chieftainship after him, for he had no part in the killing of Cathal as it is said.

There are also examples of the deposition of reigning kings who had committed murder.[78]

The fact that severe mutilations appear invariably to have been effective in debarring the victim from kingship highlights the importance of the king's role as a vigorous war-leader, able to put down disorder within his boundaries and defend the country from outside invaders. The Middle Irish poem *Cert cech ríg co réil* urges the king[79]

When you meet a foray, answer it early that you may abide for ever, like a pillar-stone:

The *Teguscc Cumscraidh* contained in the 'Battle of Airtech' advised:[80]

Be a zealous and mighty champion ... ardent, warlike, contending against foreign lands for the protection of thy great territories.

Again and again annals praise a ruler as a protecting warrior, *fer crodha cosantach*,[81] and the obituary of Conchobhar Mac Diarmata in 1297[82]

the best man for word and ward, valiance and valour, fight and fray, attack and resistance, shielding and sheltering, probity and princeliness,

presupposes a man of considerable bodily vigour.

Of course an ability to fight, together with a military following, also facilitated the forcible seizure of power. An Anglo-Irish tract of *ca* 1515 observes cynically of the Irish laws of succession: 'he that hath strongyst

[75] *Audacht Morainn*, ed. Kelly, p. 66; cf. Thurneysen, 'Morands Fürstenspiegel', pp. 103–4.
[76] ed. Dillon, p. 56.
[77] Ann. Rawl. B.488, *s.a.* 1402.11 (ed. Ó hInnse, pp. 166–7).
[78] AFM 1155; AU 1178; AConn 1258.11, 1365.8.
[79] O'Donoghue, 'Cert cech ríg co réil', p. 267.
[80] Best, 'The Battle', p. 180.
[81] ALC 1452; AConn 1265.7; AU 1426, 1482.
[82] AConn, ALC 1297.

armye and hardeyst swerde among them, hath best right and tytill'.[83] This need for a ruler who was 'fighting fit' meant that when a king fell sick, as did Muircheartach Ó Briain in 1114[84] and Aodh Ó Conchobhair in 1269,[85] his kingdom was subjected to internal disorders and external aggression. Around 1210 Cathal Croibhdhearg Ó Conchobhair was severely ill, and a chronicler records it as remarkable that 'notwithstanding his sickness Connaght received no great losses'.[86] For this reason, it seems, failing health might lead to a king's deposition in the twelfth century.[87] An alternative solution, for an aging ruler, was the association of his son in kingship. At least two eleventh-century princes had borne the title *rí ri láim a athar*, 'king by the side of his father',[88] and it was said of Aodh son of Cathal Croibhdhearg in 1244 that 'he had been king in effect (*rí ar tothacht*) by the side of his father and already held all the hostages of Connacht'.[89] This last observation is important, for the man who held the hostages held the reality of power.[90] In the case of the late fourteenth-century Niall Óg Ó Néill, who was also associated in kingship with his aging father, we are fortunate in having sufficient documentary evidence to establish that, so far from acting as his parent's deputy or second-in-command, Niall Óg wielded the supreme authority as *capitaneus de natione sua*.[91] A similarly dominant role appears to have been played by Aodh son of Feidhlim Ó Conchobhair in 1258/9,[92] by Niall Garbh Ó Domhnaill in 1418–21,[93] and by Éinrí Ó Néill in 1442 and 1449,[94] during the reigns of their respective fathers. For practical purposes a son empowered in this way *was* king. Indeed this possibility of a double rule was not confined to cases of father and son. Sometimes it was the result of a more or less amicable compromise between two rival aspirants to kingship, as with the joint-rule of the brothers Cathal and Cúchonnacht Ó Raighilligh in thirteenth-century Bréifne,[95] or the Clann Aodha Buidhe branch of the Ó Néill family in 1475 of which Finghin Ó Mathghamhna recorded that: 'Conn son of Aedh Buidhe son of Brian Ballach has control of Trian Conghail, and his uncle is Ó Néill Buidhe'.[96] Similarly, Eoghan son of Niall Óg Ó Néill of Tír Eoghain may have enjoyed some form of effective kingship during the last years of the reign

83 *State Papers, Henry VIII, Ireland 1515–38*, p. 4.
84 AI 1114.2.
85 AClon, AConn, AFM, ALC 1269.
86 AClon 1210.
87 AU 1114.2; AI 1123.6.
88 Ó Corráin, 'Irish regnal successsion', p. 36.
89 AConn 1224.3.
90 See below, pp. 97–9.
91 *CCR 1392–6*, pp. 157–8; Curtis, *Richard II*, p. 86.
92 AConn 1258.9 and 16, 1259.4–8 and 11–12.
93 AConn 1418–21.
94 AFM, AU 1442; Prene's Register, Lib.i, fo 33r; Curtis, 'The "Bonnaght" of Ulster', pp. 87–8.
95 Simms, 'The O'Reillys', pp. 311–12.
96 Stokes, 'The Gaelic Maundeville', p. 4.

of his cousin and rival Domhnall Bog Ó Néill. The Annals of Ulster state that 'Ó Néill', that is, the head of the family, led an expedition to relieve Ó Raighilligh in 1429, yet the Bréifne annals name the leader with greater probability, as Eoghan, not king but heir to the throne of Ulster, *ríoghdhamhna Uladh*.[97]

With regard to the two Irish terms generally translated as 'royal heir', *ríoghdhamhna* and *ádhbhar ríogh*, Gearóid Mac Niocaill has argued that both early and late in the middle ages they can be understood as synonymous with *tánaiste*, 'second [to the chief]', all three meaning 'individuals designated beforehand to the succession'.[98] For the later period, at least, this would seem too rigid an equation.[99] In obits the phrase *adhbhar ríogh* can be used in a loosely complimentary context, associated with personal qualities rather than legal status, as in *adbur Ríg Érenn ar uasli & ar engnam & ar enech, ar delb & ar denam* ('eligible for his nobility, valour, generosity, form and feature for the kingship of Ireland');[100] in such cases the title has much the same force as *soithech dingbala d'airdríghi* ('a worthy vessel for high kingship'),[101] or *dil Érenn do ríg* ('worthy to be king of Ireland').[102] In none of these instances would the word *tánaiste* be appropriate. Donncha Ó Corráin considers that the term *rígdamna* was applied in practice, during the tenth to twelfth centuries, to the head of the main dynastic segment not in possession of the kingship,[103] and this description perfectly fits the status of Eoghan Ó Néill in 1429. Even more convincingly, the equivalent title *adbur righ Uladh* ('royal heir of Ulster') was applied in 1411 to Eoghan's cousin, Muircheartach son of Cú Uladh Ó Néill.[104] Muircheartach was head of his own brothers, the sons of Cú Uladh Ruadh, but his father seems to have been merely the third son of the great king Niall Mór Ó Néill (*ob.* 1397),[105] and there is no evidence to suggest that Muircheartach himself or his brothers put forward serious claims to royal power. The term *tánaise* or *tánaiste* (which has been shown by Binchy to be very early[106]) Ó Corráin suggests to have been revived later precisely because *rígdamna* with the passage of time came to be applied loosely 'to the head of the most able discarded segment or to any distinguished but discarded royal considered to be worthy of the highest office'.[107] On the other hand, it seems well established that the title *adhbhar ríogh* or *ríoghdhamhna* in

97 De hÓir, 'Annála as Bréifne', p. 68.
98 Mac Niocaill, 'The "heir designate" '.
99 Doubt has been expressed even for the earlier period in Byrne, *Irish Kings*, p. 312.
100 AConn 1309.2, 1306.4, 1320.3, 1328.16; AU 1369.
101 AConn, AU 1342.
102 AConn 1461.2.
103 Ó Corráin, 'Irish regnal succession', p. 35.
104 AConn, AFM, AU 1411.
105 *CCH*, p. 147, nos 222, 240; AU 1400; Dublin, Royal Irish Academy, M.S. 1233, fo 36rb; Fleming's Register, fo 15r.
106 Binchy, 'Some Celtic legal terms', pp. 222–3.
107 Ó Corráin, 'Irish regnal succession', p. 37.

the fifteenth century could indicate a recognised position of power. For instance Muirghius Mac Diarmata, who died in 1418, is described as *degadbar rígdamna Moigi Luirc*, 'a man well qualified to be *ríoghdhamhna* of Magh Luirg'.[108] Pilib Máguidhir was called *tánaiste* of Fir Manach in 1447, but in 1457 and at the time of his death in 1470 he was styled *adhbur rígh Fer Manach*.[109] Éigneachán son of Neachtain Ó Domhnaill was created *tánaiste* of Tír Conaill in 1480 but is called *rídhamhna Cheneoil Conoill* at his death in 1497.[110] Each of these men appears to have suffered a change in status which coincided with this change in title. It was obvious from 1450 – when, during the absence of the king of Fir Manach on pilgrimage, his son and eventual successor Éamonn undertook responsibility for enforcing order as acting head of the family[111] – that Éamonn rather than his uncle Pilib was now destined heir to the kingship. In Tír Conaill, although the chief, Aodh Ruadh, had been forced to accept Éigneachán Ó Domhnaill as *tánaiste* in 1480, war had broken out between the two kinsmen in 1485.[112] Éigneachán was eventually murdered by Ó Domhnaill's son in 1497, his bard lamenting 'an inheritance which does not lay claim to its due (*oighreacht nach iarr a cána*)'.[113] In other words, *ríoghdhamhna* or *adhbhar ríogh* might describe a prince entitled to succeed to the kingship, but only the term *tánaiste* conveys that such a man's claim to act as the king's deputy and successor was sanctioned by the ruler himself.

The word *tánaiste* originally held the meaning 'the expected one' because, as the Old Irish legal tract *Críth Gablach* explained, 'the whole people looks forward to his kingship without opposition to him'; but before the end of the Old Irish period it had extended its meaning to become a translation of the Latin *secundus*.[114] A *secundus abbas* or *secnab* was a prior, 'a deputy with right of succession'.[115] In the ninth and tenth centuries the *tánaise abbad* of the great churches of Clonmacnoise and Armagh might hold power not merely as expected heir to the chief abbacy, but as abbot in his own right of lesser churches and as an influential official within the monastic *paruchia*.[116] In the same way it seems that the position of lay *tánaiste* to a king came to bring with it not merely the expectation of succession but the immediate acquisition of certain rights. The Annals of Inisfallen refer in 1176 to the 'tanist's land' (*fearann tanisteachta*), apparently mensal land attached to the office,

[108] AConn 1418.9 (Freeman's translation seems inaccurate here).
[109] AU 1447, 1457, 1470.
[110] AFM, AU 1480; AConn 1497.2.
[111] AU 1450.
[112] AFM, AU 1480 and 1485.
[113] 'Tuile ar ttrághadh trén Gaoidheal', ed. McKenna, 'Some Irish bardic poems', pp. 438, 441; AConn, AFM, AU 1497.
[114] Greene, 'Some linguistic evidence', pp. 83–4; Charles-Edwards, 'The heir-apparent'.
[115] Greene, 'Some linguistic evidence', pp. 83–4.
[116] AFM 865; AU 891.4, 896.8, 924.5, 931.2.

similar to the 'king's land' (*ferann ríg*) which occurs in the same annals under the year 1283. During the reign of the high king Muircheartach Ó Briain, his brother and eventual successor Diarmait subscribed himself *Dermeth dux, frater regis* while the clergy and people of Waterford in the same letter speak of *rex noster Murchertachus ... et Dermeth dux noster*.[117] Some sixty years later Murchadh Ó Cearbhaill, heir to the kingship of Airghialla, held during his father's lifetime the title 'king of Uí Méith and the Tríocha céad of Airthir'.[118] In 1210 Aodh son of Cathal Croibhdhearg Ó Conchobhair, while his father was still the active ruler of the province, is said to have been promised 'a charter for the third part of Connacht' from King John of England.[119] These examples apply to demonstrable heirs, but men who are not expressly recorded as bearing the title of *tánaiste*. In the fourteenth and fifteenth centuries the example of Domhnall Ó Conchobhair, *tániste Connacht uili*, 'his territory extending from the Curlieu Hills to Caeluisce',[120] is atypical, since this man was head of his own dynastic segment and only distantly related to the reigning king of Connacht. On the other hand we find that Éinrí Aimhréidh Ó Néill, brother to Niall Óg, the chief of Tír Eoghain, and described as 'tanist and next successor of the principallity of Ulster', was powerful enough in his own right to defeat MágUidhir, king of Fir Manach, and to assist Toirdhealbhach an Fhíona O Domhnaill to the kingship of Tír Conaill.[121] Two fifteenth-century MágUidhir princes who successively held the title *tánaiste Fer Manach* seem to have ruled the western shore of Loch Erne almost as a separate lordship.[122] Indeed, at the beginning of the sixteenth century an anonymous Anglo-Irish description of Ireland, after listing the sixty chieftaincies into which the country was parcelled, states unambiguously, 'also every of the said regions is devydeid and departeid bytwyxt the chyef captayne and deputye captaines of the same'.[123] It is implied in a series of ordinances promulgated under Henry VIII, as a compromise between brehon law and English common law, that in such Irish lordships there was not merely a territorial division between chief and *tánaiste* but a sharing in the profits of authority: 'for every theft under 14d a fine of 5 marks should be paid, 46s 8d to the captain and 20s to the tanister'.[124]

Edmund Spenser, who gives a most detailed description of the position of the *tánaiste* in the late sixteenth century, tells us that the tanist was nominated at the time of the election of a new chief, and by the same assembly, as a man 'next of the blood' to the chief, 'who shall next succeed him in the said captainry if he live thereunto'. While the chief

117 Ussher, 'Veterum Epistolarum Hibernicarum Sylloge', pp. 518–19.
118 Simms, 'The O Hanlons', pp. 72–4.
119 ALC 1210.
120 AConn, ALC 1307.
121 AClon 1379, 1380, 1392.
122 Simms, 'The medieval kingdom', p. 133.
123 *State Papers, Henry VIII, Ireland 1515–38*, p. 5.
124 Morley, *Ireland under Elizabeth and James I*, p. 323.

stood on the inauguration-stone and swore to preserve the ancient customs and to deliver up the succession peaceably to the *tánaiste*, the latter 'setteth but one foot upon the stone and receiveth the like oath that the captain did'. The custom, he explained, avoided the possibility of rule by a minor, for[125]

> the Tanist is always ready known, if it should happen the Captain suddenly to die or to be slain in battle or to be out of the country, to defend it and keep it from all such doubts, and dangers; for which cause the Tanist hath also a share of the country allotted unto him, and certain cuttings and spendings upon all the inhabitants, under the lord.

Although this is a late source and the writer a foreign observer, each detail in his account seems to be corroborated by earlier references. In 1342 the *tánaiste* of Connacht was nominated at the same time and by the same people as the king.[126] In 1433, when Tír Conaill was invaded in the absence of its king, Niall Garbh Ó Domhnaill, a council of nobles met and negotiated with the enemy under the leadership of Niall's brother and eventual heir, Neachtain Ó Domhnaill. In the same way Neachtain seems to have led resistance to Ó Néill during his brother's long captivity in 1434–9, although he was not inaugurated until after Niall Garbh's death.[127] The one point on which Spenser leaves some doubt concerns the tanist's absolute right to succeed. For while he points out that the heir was at hand to take the chief's place in a sudden emergency, he also states that, whenever a chief died, an assembly subsequently elected his successor. Since a chief and his *tánaiste*, being elected at the same time, were normally contemporaries, a chief who died of old age might leave a very decrepit *tánaiste* behind him, having perhaps already associated his eldest son in kingship with him for some years. A situation of this kind seems to have formed the background to civil war in Fir Manach in 1420,[128] and in Tír Conaill in 1431.[129] However, it so happens that those nobles actually styled *tánaiste* in annal-entries in the later middle ages – such as Éinrí Aimhréidh or Aodh of the Fews Ó Neill,[130] Aodh and Pilib MágUidhir,[131] and Eigneachán Ó Domhnaill[132] – all died before the chief whose designated successors they were; while it seems clear that in none of these cases could the *tánaiste* have succeeded without a sharp struggle against the claims of his predecessor's sons, the point cannot be illustrated by recorded events. In any case, where the chief and his *tánaiste* were much of an age, there was always a fifty-per-cent probability that the *tánaiste* would die first, and the *tánaiste* who never became king

125 Spenser, *A View* (ed. Renwick), pp. 7–8.
126 AConn 1342.17.
127 AFM, AU 1435, 1439; Simms, 'Niall Garbh II O Donnell', p. 18.
128 AU 1420; see Simms, 'The medieval kingdom', p. 133
129 Simms, 'Niall Garbh II O Donnell', p. 17.
130 AClon 1392; AFM 1514.
131 AU 1407, 1447.
132 AFM, AU 1480.

seems accepted as a normal figure by the Four Masters, who remark of Art Ó Néill in 1514: 'seldom, indeed had the son of a *tánaiste* been lord of Cenél Eoghain before him'.

Even the *mac ríogh*, the king's son who was not expecting to succeed, occupied an influential position in society, as Gearóid Mac Niocaill has pointed out, drawing on the thirteenth-century law-tract of Giolla na Naomh Mac Aodhagáin.[133] In the scale of honour-prices and compensations, Mac Aodhagáin equates the son of a provincial king with a reigning sub-king, or king-chieftain, while the son of a sub-king has the status of a 'chieftain without noble clients' (*taoiseach ag nach bia aireachta*).[134] This theory is borne out by the practice of the later middle ages. Cú Uladh Ruadh Ó Néill was treated as an independent chieftain in the 1390s when hostages were taken from him to be held in Trim castle, *caput* of the Irish lands of Roger Mortimer, earl of March and Ulster; but Cú Uladh was neither head of the Ó Néill family nor designated as successor to his father, the chief Niall Mór.[135] In 1425, when Brian Mac Mathghamhna, chief of Airghialla, entered into an agreement with the king's lieutenant of Ireland, two of his brothers were parties to the indenture, one being lord of Fearnmhuighe, and the other very probably lord of Dartraighe.[136] The archbishops of Armagh, when appealing to local magnates to exercise their power on behalf of the Church, might name the sons of kings other than the reigning chief and his designated successor, for instance when on 11 November, 1455, Archbishop Mey invoked the authority not merely of Éinrí Ó Néill and of his *tánaiste* Aodh of the Fews, but of their brothers Feidhlim Ó Néill and Art of Omagh.[137] Elsewhere such sons of kings are called *generosi*,[138] *nobiles uiri*,[139] or *magnates*.[140] The fact that men in this position were brought in to make their submissions to Richard II[141] and Richard, duke of York,[142] testifies in itself to their political importance. Gearóid Mac Niocaill has collected annalistic references to '*na meic ríogh*' as military leaders,[143] and drawn attention to a poem in the Book of Fenagh which demands the same tribute to St Caillín from a *mac ríogh* as from a *taoiseach* (chieftain).[144] In addition, annalistic obituaries praise the *mac ríogh* or *mac taoisigh* not only for warlike ability but for hospitality and patronage

133 Mac Niocaill, 'A propos du vocabulaire'.
134 *Ibid.*, pp. 516, 519–20.
135 *CPR 1399–1401*, p. 289.
136 *CCH*, p. 239, no. 118; AU 1432, 1457, 1486; Gilbert, *Facsimiles*, III.1, appendix v.
137 *Registrum Iohannis Mey*, edd. Quigley & Roberts, no. 326.
138 Prene's Register, Lib. iii, fo 1r.
139 *Registrum Iohannis Mey*. edd. Quigley & Roberts, no. 178; Prene's Register, Lib. i, fos 7r, 30r.
140 *Registrum Iohannis Mey*, edd. Quigley & Roberts, no. 205.
141 Curtis, *Richard II*, pp. 60–1, 79–80, 97–8, 103.
142 Gilbert, *Facsimiles*, III, plate xl.
143 Mac Niocaill, 'A propos du vocabulaire', p. 520, n. 1.
144 *The Book*, edd. Hennessy & Kelly, pp. 80, 134.

of poets,[145] suggesting a man of some substance. In 1433, when Neachtain Ó Domhnaill parleyed with Ó Néill in his brother's absence, the other members of this council were Ó Domhnaill's wife (the queen of Tír Conaill) and the *meic ríogh Conallaigh*, 'the princes of Tír Conaill'.[146] The political importance of these *meic ríogh* is as plain as the military importance of the corresponding class in the annals of thirteenth-century Connacht.[147]

In 1434 we are told that a war broke out between Niall Garbh Ó Domhnaill, king of Tír Conaill, and his brother and heir Neachtain over the death of a third brother, Eigneachán, killed by yet a fourth brother. If we disentangle the genealogical background to this incident,[148] it seems to indicate that the cadet-sons of kings, as leaders of the second rank, were grouped under the patronage of one or other of the main rulers – whether styled *rí*, *tánaiste*, or *ríoghdhamhna* – in a bond which had more to do with vassalage than with blood-ties, since Niall Garbh and Neachtain were full brothers, while their respective protégés were each only half-brothers.

A *mac mic ríogh*, the son of a king's son, might also be a man of some importance, as we learn from the obituary of Pilib son of Seáan Buidhe Mac Mathghamhna in 1517.[149] Another king's grandson, Brian son of Feidhlim Ó Néill, was invoked by Archbishop Bole in 1463 as the Church's secular arm in the rural deanery of Tullahogue.[150] On his death he was lauded as 'an eminent leader and one who ... most bought of poetry and did most of raids of borderlands that was in his time';[151] yet the war which erupted in his lifetime between his own kin-group – the sons of Feidhlim and the Great Ó Néill[152] – was part of a pattern repeated over and over again in other Gaelic lordships. The lands and power with which the sons and brothers of a former king were endowed were often taken away from their descendants to enrich the cadets of a succeeding generation of rulers. If the son of a *mac ríogh* was to avoid this decline in fortune, then instead of holding his lands and authority as a dependant of the chief he must lay claim to his father's endowments as a separate lordship, and pass them down as the inheritance of his own branch of the family under the rule of a sectional kin-leader, or *ceann-fine*. This development of a new sub-lordship, with its own chain of inheritance inside the main dynasty, was common enough and could involve quite small estates, but some of the most spectacularly successful examples were the new chieftaincy of Ó Néill of Clann Aodha Buidhe, set up in the

145 AConn 1298.5, 1314.7, 1333.6, 1418.2, 1443.3; AU 1206, 1329, 1372, 1374, etc.
146 AU 1433.
147 AConn 1232.6, 1247.8 and 9, 1249.9 and 10, 1256.11, 1262.6, 1272.2.
148 AFM, AU 1433, 1434; *Beatha Aodha Ruaidh*, ed. Walsh, II.168.
149 AU 1517.
150 Prene's Register, Lib. i, fo 194v.
151 AU 1482.
152 AFM, AU 1479, 1480, 1481.

mid-fourteenth century[153] and eventually spreading to cover most of Antrim and Down; the lordship of Ó Néill of the Fews in south Armagh;[154] and the lordship of Clann Philib MhéigUidhir in western Fir Manach.[155] In each of these three cases the new kin-group, soon after its organisation as a separate entity, had succeeded in installing one or more of its own kin-leaders in the chieftainship of the whole dynasty. This brief spell of supreme power may have been a decisive factor in confirming such kin-groups in their landed possessions. Many internal wars which developed into succession-struggles, such as the Uí Néill war between the chief Niall Óg Ó Néill (*ob.* 1403) and the sons of his *tánaiste*, Clann Éinrí Aimhréidh,[156] or the Uí Dhomhnaill feud between the sons of the dead chief, Niall Garbh, and their uncle Neachtain Ó Domhnaill,[157] can be plausibly interpreted as originating in the determination of a prince's sons to retain their father's portion as against the desire of a new chief to have all the lands at his disposal. In this situation a kin-group within the ruling dynasty could simply use its leader's claim to the royal succession as a weapon in its own defence. Such claims undoubtedly added venom to the original quarrel, and since they were made possible by a general acceptance of the principle *feabta la flaith*, that power took precedence over primogeniture, it is possible to argue that the Irish succession-system bore responsibility for the endemic civil wars within the Gaelic lordships.

This is neither a full nor an adequate explanation, however. The real problem would seem to have lain deeper still, in a system of land-tenure which appears to have given the princes overlordship rather than ownership of their allotted area,[158] such that they required kern and galloglass to maintain their influence, and could be driven out at any time by a stronger intruder. Such overlordship without ownership is most clearly demonstrated in the demands made by the Ó Néill princes for tributes and services from the ecclesiastical tenants of Armagh, since the estates in these cases clearly belonged to the Church.[159] The forcible imposition of lordship was not confined to the chieftaincy itself, but applied throughout the noble grades in a society which could not function without violence. Violence was the sanction which ensured authority, justice, peace, and protection.[160] The customs and practice governing succession to the kingship were not an anachronistic flaw in the system, bringing turmoil into the Gaelic territories. The turmoil was already there. Rather, the institutions of kingship reflected the society which had created them.

153 Hogan, 'The Irish law', pp. 226–7.
154 Ó Fiaich, 'The O'Neills', pp. 1–24.
155 Simms, 'The medieval kingdom', p. 133.
156 Simms, 'Niall Garbh II O Donnell', pp. 10–11.
157 AU 1452.
158 See above, pp. 39–40, and below, pp. 113–14.
159 Simms, 'The archbishops'.
160 See above, pp. 25, 51, and below, pp. 106–7.

V

THE KING'S COUNSELLORS

Old Irish tracts on law and the duties of kingship lay considerable emphasis on the need for the inhabitants of a *tuath* to meet together frequently in assemblies presided over by their king, the *rí tuaithe*. The various terms which they use may be intended to distinguish different kinds of meeting, but there seems to have been a considerable overlap. Broadly speaking, the *oenach* was the most general gathering of the inhabitants, held at regular intervals for athletic, commercial, and legal activities and for the proclaiming of special ordinances by the king in certain recognised emergencies.[1] In origin the *airecht* may have been similarly open to every freeman (*aire*), but it came to be particularly associated with the hearing of law-suits.[2] *Dál* and *terchomrac* were more general terms for a meeting or mustering and sometimes had military connotations, although *dál*, like *airecht*, could also mean a law-court.[3]

It is not clear whether any such assemblies were accustomed to take counsel with the king before important decisions were reached affecting the public good. The legal tract *Críth Gablach* speaks obscurely of the king's need for some form of popular consent in relation both to the summoning of an *oenach* and to the definition of legal custom (*fénechas*).[4] *Tecosca Cormaic* recommend the king to hold abundant assemblies of every kind: 'a *terchomrac* of nobles, frequent *dála* ... an *airecht* according to the rules ... a lawful synod ... let him be an entertainer of a *dál* and an *airecht*'; but at the same time the text warns that consultation should be selective: 'listening to elders, turning a deaf ear to the rabble ... let him be attended by a host in gatherings (*i ndálaib*), let him be attended by few in secret councils (*i sanasaib*)'.[5] Consultation with a restricted élite is also implied in the seventh-century Life of St Patrick by Muirchú, when King Loíguire is represented as discussing his conversion with 'the elders and his whole council' (*senioribus et omni senatu suo*).[6] Similarly, in the Old Irish saga of Fergus mac Léti, preserved in legal manuscripts, it is 'the

[1] Binchy, 'The Fair', p. 124.

[2] Binchy, *Críth Gablach*, p. 73.

[3] *Dictionary*, ed. Quin, *s.v.*

[4] Binchy, *Críth Gablach*, lines 493–505, 514–16 (pp. 102, 104).

[5] *Tecosca Cormaic* (ed. Meyer), §§ 3 and 6.

[6] Bieler & Kelly, *The Patrician Texts*, p. 96. I owe the references in this and the next two footnotes to my husband, Kim McCone.

decision of the wise men of Ulster' (*comairle gaeth nUlad*) which allows the blemished king to remain in office.[7] Moreover, the importance of the king's deferring to the counsels of the wise (*gaeth*) is a theme occurring in both *Togail Bruidne Da Derga* and *Briathartheccosc Con Culaind*.[8] At the same time, it is perhaps significant that in *Tecosca Cormaic* the king should need to be warned to turn a deaf ear to the rabble (*fri daescarshlúag*). Certainly, many sagas speak as if political decisions were taken at assemblies of all the free-warrior class in a particular territory. Instead of using technical terms like *oenach* or *airecht*, *De shíl Chonairi Moir* (as we have seen in an earlier chapter) tells us that the choice of a new king of Tara was discussed by 'the men of Leinster and the race of Conn Cétchathach' and in *Scéla Conchobair* succession to the throne of Ulster was decided by 'the Ulstermen'.[9] However, it is made clear that even these saga-writers did not envisage a turn-out of the entire population on such occasions: we read in *Serglige Con Culaind* of a great assembly (*mórdál*) of four provinces of Ireland which met 'in the house' of Erc mac Corpri Niad Fer to choose another king of Tara.[10] The early twelfth-century history of Brian Bóroimhe, *Cogadh Gaedhel re Gallaibh*, depicts a number of meetings summoned by kings to discuss a great variety of topics. Here, too, the impression is of a general gathering of the warrior class:[11]

> ... all the Dál Cais were assembled to one appointed place before Mathgamhain and he asked them what decision they wished to come to, namely whether they would have peace or war with the foreigners, and with the Danars. Then they all answered, both old and young ['War'] ... and this was the voice of hundreds as the voice of one man.

Later in the same story Aodh Ó Néill summoned the Cineál Eoghain and asked them if he should ally with the high king Maoilsheachlainn against Brian. They raised certain objections, and he advised them to retire from his presence and discuss the question in secret council (*i comarli ocus i cocur*). Cineál Eoghain decided to exact impossibly high concessions from Maoilsheachlainn. At the news of this rebuff, Maoilsheachlainn consulted his own kin-group, Clann Cholmáin, which advised him to submit to Brian, as he then did.[12] It is now recognised that the *Cogadh* was the work of political propaganda,[13] but since it was presumably written to enhance the prestige and authority of later Ó Briain rulers it seems unlikely that the powerful position of the assembled counsellors in relation to their respective kings would have been deliberately over-stressed.

[7] Binchy, 'The saga', pp. 36, 38.
[8] Knott, *Togail Bruidne Da Derga*, lines 166–7; Dillon, *Serglige Con Culainn*, line 287.
[9] See above, p. 42, nn. 6–7.
[10] Dillon, *Serglige Con Culainn*, lines 239–40.
[11] Todd, *Cogadh Gaedhel*, p. 68.
[12] *Ibid.*, pp. 128–31.
[13] Ó Corráin, 'Caithréim Chellacháin Chaisil', pp. 5, 69.

Indeed, the Annals of Inisfallen during the reign of Brian's brother Mathghamhain speak of three ordinances being enacted 'by the counsel of the nobles of Mumu'.[14]

All pre-Norman chronicles have frequent references to assemblies, distinguishing between *oenach*, *dál* and *airecht*. The *oenaig* which they mention are the great province-wide gatherings, especially *Oenach Tailten* held among the southern Uí Néill.[15] Until the ninth century these reunions were (it is assumed) annual events, only worthy of note if they were broken up by fighting among the participants (*cummasc oenaich, commixtio agonis*)[16] or if they were the scene of some startling event or miracle.[17] After 872, however, *Oenach Tailten* gradually fell into disuse; the *oenach* of Roighne in Ossory had already been discontinued prior to 859,[18] and it would seem that these recorded instances of neglect were part of a more general trend. From the late ninth century to the twelfth there were sporadic attempts to renew the celebration of Tailtiu and other *oenaig*,[19] but these were evidently single occasions on which a king gave a public demonstration of his newly extended authority.

Instead, the great ecclesiastical settlements became a general meeting place for the surrounding populations on the occasion of the main Church-festivals. Already in the second half of the seventh century the monk Cogitosus is able to tell us of the innumerable peoples from all provinces who streamed into Kildare on St Brigit's Day (1 February), some of them apparently to enjoy the banquets and admire the crowds rather than for any strictly religious purpose.[20] From the ninth century onwards, assemblies at such ecclesiastical sites began to be mentioned by annalists just at the time when the *oenach* was falling into decay. The faction-fighting at Armagh on Whitsunday,[21] or at Clonmacnoise on St Ciarán's Day,[22] is reported in the same terms as the earlier *cummasc oenaich*, disturbance of an *oenach*. Indeed, the Old Irish Triads explicitiy list as the 'three *oenaig* of Ireland' (*par excellence*) the *oenach* of Tailtiu, the *oenach* of Cruachan, and the *oenach* of St Colmán of Lann Ela.[23] Although the Royal Irish Academy's *Dictionary* would explain the third *oenach* as a reference to St Colmán's crowded religious community, the later Irish Life of Colmán Ela does not support this interpretation. According to this the *oenach* was a duty which the population surrounding Lann Ela, the Fir Chell, must perform for the saint on pain of

14 AI 972.1.
15 Binchy, 'The Fair'.
16 AU 717.6, 774.7, 789.17, 827.5–6, 831.5.
17 AFM 539, 767, 784, 806.
18 AFM 859.
19 AFM 859, 894, 915, 954, 1006, 1033, 1120, 1168; Ó Corráin, 'Nationality', p. 20.
20 Cogitosus, *Vita Brigidae* (ed. Bollandus), § 39.
21 AU 819.8, 893.2.
22 AFM 998, 1038.
23 § 35 (ed. Meyer).

malediction, and its essence consisted in paying tribute to Colmán's crozier,[24] as those who came to Kildare on St Brigid's Day were said to bring great gifts with them. Similar references to the *oenach* at Glendalough appear in the Irish Lives of St Coemgen.[25] Indeed, as late as the nineteenth century the 'Festival of the Seven Churches, Glendalough' is painted by Joseph Peacock as a popular gathering markedly secular in tone.[26] It could well be that the survival of the word *aonach* meaning simply 'a fair' in Modern Irish is due to the mediaeval observance of local saints' days.

This evolution from a secular to an ecclesiastical *oenach* meant that such gatherings were no longer presided over by a king and thus lost whatever political significance they had once possessed. A rather different fate awaited the reforming synods of the Irish Church in the twelfth century, sometimes referred to in annalistic texts by the secular terms *dál*, *comdál*, or *mórdál*.[27] Like the eighth-century Frankish synods or tenth-century Anglo-Saxon Church-councils, they were usually summoned by a king and attended by the lay nobility as well as by clerics.[28] This involvement of secular rulers in ecclesiastical affairs might seem rather anachronistic by the twelfth century, but it had been recommended to the Irish Church by Lanfranc, archbishop of Canterbury, whose own synods were notoriously subject to the authority of William the Conqueror, though not actually attended by the Norman king.[29] From the first the Irish kings used such assemblies to promote their own political interests, as when Muircheartach Ó Briain granted the Rock of Cashel, chief place of the rival Eoghanacht dynasty, to the Church at the First Synod of Cashel, in 1101.[30] Under the influence of Cistercian ideals, St Malachy of Armagh and his followers went some way towards breaking this tradition by holding the Synod of Inispatrick in 1148 and the Synod of Kells in 1152 without obvious royal patronage.[31] However, a further mixed assembly of clerics and laymen was held in 1161 – under the control of Muircheartach MacLochlainn, the northern 'high king with opposition' – and showed clear political motivation by promoting the interests of Derry in the North at the expense of the rest of the Irish Church.[32] Finally, in 1167, a gathering held under the last high king, Ruaidhri Ó Conchobhair, was arguably concerned as much with secular as with ecclesiastical affairs, since it is said to have 'passed many good

[24] *Betha Cholmáin Eala* (ed. Plummer), §§ 25, 28, 30, 31.
[25] *Betha Caoimhgin* (II) (ed. Plummer), § 11; (III), § 22.
[26] De Breffny, *The Irish World*, p. 174.
[27] AFM, AT 1101; AI 1111.3; AU 1161.
[28] Nelson, 'National synods', p. 43; McKitterick, *The Frankish Church*, p. 12; Duckett, *Anglo-Saxon Saints*, pp. 422–4; Whitelock, *English Historical Documents* pp. 68–9.
[29] Brooke, *The English Church and the Papacy*, pp. 132, 136–7. See above, p. 26, n. 21.
[30] Gwynn, *The Twelfth-century Reform*, pp. 9–10.
[31] *Ibid.*, p. 51; AFM 1148, 1152.
[32] AU 1161.

resolutions ... respecting veneration for churches and clerics, and control of tribes and territories'.[33] Just such mixed councils of clerical and lay leaders have been seen, rightly or wrongly, as the forerunners of the *cortes* or parliamentary assembly in Spain.[34] In Ireland, however, this involvement of lay chieftains in synods was to end with the Norman invasion, followed by the Second Synod of Cashel held in the winter of 1171/2 at the command of the English king, Henry II.[35]

The annalistic evidence indicates that the one political assembly in the pre-Norman period which contained the seeds of future development was the *airecht* or *oireacht*. As the annalists use the term, it was an institution with wider functions than a law-court, the scene for parleys between warring territories or between vassal-kings and their overlords. Sometimes it is spoken of as belonging to all the people of a certain kingdom, as in 1023, when the earliest annalistic occurrence of the word refers to an assembly of the Dublin Norsemen:[36]

Donnchadh Ua Duinn, lord of Breagh, was treacherously seized upon by the foreigners at their own *airecht*; and he was carried eastwards over the sea, in violation of Colum Cille, whose successor was his guarantee.

At other times, however, the *airecht* is said to belong not to the people but to the ruler. In 1026 'Muiredhach Ua Céle was betrayed by Domhnall Ua Ceallaigh, who slew him in his own *aireacht*',[37] and in 1053 'Curian Ua Maeldúin, lord of Feara Luirg, was treacherously killed by Mac-na-hAidhche Ua Ruairc, at his own *aireacht*'.[38] As these entries show, violent death at such a meeting is invariably described as treachery or betrayal, implying that an *airecht* was by definition a peaceful occasion, intended for discussion rather than armed confrontation. In entries for the late eleventh and early twelfth centuries the phrase '*x* came into the *airecht*' of some powerful king appears tantamount to saying that he 'joined forces with' or even 'submitted to' an overlord.[39] This is made explicit in an entry for 1118, when the high king Muircheartach Ó Briain was deserted by his allies:[40]

Toirdhealbhach Ó Conchobhair, Murchadh Ó Maoil Sheachlainn and Aodh son of Donnchadh Ó Ruairc came into the *oireachtas* of Tadhg son of MacCarthaig and made an enduring treaty with him and with Cormac, his kinsman, against Muircheartach.

The word employed here, *oireachtas*, is an abstract noun derived from

[33] AFM 1167.
[34] Merriman, *The Rise*, I.218–19; King, *Law*, pp. 125–9.
[35] Watt, *The Church in Medieval Ireland*, p. 34.
[36] AFM, ALC, AU 1023. See also AFM 1163.
[37] ALC, AU 1026.
[38] AFM 1053.
[39] AI 1093.2 (above, p. 42, n. 9); AU 1114.3.
[40] McC 1118.3.

airecht or *oireacht* and it foreshadows a subtle change of usage in the later twelfth century. Thereafter *oireachtas* described the assembly itself and *oireacht* was reserved for the people who attended it. In 1184, for instance,[41]

> Art Ó Maelsechlainn, king of Midhe, was slain by Diarmaid Ó Briain at a meeting (*a conne*) at Druim Chuilinn, after having come from the midst of his own *airecht* to speak apart with the son of Ó Briain, and the son of Ó Briain deceived him.

Rather than of events taking place 'in the *airecht*', we hear instead of decisions taken 'by the *airecht*',[42] even of chieftains assassinated by their own *airecht*.[43]

This shift in meaning allows us at last to seek an answer to the question of what kind of people constituted an *airecht* or *oireacht*. During the late twelfth and early thirteenth centuries there are scattered annal-entries identifying certain noblemen as belonging to the *oireacht* of the Ó Conchobhair kings of Connacht. Apart from princes of the royal family of Ó Conchobhair, the families named are Ó Fiannachta, Mac Diarmata, Ó Maoilmhíchil, Ó Floinn, Ó Flannagáin, Ó Taidhg.[44] All these surnames figure in the list of the twelve sub-chieftains from Ó Conchobhair's home territory of Síol Muireadhaigh who were traditionally entitled to assist at his inauguration, each of their families having the hereditary right to supply a particular official to serve in Ó Conchobhair's household and army.[45] Indeed, while the Four Masters' version of the events of 1189 tells us that the Ó Conchobhair king was slain by a section of his own followers and his *oireacht*, the Annals of Ulster and of Loch Cé say that he was killed by his own officials (*d'a lucht grádha féin*).[46] Not all the nobles named in these entries are definitely identifiable as reigning sub-chiefs, and it is certain from other contexts that men chosen as royal officials were not invariably the heads of their kindreds.[47] A charter drawn up in 1224 to record a grant by Aodh Ó Conchobhair, king of Connacht, to the Cistercian order ends with a list of witnesses comprising prelates, sub-chieftains, and royal officials. In this case the officials – Torbert Mac Gallghaeidhil, the king's seneschal or *reachtaire*, and 'Concors' his chancellor – do not seem to have been members of the hereditary nobility at all, but four of the five sub-chieftains named figure in contemporary annals as members of the *oireacht* and the same status is implied for the son and heir of the fifth Irish chieftain.[48]

41 ALC 1184.
42 AConn 1225.5, 1262.9, 1296.2, 1317.10.
43 AFM 1189, 1407, 1465; AU 1214; AConn 1306.3.
44 AFM 1189; AConn 1225.5 and 18.
45 Dillon, 'The inauguration', p. 189.
46 See below, p. 85, n. 54.
47 For example, AConn 1225.30 and 31.
48 AConn 1225.4, 5, 18. Orpen, 'Some Irish Cistercian documents', pp. 304–6.

This encourages one to look more closely at similar lists in other thirteenth-century royal grants. Two charters of the thirteenth-century kings of Thomond were witnessed by the clerks of the kings' household and by a list of men bearing the surnames of the hereditary sub-chieftains of Thomond,[49] although the evidence to identify them positively as heads of their families is unfortunately lacking. More satisfactory is a document emanating from Airghialla (the Co. Monaghan area) in 1297. Here we have an affirmation of the immunity of churchmen and Church-land from assault or lay taxation; this is accompanied by regulations to ensure the observance of such immunity, jointly agreed to by the local king, Brian Mac Mathghamhna, a named list of his sub-chiefs, 'and the rest of the other nobles of Airghialla'. Appended to the main text are statements that the primate of Armagh had requested and obtained the same concessions from two other assemblies, that of King Domhnall Ó Néill and the magnates of Tír Eoghain, and that of Donn MagUidhir, king of Loch Erne, with his magnates and chieftains.[50]

The apparent contrast – between the passive role of the nobility as witnesses to the grants in Connacht and Thomond and their active participation in the northern agreements – probably reflects the nature of the documents rather than any regional variation in political custom. The Connacht and Thomond charters granted an annual sum of money to the monastery of Cîteaux in the name of the king himself and his immediate family. In Thomond this was followed by a series of separate grants from each of the chief nobles and their wives, drawn up in an additional charter sealed with the seal of their overking, Donnchadh Cairbreach Ó Briain, 'cum sigilla propria non haberemus'.[51] Since the initial donations came from the provincial kings as individuals, there was no reason for the direct participation of their vassals. In Ulster, on the other hand, the grant of immunity to Church-lands and personnel was explicitly stated to concern the jurisdiction of the local chieftains, 'that one of us who in time past was accustomed to receive the amend for theft, spoils or any other similar transgression'. The authority of the king of Airghialla was only to be invoked when his vassal failed to take action over an ecclesiastic's complaint.[52] In this society, it seems clear, the king was far from occupying the role of the emperor in Roman civil law as the 'fount of justice', delegating his powers to the local rulers as to his agents and representatives. Here, jurisdiction over a particular locality was the customary right of its own hereditary chieftain, and it would appear from what follows that the king's supervisory powers were based on his lordship over the chieftain himself through a personal contract of vassalage.

Among the sub-chieftains of Airghialla named in this 1297 agreement are Ó Dubhthaigh, chief of Teallach Gealagain, Mac Cionaetha, chief of

[49] D'Arbois de Jubainville, 'Chartes', pp. 83–5.
[50] Nicholls, 'The Register', pp. 410–15, 422–3.
[51] D'Arbois de Jubainville, 'Chartes', pp. 85–6.
[52] Nicholls, 'The Register', p. 417.

the Triocha Céad, and the lord of Dartraighe whose title was at this time held by the king's own brother, Roalbh Mac Mathghamhna, although it had earlier been hereditary in the Ó Baoighealláin family. As far as we know, Uí Bhaoigheallain never recovered control of Dartraighe after this date, and even the Ó Dubhthaigh family lapsed into political obscurity, a fact which imparts a striking air of antiquity to one passage in an early seventeeth-century tract on the rights and customs of Mac Mathghamhna.[53]

The three principal chieftains of the Oirghialla in the time of Brian Mór son of Ardghal [*sic*, ob. 1442] were Ó Buidhellan of Dartraighe, MacCeanaith in the Triucha and Duthach [*sic*] in Teallach Gealagáin; and these chieftains are by right stewards [*maoir* = tax-collectors] of their own territories and Ó Connalaigh is the chief marshal of all Oirghialla. And at the inauguration of MacMathghamhna each of these (three) chieftains receives either a rider's suit or forty marks of old silver in its stead. They and Ó Connalaigh and the comharba of Cluain Eois are the five lawful members of the council of Oirghialla (*an cuigear dligheas comhairle Oirghiall do beith acu*)

The statement here that these three hereditary sub-chieftains received ceremonial gifts at the inauguration of their overking, and that together with two leading office-holders, one lay and one ecclesiastical, they formed a kind of *quorum* of the territorial council, recalls the mid-thirteenth-century poem quoted in an earlier chapter, in which Ó Catháin's chief poet recollects playing at inaugurations with his patron when they were both children:[54]

> His stipend (*a thuarastal*) to me was always coming to us,
> Just as if we were his *oireacht*.

The word *tuarastal*, as well as applying to the ordinary wages of mercenary soldiers, was used of the ceremonial gift bestowed by an overlord on his vassal at the time of submission.[55] Clearly the author of this poem, composing about the year 1260, regarded the *oireacht* as typical recipients of such a gift. Rather than denoting a law-court, or an assembly of counsellors, the word in this context is used primarily as a collective term for the king's vassals, his subject nobility.[56] Some entries in thirteenth- and fourteenth-century annals show this semantic shift, and extend it to include not only a king's vassalage but his subject territory also. Thus a muster of local fighting-men in 1225 is termed *tinól oirechta* (? 'a territorial levy').[57] In 1311, we are told, 'battle was given by Donnchadh Mac Conmara and by his *oireacht*, namely, by the cantred of

[53] Ó Dufaigh, 'Cíos Mhic Mhathghamhna', p. 132.
[54] Above, p. 23, n. 11.
[55] Below, p. 101.
[56] For Mac Niocaill's translation of *aireachta* as 'clientèle noble' see above, p. 57, n. 134.
[57] AConn 1225.8.

Uí Chaisin'.[58] In some entries the word seems to denote noble vassals other than the sub-chieftains themselves, as in 1306: 'Great war between Aed son of Eogan Ó Conchobair, king of Connacht, with the nobility of Sil Murray on his side, and Aed son of Cathal Ó Conchobair, with many of the kings' and chieftains' sons of Connacht and the chieftains and *oirechts* of Bréfne ... on his'.[59] We hear that in 1315,

> [MacDiarmada] plundered from the Sinainn to Caraidh-Cúla-Cuirc, where the *oirechts* of the three Ciarraidhe were, viz. Ciarraidhe iartharach, and Ciarraidhe-Mhaige and Ciarraidhe-Airtigh, with all their flocks and cattle.

Although these contexts take us a long way from the council-chamber, yet at this period there was still a sense of legal entity, a corporate authority, vested in the term, which surfaces in accounts of the making and deposing of kings. In 1262, for instance,[61]

> A great depredation was committed by the Foreigners of Midhe on Gilla-na-naemh O Ferghail, chieftain of the Anghaile; and his own *oirecht* forsook him and went over to the Foreigners; and he was deposed by them, and the son of Murchadh Carrach Ó Ferghail was made chieftain in opposition to him.

In 1296 'Aed son of Eogan Ó Conchobair was deposed by his own *oirecht* and the Clan Murtagh were brought in to replace him, the lordship and hostages of the country being given to Conchobar Ruad son of Cathal Ruad Ó Conchobair'.[62] Again in 1309,[63]

> Maelruanaig MacDiarmata ... came with his household muster about him into the heart of Sil Murray, to uphold the kingship and rule for his foster-son Fedlimid O Conchobair ... and he encamped stoutly and sturdily at Fiad Ratha Cruachan among the trains of the district (*a mesc imircech an tiri* = 'the migrating bands of the land'), keeping them together; for his great fear was that those *oirechts* should come to an agreement with Aed Brefnech son of Cathal. And he took personally the lordship of the chieftains and the submission of the sub-kings and exacted their rents and stipulated tributes and all the family and regal jewels of the king of Connacht, and all Sil Murray made oath and gave security that they would not yield the lordship to any other [but to Fedlimid].

This picture of the *oireacht* wielding joint-powers and taking a joint-oath is interestingly borne out in a series of Anglo-Norman documents from the early fourteenth century. In 1310, after a truce negotiated by Richard D'Exeter, justice of the King's Bench at Dublin, the king issued letters of pardon to *Maghoun McMaghoun et omnibus Hibernicis de eraghto suo* for

58 AConn, ALC, AU 1311.
59 AConn, ALC, Ann. Rawl. B.488: 1306.
60 AConn, ALC 1315.
61 AConn 1262.9.
62 AConn 1296.2.
63 AConn 1309.3.

their raids against the inhabitants of Co. Louth.[64] Mac Mathghamhna and his *oireacht*, or 'eraght', became jointly responsible for paying a fine of £10,[65] and as surety for the payment they gave three hostages.[66] At the same time a similar pardon was negotiated with Mathghamhain Mac-an-Chaoich Uí Raighilligh, *pro se et eraghto suo*, when two hostages were handed over in pledge for a fine of ten marks.[67] Since the justiciary roll's account of these transactions implies that Mac Mathghamhna's *oireacht* took part in the negotiations ('they would ... satisfy all who wished to complain of them ... Maghoun McMaghoun and his men ... found pledges', etc.), the word would seem to refer here to an actual council or assembly of nobles. As an instance of the use of the word in the more general sense of 'vassal-nobility', we find the Irish Close Roll of 1358 recording that 'Art' Kevenagh McMurgh et Donenald Revagh cum aliis de Iraghto suo et aliis complicibus de guerra insurrexerunt',[68] where the *oireacht* seems distinguished on the one hand from Mac Murchadha's kinsman, Domhnall Riabhach, and on the other from his external allies.

However, from about the mid-fourteenth century, *oireacht* more or less ceased to be used as a collective noun. It occurred instead as a simple plural *aireachta* ('nobles', 'vassals') and it is significant to find that in the early seventeenth century the Four Masters substituted this plural form when rewriting in their Annals entries where the earlier Annals of Connacht and Annals of Ulster either read *airecht* or *oirecht* (in the singular) or give the names of individual sub-chiefs.[69] *Aireachta* in the plural may well be the basis for the sixteenth-century Anglo-Irish term 'urraghts', applied to the vassal-chiefs of Ó Neill or some other paramount lord,[70] although the variant forms 'euraghe' and 'urriaghe' suggest some influence from a separate word, *uirrighthe*, 'sub-kings'.

Oireacht as a noun in the singular survives mainly as a component meaning 'lordship' or 'territory' in place-names formed during the fifteenth and sixteenth centuries, as in Oireacht-Uí-Chatháin, 'the lordship of Ó Catháin' comprising most of the modern Co. Derry,[71] or Iraghticonnor, a barony in the north of the present Co. Kerry. There was also in use a curious phrase, *duine maith oireacht* ('a good man of *oireachta*'), which crops up in annalistic obits in this later period to

64 *CCH*, p. 18, no. 112; *CJRI 1308–14*, p. 161.

65 *PRI rep. DK* no. 39, p. 36. The printed calender of the pipe-roll reads here 'Mahoun M'mahoun and *totus creghus suus*', but Betham's manuscript-excerpt from the same lost original (Dublin, National Library of Ireland, MS.760, p. 292) seems to read *totus eraghus* and, in view of the reading *eraghtus* in the calendered Irish patent roll (n. 64 above), Betham's version is to be preferred.

66 *CJRI 1308–14*, p. 161.

67 *Ibid.*; *CCH*, p. 18, no. 113.

68 *CCH*, p. 68, no. 34. See also Mac Niocaill, *The Red Book*, no. 169.

69 Compare AConn 1225.5 and 25, 1262.9, 1296.4, and AU 1366 with AFM for those years.

70 Nicholls, *Gaelic and Gaelicised Ireland*, pp. 22–4, 187–8; Brewer & Bullen, *Calendar of the Carew Manuscripts*, II.11, 15–16, 384.

71 Ó Ceallaigh, *Gleanings*, p. 48.

describe men of noble family who did not hold any official title. The context is often one of vassalage – a *duine maith oirecht* 'of the people of the sons of Philip MagUidhir', 'of the people of Ua Neill', 'of the people of the sons of Ua Ruairc' [72] – and the usage may reflect the distinction occasionally drawn as early as the end of the thirteenth century[73] between sub-chieftains and the other vassal nobility of an overlord.

In effect, then, the meaning originally attached to the word as a corporate body of counsellors became obsolete from the mid-fourteenth century onwards. Nevertheless, it is clear that consultations continued to take place between kings and their subjects on the eve of important political decisions. We have contemporary documentation of one such occasion in the Ó Néill lordship of Tír Eoghain in the spring of 1395. News of the landing of King Richard II and his army in the previous October and of his military defeat of the Leinster chieftains had prompted Niall Óg Ó Néill, 'governor of the Irish of Ulster', and his elderly father, Niall Mór Ó Néill, to send conciliatory letters to the king early in January.[74] On the 19th or 20th of that month Niall Mór appeared before Richard in Drogheda, took an oath of allegiance on his own behalf and that of his powerful son and exhibited a document from Niall Óg formally authorising his father to negotiate a truce with the English which would bind 'meque et nacionem patriamque et omnia bona mea ... ad emenda seu satisfacciones prestandas'.[75] The Irish considered these negotiations to involve not only members of the Ó Néill kindred or surname (*natio*) but also the sub-chieftains of Tír Eoghain. One of their number, Maghnus Ó Catháin, wrote subsequently: 'Ó Néill, as he asserts, made peace both for himself and for his vassals, and so it was against the king's peace that my men were preyed'.[76] Interestingly, it would appear that neither Ó Catháin nor the other sub-chieftains had been formally consulted before the letters were sent off, allegiance sworn, or peace concluded. It transpired, however, that in spite of his letters of authorisation Niall Óg did not consider himself fully committed by his father's embassy, and Richard insisted that he should come to do homage in person. Still hesitating, Niall Óg wrote to the English archbishop of Armagh: 'According to your sage counsel, we made to come to us all the great men [obedient to us] among the Irish of Ulster to consult and deliberate with them about my going to the King's Court'.[77] Concerning the council itself, we have only strong presumptive evidence that it was attended by Ó Catháin and the Scottish constable of Ó Néill's galloglass,

72 AU 1474, 1485, 1486.
73 Above, n. 59.
74 Curtis, *Richard II*, pp. 129–32. The letters themselves are undated, but Richard II wrote on 8 January that he had received Ó Néill's offer of submission (Legge, *Anglo-Norman Letters*, p. 209).
75 Curtis, *Richard II*, pp. 86–7, 106–7, 145.
76 *Ibid.*, p. 220.
77 *Ibid.*, p. 221 (words in square brackets are in the Latin text but omitted from Curtis's translation).

both of whom favoured submission to Richard II. As well as the nobles of Tír Eoghain, Ó Néill may also have consulted his subordinate allies, leading members of the Mac Mathghamhna family of Airghialla and the Uí Anluain of Airthir, who came to do homage to Richard in the same week as Niall Óg himself.[78] Nevertheless, Niall Óg's eventual decision to submit was apparently seen by the Irish as a personal rather than a communal responsibility. He subsequently wrote to Richard: 'I cannot trust my own people since they see me turning away from them to your Majesty'.[79]

Perhaps this emphasis on the individual will of Ó Néill in the late fourteenth century may be usefully contrasted with a similar episode in the early thirteenth century when the king of Connacht's council took a more active role in dictating the terms of submission and suffered in person for their error of judgement:[80]

> Johannes ... the king of the Saxons told the king of Connacht to come to meet him at the end of a fortnight. He promised that he would, and that he would bring his son with him, i.e. Aedh, son of Cathal Crobhderg; (and it was not the king who requested this). 'Bring him,' said the king, 'that he may receive a charter for the third part of Connacht.' When Ó Conchobhair arrived at his own place, the counsel which he, and his wife, and his people adopted was, not to take the son to the king, although this was the worst counsel. However, when Ó Conchobhair went to the king of the Saxons and did not take his son with him, Diarmaid, son of Conchobhar MacDiarmada, king of Magh-Luirg, and Conchobhar Ó hEghra, king of Luighne of Connacht, and Find Ó Carmacan, a man of trust (*fer grádha*) to Ó Conchobhair, and Toirberd, son of a Gall-Gaeidhel, one of Ó Conchobhair's stewards (*reachtaire*), were apprehended by the king of the Saxons. The king of the Saxons went across afterwards, and took these chieftains with him to Saxon-land.

Returning to the later period, we find that, since Niall Óg had issued a written authorisation to his father to negotiate a truce binding on his 'nation and fatherland' before consulting the magnates obedient to him, there must be some doubt as to what discussions, if any, lay behind other claims to full authorisation in connexion with similar treaties during the fifteenth century. For instance, in 1401, in an indenture with Prince Thomas of Lancaster, then King's Lieutenant in Ireland, the young Eoghan Ó Raighilligh, chief of East Bréifne, claims when renewing the terms of his father Seaán's submission to the English that he has 'a general power and special command from all his subjects and adherents or allies, of proceeding with, accomplishing, and observing the following articles'.[81] Yet the contemporary annals of Aughuistín Magraidhin state that in 1401 'the son of Seaán' Ó Raighilligh had been imposed on his subjects by the English and was subsequently expelled and the chieftain-ship awarded

[78] *Ibid.*, pp. 60, 68, 70, 97–8, 102–3.
[79] *Ibid.*, pp. 213–14.
[80] ALC 1210.
[81] Hardiman, 'A statute', p. 88, n. 6.

to a rival kinsman.[82] In the same way, Éinri Ó Néill, in his indenture with the Duke of York in 1449, claimed to possess 'plenam potestatem pro dicto patre suo filiis et fratribus suis et omnibus sibi subditis',[83] but there is no explicit reference to prior consultation.

On the other hand, in 1433 when Niall Garbh Ó Domhnaill, king of Tír Conaill, had departed with his army to wage war against Ó Néill and his enemies took advantage of his absence to invade Tír Conaill itself, a meeting (*comdháil*) was held at Inis Eoghain at which Ó Domhnaill's wife, his brother Neachtain, and the 'princes of Tír Conaill' (*meic rígh Conallaigh*) parleyed with the invaders 'and peace was made between them without permission from Ua Domnaill'.[84] The presence of the chief's wife at this conference is consonant with the earlier participation of Ó Conchobhair's wife in debating the terms of her husband's submission to King John, and with the later presence of Aodh Dubh Ó Domhnaill's wife at the council of nobles which elected her son Aodh Ruadh to succeed to his father's authority.[85] Within the government of an Irish lordship a queen held a recognised position comparable to that of the *tánaiste*, being endowed like him with certain lands and revenue from taxation.[86] The attendance of the queen *ex officio* at the 1433 meeting suggests a formal council held in accordance with tradition rather than an *ad hoc* discussion between the opposing military commanders.

Even in the sixteenth century the right of a chieftain's noble vassals to participate in important political decisions receives recognition on a number of occasions. In 1541, when Sir Anthony St Leger asked Murchadh Ó Briain to accede to certain articles of submission,[87]

> he requyred, forasmiche as he was but one man, allthogh he were capytayne of his nation, that he moght have time till Shrofetide, to consulte with his kinsfolke and frendes, and then to make answer.

In 1564, when Sir Henry Sidney restored *an Calbhach* Ó Domhnaill to power in Tír Conaill, the articles of his submission were not merely witnessed but confirmed (*his predictis concessiones suas dederunt et affirmauerunt*) by a list of local nobles comprising Ó Domhnaill's own brother and uncle, the bishop and the 'official' of the diocese of Raphoe, Ó Dochartaigh, Ó Baoighill, Ó Gallchobhair, the three Mac Suibhne chieftains *et ceterorum generosorum Conalie*.[88]

In all these examples, from the late thirteenth century onwards, of consultation between an overlord and his subjects the counsellors have been unambiguously identified as aristocrats, *nobiles*, *magnates*, *generosi*.

[82] Ann. Rawl. B.488 (ed. Ó hInnse), 1401.11, 1402.33.
[83] Curtis, 'The "Bonnaght" of Ulster', p. 87.
[84] AU 1433.
[85] Above, n. 80; Walsh, *Beatha Aodha Ruaidh*, I.40.
[86] Simms, 'The legal position', pp. 108–9.
[87] *State Papers, Henry VIII, Ireland 1538–47*, p. 288.
[88] Betham, *Irish Antiquarian Researches*, p. 197.

Sometimes an even more restricted group of advisers is indicated, as with the 'five lawful members of the council of Oirghialla',[89] or the five chief vassals entitled to elect MacWilliam Burke of Mayo.[90] Yet references, from the fourteenth century to the late sixteenth, to meetings of the *oireachtas*, the political assembly held by an overlord, indicate that such an élite-group of noble vassals might often convene on the occasion of a more general gathering, resembling the *oenach* in that it was held at regular intervals and attended by the population at large, and resembling the old *oireacht* in that it dealt with legal disputes between territories or between individuals. The annalists' use of the word *oireachtas* tells us only that ruling chiefs summoned the nobles of their territory to attend it,[91] that it provided the occasion upon which rebellious vassals might tender their submission or hostile neighbouring chieftains might parley for peace-terms, and that to assassinate an old enemy in these circumstances was 'ugly treachery'.[92]

The annalists also quote a proverbial saying of candidates for chieftainship who died before they were formally inaugurated – *escur i mbeol airechtais*, which could be interpreted as 'a fall on the assembly-threshold'.[93] This would suggest that formal reception by the assembled territorial council may have been an integral preliminary to the inauguration-ceremony, a possibility consistent with the power of the thirteenth-century *oireacht* to make and depose kings, with the references in the Life of Aodh Ruadh Ó Domhnaill to the election of chiefs by a council of nobles,[94] and with the vaguer allusions in the fifteenth-century Annals of Ulster to kings being made 'unanimously, by will of God and by the laity and clergy and elders and ollams and yeoman and hospitallers (*le brughadhaibh & le biatachaibh*)'.[95] On the other hand, it must be recognised that *oireachtas* acquired the secondary meaning of 'sovereignty', 'power' – the abstract counterpart of *oireacht* in the sense of territorial lordship – and thus the proverbial phrase in question could be less colourfully translated as simply 'a fall at the very beginning of sovereignty'.[96]

More explicit information comes from sixteenth-century sources. In 1526 a written covenant was drawn up in Irish between two chieftains in Westmeath, Mac Eochagáin and his vassal *An Sionnach* ('the Fox'). One clause stipulated that 'Every Allhallowtide or May *oireachtas* that shall take place in Mageoghegan's country shall be convened at the town of Ath-an-urchair or Corrna-sgean, and the Fox and the chieftains of his

[89] Above, n. 53.
[90] Above, p. 48, n. 50.
[91] Ann. Rawl. B.488 (ed. O hInnse), 1404.8, 1406.16.
[92] AConn 1342.4, 1366.2; AU 1382, 1384; AFM 1403; Ann. Rawl. B.488 (ed. Ó hInnse), 1392.9.
[93] AConn 1410.2, 1418.3.
[94] Above, p. 48, n. 50; Walsh, *Beatha Aodha Ruaidh*, I.40.
[95] AU 1430, 1432.
[96] *Dictionary*, ed. Quin, *s.v.* '*airechtas* (b)', and '*bél* iii(a)'.

country (*maithe a thíri*) shall come with him thither'.[97] The first day of May and the first day of November were significant dates for the general population as well as for the aristocracy. They followed bonfire-nights, folk-festivals originating in the pagan period.[98] They marked the beginning and end of the transhumance-period, the summer-pasturing of the cattle in the mountains,[99] and perhaps for that reason were the days on which cattle were counted for taxation-purposes, and on which rents and tributes fell due.[100] The idea that a lord's *oireachtas* may have involved a more general gathering than an exclusive council of nobles is found in a sixteenth-century comic romance, *Cetharnach Uí Dhomhnaill*, which describes Lord John FitzGerald of Desmond as holding his '*aonach* and high *oireachtas*' on the green outside his castle. He is approached on this occasion by a very down-at-heel kern, or unemployed mercenary soldier, whom he welcomes warmly and invites to play the harp.[101] For this author the *oireachtas* is apparently a time of festivity, including musical entertainment, at which the overlord plays host not only to the nobility but to the common people, even to vagrants. This may be the kind of occasion witnessed by Count John de Perilhos when he visited Niall Óg Ó Néill in 1397:[102]

> on Christmas day, according to what the interpreters and some others who could speak Latin were saying, the king held court ... All the clerks and knights, bishops and abbots, and great lords ... And there were with the king three thousand horses, and many poor people to whom the king gave great alms of oxflesh.

The political connotations of the *oireachtas*, are brought out in the terms of Sir Seaán Ó Raighilligh's submission in 1584. In one article of this document he undertook not to 'assemble the Queen's people upon hills, or use any Iraghtes or parles upon hills'.[103] This reiterated insistence that such public gatherings of the chief's subjects took place on hills identifies the institution described by Edmund Spenser as an *oireachtas*:[104]

> There is great use among the Irish to make great assemblies together upon a Rath or hill, there to parly (as they say) about matters and wrongs between township and township, or one private person and another ... to them do commonly resort all the scum of loose people, where they may freely meet and confer of what

[97] O'Donovan, 'Covenant', p. 193.
[98] Danaher, *The Year*, pp. 95, 209; Binchy, 'The Fair', pp. 128–30.
[99] Danaher, *The Year*, pp. 86, 206.
[100] *CSPI 1608–10*, p. 533; Nicholls, *Gaelic and Gaelicised Ireland*, pp. 61–2, 67. The terms of St Martin and 'Beltone' (*Bealtaine* or Mayday) are given as rent-days in thirteenth-century Anglo-Norman Ulster (*PRI rep. DK* no. 39, p. 51).
[101] O'Grady, *Silva Gadelica*, I.279, II.314–15.
[102] Mahaffy, 'Two early tours', pp. 7–8.
[103] Hardiman, *Irish Minstrelsy*, II.159.
[104] Spenser, *A View* (ed. Renwick), pp. 77 and 79.

they list, which else they could not do without suspicion or knowledge of others. Besides, at these parlies I have diverse times known many Englishmen and other good Irish subjects have been villainously murdered, by moving one quarrel or another amongst them, for the Irish never come to those raths but armed, whether on horseback or on foot ... dangerous are such assemblies, whether for cess or aught else.

Spenser's reference here to 'cess' seems to apply exclusively to the taxation or purveyance exacted for the support of the English army in Ireland,[105] in which case he is objecting to a native Irish institution being supported and encouraged for the administrative convenience of his own government, but he may also have been thinking more generally of taxation imposed locally by Irish chiefs. Kenneth Nicholls has already drawn attention to Justice Luttrell's reference in 1537 to lords and great men of the marches making 'penal laws upon hills to poll (tax) the poor people, and if any poor man offend that law he shall pay the penalty without any forgiveness'.[106] There are too many reports from other observers that Irish taxes were 'imposed by extortion and strong hand',[107] that chieftains had 'power to cut upon all the inhabitants high or low ... which argues they held their lands of the chief lord in villeinage',[108] to allow one to posit that such assemblies could have possessed a realistic power to withhold consent to taxation, but it is not impossible that arrangements for allotting and levying the required sums could have been subject to discussion and negotiation, as in the Provincial Estates of early modern France.[109] As quoted above, a right of the three hereditary chieftains who were among the 'lawful members of the council of Oirghialla' was to be *maoir*, or tax-collectors of their own territories, and the same tract continues: 'Every expense sustained by the territory must be paid for or levied by them'.[110] Sub-chieftains who levied tax on behalf of an overlord were entitled to retain a proportion of the yield as a reward for their trouble.[111] In this context, therefore, the issue of taxation may well have been discussed at the periodic assemblies of the vassal nobility in an Irish lordship, but the absence of the all-important power of consent or otherwise to the lord's financial demands reduces the significance of this point from the perspective of constitutional history.

The experience of assemblies elsewhere in mediaeval Europe suggests that where subjects have failed to achieve control of the purse-strings of government they must also fail to exert a decisive influence on the legislative process because they cannot use economic pressure to compel the executive to pass measures designed to alleviate their

[105] *Ibid.*, pp. 79–81; Brewer & Bullen, *Calendar of the Carew Manuscripts*, II.66–7.
[106] Nicholls, *Gaelic and Gaelicised Ireland*, p. 46.
[107] Butler, *Gleanings*, p. 20.
[108] Morley, *Ireland under Elizabeth and James I*, p. 386.
[109] Mettam, *Government*, p. 33.
[110] Ó Dufaigh, 'Cíos Mhic Mhathghamhna', p. 132.
[111] See below, p. 137.

grievances.[112] While the main body of Irish law was seen as immemorial custom, there are some references from pre-Norman Ireland to ordinances being issued at councils or assemblies.[113] These allusions are less frequent in the later middle ages. The regulations accepted by the chiefs of Oirghialla in 1297 for the protection of Church-personnel and Church-property were the result of an entirely ecclesiastical initiative.[114] In the southern kingdom of Thomond, ruled at about the same date by Toirdhealbhach Ó Briain (*ob.* 1306), we are told in a fourteenth-century tract, 'The Miracles of Senán', that[115]

> An ordinance and law was set up (*do toccbadh nos & dlicched*) ... that if any man should slay another in the land, and the full eric was not got from him, that it should be exacted from his family, and if it were not obtained from them, it was to be exacted from his *tuath*...

In the event, this regulation was to prove contrary to ecclesiastical interests, and the use of a passive verb in connexion with its enactment may be an indication that it was decided in council, although it was the king, Toirdhealbhach, who was said to bear in person the brunt of St Senán's indignation. At first sight, we seem to have much clearer information about a later ruler in East Bréifne, Eoghan Ó Raighilligh (*ob.* 1449), of whom an eighteenth-century compilation of annalistic and traditional fragments records:[116]

> It is this Eoghan who, with lay and ecclesiastic consent (*do thoil tuaithe agus eaglaise*) composed the statutes (*na statuide*) by which the men of Bréifne abide.

There is nothing intrinsically unlikely about this account. The adoption of the English word 'statutes' suggests conscious imitation of English parliamentary legislation. Eoghan's contemporary, James Butler, the 'White Earl' of Ormond, had called the ordinances which he promulgated in his palatine jurisdiction of Tipperary 'statutes and corrections', and he claimed the right to summon the local inhabitants, spiritual and temporal, to his sessions, 'as well as the kyng may hole hys parlement'.[117] A number of the royal parliaments held during the fifteenth century by the chief governors of Ireland sat in Trim (Co. Meath) on the borders of Ó Raighilligh's territory, and at one of these Eoghan was accused of aping English practice to his own advantage in another way, by circulating his own bastard-coins, 'le money del O Raylly', which devalued the official currency.[118] The fact that the extract cited above refers in the present

112 Myers, *Parliaments*, pp. 29–30.
113 Above, nn. 4, 14, 33; Ó Corráin, 'Nationality', pp. 22–3.
114 Above, n. 50.
115 Plummer, 'The Miracles', pp. 8–9.
116 Carney, *A Genealogical History*, pp. 19–20.
117 Empey & Simms, 'The Ordinances', p. 186.
118 Berry, *Statute Rolls.. Henry VI*, pp. 91, 450; Dolley & Seaby, ' "Le Money del Oraylly" '.

tense to 'the statutes by which the men of Bréifne abide', suggests the survival into a later period of some recognised collection of laws ascribed to the fifteenth-century Eoghan.

However, it has to be borne in mind not only that the fragment is apparently based on oral tradition but that Irishmen in the early modern period acquired a new interest in constitutional niceties, which led them to reinterpret past assemblies and legislation in a quasi-parliamentary light. Geoffrey Keating's exposition of the prehistoric ritual *Feis Teamhra* as [119]

> a general meeting of kings like a Parliament .. when the entire assembly sat for the purpose of determining and completing the laws and customs of the country, the great Teach Miodhchuarta was their hall of public debate ... each king accompanied by a party of real nobles of his own province

bears a kind of prophetic relationship to the imminent Confederation of Kilkenny, much as Sir Edward Coke's view of the Anglo-Saxon 'Witan' foreshadowed developments in the 1642 parliament in England.[120] A sixteenth- or early seventeenth-century addition to a Latin version of the Annals of Ulster recounts of the thirteenth-century King Domhnall Mór Ó Domhnaill that he lessened the taxes and other burdens on his subjects and introduced during his lifetime, by the counsel of his nobles, certain useful constitutions made and confirmed for common use between lords and subject tenants.[121] As with the information concerning Eoghan Ó Raighilligh, the tradition which attributed certain regulations to the initiative of these kings may or may not have had foundation in fact, but the emphasis laid on counsel and consent in recording this tradition is almost certainly a late embellishment. Contemporary evidence for the role of mediaeval Irish nobles in legislation is unfortunately lacking. The main reason for this silence may well have been a conviction that Irish law was fundamentally a body of unchanging custom, such that any new ordinances issued from time to time were merely definitions or explanations of existing principles; but it also suggests an absence of notorious disagreements between lord and vassals on as abstract an issue as legislation, although individual and group-rebellions over more practical grievances were common.

Annals and contemporary documents consistently demonstrate that the main business of the *oireachtas*, or of less formal assemblies of noble vassals to consult with their lord, was the settling of disputes – disputes between the lord himself and rebellious subjects, or disputes with neighbouring territories, submission to an overlord, alliance between friends, or peace-terms at the end of hostilities. In terms of function, then, the *oireachtas* to the end of the sixteenth century was comparable as

[119] Keating, *Foras Feasa*, I.26 and II.4 (edd. & transl. Comyn & Dineen, II.132–3, III.36–7). See Binchy, 'The Fair', p. 127.

[120] Hill, *Puritanism*, pp. 57 and 65.

[121] AU 1241 (edd. Hennessy & Mac Carthy, II.298[–9], n. 3).

an institution of government to the High Court of Parliament in early thirteenth-century England before the addition of representatives of the commons and the subsequent preoccupation with taxation and communal legislation,[122] although the open-air site and the attendant crowds of plebeians mentioned by Spenser indicate a rather different atmosphere.

[122] Richardson, 'The origins', pp. 149–68; Marongiu, *Medieval Parliaments*, pp. 80–8.

VI

THE KING'S ADMINISTRATION

The primary political unit or 'kingdom' of the Old Irish law-tracts, the minuscule *tuath*, is credited with a proportionately minuscule administration. Only two royal officers are named, the king's *brethem* or judge, and his *rechtaire* or seneschal. In a society where the concept of public law was in its infancy, most cases were contested privately between one kin-group and another, with a hereditary class of learned custodians of the law to act as arbitrators. The king's *brethem* was only a particular member of this class who had been retained to judge cases involving the king's own rights against his subjects, for example rebellion or failure to come on hosting when summoned,[1] or alternatively to provide the king with legal advice when he delivered judgments in person.[2] The word *rechtaire* derives from *recht* meaning 'rule' or 'right', and later literary sources suggest that such a man was overseer not only of the collection of the king's tribute or food-rents[3] but of their subsequent distribution at royal banquets.[4]

The law-tracts, however, are notoriously conservative. Even as they were being written down in the early eighth century, the little independent *tuatha* fundamental to their framework of reference were being subsumed into larger conglomerate territories, each under the authority of a powerful overking,[5] and this trend was subsequently to accelerate, so that during the tenth, eleventh, and twelfth centuries Ireland as a whole consisted of no more than a dozen overkingdoms, some of which had themselves become subordinate to dominant neighbours by the end of the period.[6]

These later kings, wielding authority over a wider area, had need of a more numerous administrative staff, and evidence for such expansion can be gleaned from the annals,[7] from the lists of witnesses in the twelfth- and early thirteenth-century charters,[8] from certain tracts on the customary

[1] Binchy, *Celtic and Anglo-Saxon Kingship*, pp. 18-19.
[2] McLeod, 'The concept', p. 357.
[3] Binchy, *Celtic and Anglo-Saxon Kingship*, p. 18.
[4] Below, n. 17.
[5] Binchy, 'Distraint', p. 60; Ó Corráin, *Ireland before the Normans*, pp. 28–32.
[6] Ó Corráin, 'Nationality', p. 11.
[7] *Ibid.*, pp. 26–30.
[8] Above, pp. 65–6, nn. 48–49; below, nn. 13–14.

rights of various kings – which deal with the pre-Norman period, though they survive only in later mediaeval recensions[9] – and from Middle Irish commentaries appended to the Old Irish law tracts themselves.

An example of the last-named source is a passage of commentary on the Old Irish tract *Uraicecht Becc.* The original text states that the honour-price of every man's wife, the son who supports him, his *rechtaire* (in the case of a king) or his deputy-abbot (in the case of an ecclesiastical head) is to be estimated at half the level of his own honour-price. In the fourteenth-century N.L.I. MS. G.3, a Middle Irish commentary on this text points out that the king may have more than one *rechtaire* in his service, and these must share the half honour-price between them, while at the same time he employs other servants of much higher status, each one protected by the full honour-price of the king himself: 'the hireling of secret [confidence], of speech and converse'.[10] A lengthier recension of the same commentary appears in the Yellow Book of Lecan, in the Book of Ballymote, and in T.C.D. MS. 1337: this mentions hirelings who share the king's house, hirelings who are billeted out, servant-boys who travel, tend dogs, hold horses, and sweep the floor, one or more *maoir* or collectors of dues, and privileged hirelings from foreign parts who, like the confidential servants, are protected by the full honour-price of the king himself.[11] The language of this fuller version is, however, corrupt, less clearly assignable to a Middle Irish period (twelfth-century or earlier), and it may possibly represent a fourteenth-century elaboration on the original commentary.

It remains true, however, that all the classes of servitor mentioned even in the fuller version of this passage can be shown from other sources to have been maintained by Irish kings during the twelfth century and into the first half of the thirteenth. The confidential servant, the hireling who enjoyed equal honour-price with the king himself, is most easily identified with men like the royal chancellors. In 1175 Master Laurence, chancellor to Ruaidhri Ó Conchobhair, king of Connacht, was sent to England on his master's behalf together with the Archbishop of Tuam and the Abbot of St Brandon to negotiate the treaty of Windsor,[12] a clear indication of the confidence reposed in him. Diarmait Mac Murchadha, king of Leinster, is also said to have had a chancellor, 'Florentius',[13] and as late as 1224 one 'Concors' is described in a charter as chancellor to Aodh Ó Conchobhair, king of Connacht.[14]

The idea that one king might employ a number of *rechtairi* is borne out in the case of Toirbert Mac Gallghaeidhil, described in the charter of

[9] O'Donovan, *The Tribes and Customs*, pp. 62–93; O'Flaherty, *A Chorographical Description* (ed. Hardiman), pp. 368–72; Dillon, 'The inauguration', pp. 188–98.

[10] Binchy, *Corpus*, VI.2273.

[11] *Ibid.*, II.653, IV.1607, VI.2323.

[12] Stubbs, *Chronica Magistri Rogeri de Houedene*, II.84.

[13] Dugdale, *Monasticon Anglicanum*, VI.2, p. 1142. See Flanagan, 'Monastic Charters', pp. 129–47 for discussion of this document.

[14] Above, p. 65, n. 48.

1224 as the king's *senescallus*, and earlier, in the annals, as *reachtaire do reachtairibh hI Conchobhair*, that is, as *one* of Ó Conchobhair's *rechtairi*.[15] One reason for the king having more than one officer with this title was the *rechtaire's* role as majordomo. In the eleventh- and twelfth-century annals such men are associated with particular palaces or strongholds within their masters' domains – the city of Limerick and the fortress of Dún na Sciath in the kingdom of Thomond, or the hill-top rath of Tulach Óg in the northern kingdom of Tír Eoghain.[16] The domestic side of this office is stressed in a Middle Irish 'historical' tract, *Suidigud Tellaig Temra*, which describes a feast held by the sixth-century king of Tara, Diarmait mac Cerbaill, with[17]

> choice fruit and oxen and boars and flitches for kings and ollaves, and for the free noble elders of the men of Ireland likewise: stewards and stewardesses carving and serving for them (*rechtairi & banrechtairi ic roind ⁊ ic dáil dóib sidhe*).

The implication here that it was a duty of the *rechtaire* to be *ic roind*, 'carving', 'sharing out', 'dispensing' food at the banquet, has a number of echoes elsewhere. In 1133 Giolla na Naomh Ó Beirn, a subject of Toirdhealbhach Mór Ó Conchobhair, king of Connacht and high king of Ireland, is described in the annals as *righreachtaire Ereann*, 'chief *rechtaire* of [all] Ireland',[18] yet in a tract on the inauguration of Ó Conchobhair the Ó Beirn family is said to hold the hereditary title of *ronnadóir*, 'carver' or 'dispenser' to the king. A fifteenth-century poem based on the contents of this tract combines both terms by stating that Ó Beirn has 'the hereditary office of dispensing and ordering (*re roinn is re reachtas*).[19]

In spite of this domestic role, some of the men described as *rechtairi* to the various overkings of the eleventh and twelfth centuries are clearly powerful nobles in their own right. Donnsléibhe Ó hÓgáin, hereditary *rechtaire* of Tulach Og in Tír Eoghain, was also hereditary chieftain of Cineál Fearghusa, a branch of the main Cineál Eoghain dynasty.[20] Giolla Aonghusa Mac Giolla-easpaig, *rechtaire* of Cath Monaigh in the kingdom of Ulaidh, also bore the title, 'chief of Clann Aoilabhra'. When he was murdered by Donnshléibhe Ó hEochadha, the king whom he had earlier helped to seize power, the nobility of Ulaidh, who had guaranteed Giolla-Aonghusa's safety, put the king to death in retaliation.[21] According to Ó Corráin's interpretation of an ambiguous entry in the Annals of Ulster, Domhnall Ó Coindealbháin, hereditary sub-king of Cineál Laoghaire

[15] Above, p. 71, n. 80.
[16] AI 1031.6, 1108.7; AU 1056.7, 1103.4.
[17] Best, 'The settling', pp. 124–5.
[18] AFM 1133.
[19] Dillon, 'The inauguration', pp. 190, 196, 198, 202; Simms, ' "Gabh umad a Fheidhlimidh" '.
[20] AFM 1122. See AU 1056.7, 1081.3, 1103.4.
[21] AFM 1171, 1172.

in the province of Meath, was *rechtaire* to Maoilsheachlainn II, king of Meath and high king of Ireland.[22] The Ó Beirn family mentioned above was to acquire the sub-kingdom of Tír Briúin na Sionna in Connacht during the course of the thirteenth century,[23] though here territorial authority may have been achieved as a result of high office rather than co-existing with it.

The apparently incongruous combination of an office which in origin at least involved serving at table with high political status is parallelled by the case of the *dispensator regis* at the twelfth-century Scottish court. Ailred of Rievaulx, who was *dispensator* to King David, was described as[24]

> a second lord and prince over a host of officials and all the men of the court ... *echonomous* of the royal household. Nothing, inside or out, was done without him ... he was chief steward of the royal table, he stood in the presence of the King at dinner, serving the dishes and dividing the food in turn to the eaters.

Another high official who was listed as witness to the Connacht charter of 1224 besides the king's *rechtaire* and chancellor was Fearghal Ó Taidhg, 'chief of the household' (*dux luchta tighe*).[25] Elsewhere the annals identify him as a noble of the *oireacht*,[26] and the traditional tract on Ó Conchobhair's inauguration speaks of his office as hereditary in the Ó Taidhg family, using here the synonymous titles of *taoiseach teaghlaigh* and *marusgal tighe*.[27] This appointment appears to have been primarily a military one, since the king's 'household', his *teaghlach* or *lucht tighe*, figures prominently in annalistic descriptions of battles from the eleventh to the early fifteenth century.[28] Ó Corráin has drawn attention to an entry indicating that the *lucht tighe* of Maoilsheachlainn II included two of his own kinsmen and three sub-kings.[29] In such contexts we are dealing, it would seem, not so much with hirelings (*amuis*) in the king's pay as with hereditary functions or even privileges assigned to different families among his vassal nobility. The traditional tracts abound in such titles: 'chieftainship of the horse' (*taoisigheacht scuir*), 'command of [the king's] foot' (*cennus a chosi*), 'command of the fleet' (*cennus cabhlaigh*), 'guardianship of hostages and prisoners' (*coimhét giall ⁊ brághad*), 'rearguard' (*cúlchoimed*), 'standard-bearers' (*fir brataighe*), 'chief of the treasures' (*taoiseach séd, taisighecht eallaigh*), 'chief of the banquet' (*taisech comoil*), doorkeeper (*doirseoir*), dog-keeper (*conmhaor*), bee-keeper

[22] AU 1018.6: 'Domnall H. Caindelbain ri Loegaire, ⁊ Cais Midhe rechtaire Mael Shechlainn do marbad'; see Ó Corráin, 'Nationality', p. 29.

[23] AConn 1249.12, 1268.11, 1287.5, 1311.6.

[24] Powicke, *The Life*, pp. 3–4, and 'The *dispensator*'.

[25] Orpen, 'Some Irish Cistercian documents', p. 306; AConn, ALC 1226.

[26] AConn 1225.18.

[27] Dillon, 'The inauguration', pp. 190, 198.

[28] AFM 1012, 1101, 1303, 1435; AConn 1309.2 and 3, 1315.13, 1316.3, 1322.8, 1336.8, 1355.11.

[29] Ó Corráin, 'Nationality', p. 29; AU 1013.2; AFM 1012.

(*beachadóir*), even hereditary latrine-cleaning (*denum an chamra & a chartadh*).[30]

In such tracts the word *maor*, a bailiff or collector of dues, occurs frequently as part of an honorific title (*ardmhaor, conmhaor, maor each*), but its use in the annals is more restricted. In most pre-Norman instances the reference is clearly to an important ecclesiastic, collecting the dues of a great church from the particular territory to which he has been assigned. He is called, for instance, '*moer* of Bregh on the part of [St] Patrick',[31] '*maor* of Adomnán's law [*or* tribute]',[32] 'Patrick's *maor* in Munster',[33] or '*moer* of the "family" of Ard Macha from Belach Dúin to the sea and from the [river] Boinn to Cossan'.[34] It is just possible, however, that a few more cryptic allusions during the eleventh and twelfth centuries to the *maor* of Dál gCais or of Airmumha refer to officers of the Ó Briain high kings rather than to ecclesiastical tax-collectors.[35] An early Latin entry in the Annals of Ulster gives us the curious information that the *exactatores* of the Pictish king Nechtan were killed in the battle of Monith Carno.[36] *Exactatores* would represent a natural latinisation of the Irish *maoir* or *mair*, but a less apt translation for *mormhair*, the military commanders under the Scottish kings whose title seems to have derived independently from a word of Pictish origin, but came to be understood by Irish scribes as meaning *mór-mhaoir*, 'great stewards' or 'bailiffs'.[37] This entry on the battle of Monith Carno may indicate confusion between the two terms as far back as the eighth century.

In the later mediaeval annals it is notable that men described as *maoir* are never given formal obituaries of the kind accorded to sub-chieftains, or royal officers of high status. They are mentioned only incidentally, mostly in discreditable circumstances, as ill mannered, treacherous, or murderous, though in one case because the son of a *maor* merited a brief obit.[38] The implication that these *maoir* were recruited from a comparatively low social class receives support in a tale which the Four Masters insert in their annals under the year 1213, apparently drawing on a literary source:

> Fiond Ua Brolcháin, *maor* of Ó Domhnaill [Domhnall Mór] went to Connaught to collect Ó Domhnaill's tribute. He first went to Carbury of Drumcliff, where with his attendants, he visited the house of the poet Muireadhaigh Ó Dalaigh of Lissadill; and, being a plebeian representative of a hero, he began to wrangle with the poet

[30] Above, n. 9.
[31] AU 814.1.
[32] AFM 927.
[33] AFM 1053.
[34] AU 922.1.
[35] AU 1053.3, 1108.4; AI 1095.13; Ó Ceallaigh, *Gleanings*, p. 12. These men are, however, listed as ecclesiastics by Gwynn, 'Brian in Armagh', pp. 48–50.
[36] AU 729.2.
[37] *Dictionary*, ed. Quin, *s.vv.* '*maer*', '*mormaer*'.
[38] AFM 1213; AConn 1245.2, 1439.10, 1452.5.

very much (although his lord had given him no instructions to do so). The poet, being enraged at his conduct, seized a very sharp axe, and dealt him a blow which killed him on the spot, and then, to avoid Ó Domhnaill, he fled into Clanrickard.

A poem ascribed to the hero of this adventure contains the lines: 'that a churl [*bachlach*] was abusing me and that I killed the serf [*mogh*], O God! is this a ground for enmity?'[39]

In theory, then, quite a sharp distinction could be drawn between aristocratic vassals fulfilling hereditary functions at the court of their over-king and paid professional servants of plebeian origin. In practice, however, the distinction was blurred in a number of ways. As will have been noted already, the kings of Connacht did not always recruit their chief *rechtaire* from the Uí Bheirn who claimed the hereditary right to this post,[40] and where the king drew on a traditional family for his retinue he did not always enlist the head of the kindred in question.[41] Annalists used terms like *feadhmannaigh*, 'functionaries', and the more ambiguous *aos grádha*, perhaps best translated as 'retainers', to cover a wide social spectrum of royal servants. Such *aos grádha*, rather than being a fixed team of administrators for the territory in question, like a modern civil service, were the personal adherents of one particular king or great man. During the Bruce wars, two rival claimants to the kingship of Connacht, Feidhlim and Ruaidhri Ó Conchobhair, each had a following of *aos grádha*[42] and in 1230 we hear of the *aos grádha* of Muircheartach son of Maghnus Ó Conchobhair,[43] a dynast who never attained kingship in Connacht at all.

Aos grádha is a somewhat mysterious phrase, because the Irish *grádh* could mean 'grade', 'rank', '(clerical) order', from the Latin *gradus*, or it could be the native word *grádh* meaning 'love'. Technically the word of Latin origin gave rise to a noun with '*o*-stem' inflection and a genitive singular *gráidh*, while the native Irish word is thought to have originated as a '*u*-stem', giving genitive singular *grádha*.[44] It is noticeable that those annals whose surviving manuscripts date from the fifteenth and sixteenth centuries or earlier have a tendency to distinguish between the *aos gráidh* who are mentioned in clerical contexts,[45] and *aos grádha*, the followers of secular kings.[46] However, examples of this kind are not numerous enough to prove a consistent rule, and the seventeenth-century Annals of the Four Masters use the forms *aos grádha* and *aos gráidh*

39 Bergin, *Irish Bardic Poetry*, pp. 90, 253; Ó Cuív, 'Eachtra Mhuireadhaigh Í Dhálaigh'.

40 Above, p. 65, n. 48, and p. 71, n. 80; AConn 1301.7.

41 AConn 1225.30 and 31, 1269.2, 1271.4, 1277.3.

42 AConn 1315.11, 1316.4.

43 AConn, ALC 1230.

44 *Dictionary*, ed. Quin, *s.vv.* '*grád*' (1) and '*grád*' (2).

45 ALC 1048; AI, AT 1111; AConn 1249.16.

46 AT 1097, 1136; AI 1310.2; AU 1189, 1291, 1456; ALC 1014, 1187, 1210, 1225, etc.; AConn 1225.5, 16, 17, 30, 1230.2 and 3, 1245.2, etc.

interchangeably.[47] Even in Middle Irish texts where the context is clearly secular, translators have hovered uneasily between 'orderly'/'servant' and 'favourite', sometimes settling on the ambivalent 'minion' by way of compromise.[48] *I ngrádhaibh rígh* can be rendered as 'in the ranks of the king',[48a] 'in office under the king',[49] or 'in favour with the king'.[50] It is no assistance towards solving the confusion to note that Piers Gaveston, courtier, King's Lieutenant in Ireland and personal favourite of Edward II, was described in the annals as *lanfer grádha ri Saxan*,[51] 'the King of England's high man of *grádh*', but the notice of a battle in 1187 when 'six score men of the *oes grádha* of the son of Maelsechlainn were slain'[52] can hardly be cited as evidence for rampant homosexuality among Irish rulers.

Whether or not the original meaning of *fear grádha* and *aos grádha* was 'favourite' and 'favourites', the words as they occur in annal-entries from the eleventh to the early fifteenth century denote employees of the king. Sometimes these are employees of low rank – a *giolla grádha*[53] can only refer to a gillie or serving boy; at others they are those hereditary chieftains mentioned in the tracts as holding honorific offices about the king – as for instance when in 1189 the O Fiannachta chief is listed among the *lucht grádha* who killed the king of Connacht, while the Ó Conchobhair inauguration-tract calls the chief of this family the king's doorkeeper (*dóirseoir*).[54] However, for the majority of such men named in the annals it would appear that holding office under the king was their main claim to fame, and that they belonged to a kind of upper middle class sometimes specified as *óglaoch* (military vassal) or *brughaidh* (hospitaller, wealthy landowner).[55] Normally they appear to have been among the most faithful of the king's subjects;[56] their advice was influential;[57] holding them hostage was an effective way of pressurising their master[58] and as a group they were a prime target for enemy-raids,[59] whether because of their loyalty or their wealth or both.

47 AFM 1225.
48 ALC 1014, 1187, 1189; AU 1189.
48a Dillon, *Lebor na Cert*, p. 37, and p. 31, n. 4.
49 O'Donovan, *Leabhar na gCeart*, p. 78, line 12.
50 E. Gwynn, *The Metrical Dindsenchas*, III.301, line 25.
51 AConn, ALC 1308.
52 ALC 1187.
53 ALC 1014.
54 ALC 1189; Dillon, 'The inauguration', pp. 190, 196. Annal-entries suggest that the *doirseoir* was a military leader (ALC 1200; AU 1436; AConn 1543.8). As the man responsible for excluding strangers from the king's house (O'Grady, *Silva Gadelica*, I.276, II.312; Bergin, *Irish Bardic Poetry*, pp. 76–9, 246–7) he may have been captain of the palace-guard.
55 AFM 1097, 1131; ALC 1210, 1223; AConn 1225.30, 1230.3, 1269.2, 1271.4, 1277.3, 1404.32, 1412.13.
56 AFM 1136; AConn 1225.5, 1245.2, 1291.7, 1315.11.
57 AConn 1230.2.
58 ALC 1210, 1211; AConn 1225.17.
59 AFM 1225; AI 1310.2; AConn 1316.4, 1328.11.

The obit of Fionn Ó Carmacáin, 'agent and great landholder to the King of Connacht',[60] raises the possibility that the wealth of some at least of these men was based on lands held from the king in right of office. Most land within an Irish kingdom belonged to its landed gentry, the 'hereditary proprietors' (*dúthchasaigh*),[61] and the sub-chieftains who occupied honorific posts in the king's service were also said to possess their lands by inheritance (*do dhúthaigh*),[62] so that one would expect any further grants by the king to relate to the employment of non-hereditary officials and to come out of his own mensal lands. It may be as a result of such a situation that in 1310 Mac Carthaigh's 'freemen and *aos grádha*' all held their lands in the district of Uibh Ráthach.[63] The Mac Carthaigh chiefs themselves appear to have occupied strongholds in that area during the early fourteenth century[64] and as late as 1597 it was noted of the inhabitants: 'these are freeholders of the sept of the MacCarties discended from MacCartie Mores house and were his frendes'.[65] From sixteenth- and early seventeenth-century sources it appears that the mensal lands of the Great Ó Néill lay between Tullahogue and Dungannon in Co. Tyrone, and not only were they occupied by families traditionally known as his 'horsemen' or *lucht tighe*,[66] but Aodh Mór Ó Néill, the Great Earl of Tyrone, seems to have planted a number of new followers in the area, drawn from the citizenry of Dundalk and Drogheda, including his foster-brother and secretary, Henry Hovenden (or Ovington), the Westons, of whom one, Richard Weston, was said to audit his accounts throughout Tír Eoghain, John Bath, who was employed by Ó Neill on a number of embassies, and others.[67] However, the line between tenants and hereditary proprietors is not always easily drawn. In Fir Manach the Mic Mhaghnusa were legally tenants on the mensal lands of their overlord Mag Uidhir, and distinguished members of this family were given the comparatively humble title of *brughaidh* or *biatach* in their own compilation of annals,[68] but they were a long-established and powerful clan, and in the fifteenth century their leader is said to have been 'made

[60] ALC 1223.

[61] O'Donovan, *The Genealogies*, p. 162; O'Flaherty, *A Chorographical Description* (ed. Hardiman), p. 368; Morley, *Ireland under Elizabeth and James I*, pp. 363, 372–3.

[62] 'Atáid immorro ceithre bhaile fichit do dhúthaigh ag gach taoiseach díbh sin lena fheadhmantus féin ó Ua Conchabhair.' This is to differ somewhat from Dillon's translation: 'Each of those chieftains has twenty-four townlands of estate from Ó Conchubhair *by right of* office' (my italics) – Dillon, 'The inauguration', pp. 190, 198.

[63] AI 1310.2.

[64] AI 1317.8.

[65] London, Lambeth Palace Library, MS. 625, fo 32r.

[66] Ó Doibhlín, *Domhnach Mór*, pp. 43–62; *CSPI 1608–10*, p. 533.

[67] Morrin, *Calendar*, p. 373; *CSPI 1608–10*, pp. 538, 543, 544; Canny, 'Hugh O Neill', p. 9; Ó Fiaich, 'Richard Weston', pp. 269–82; De Barra & Ó Fiaich, *Imeacht na nIarlaí*, pp. 13–18.

[68] AU 1342, 1371, 1382, 1498; Simms, 'Guesting', p. 72.

Mac Maghnusa', that is, inaugurated as chief of his kindred, by Mag Uidhir and the nobles of Fir Manach.[69]

A similar ambiguity applies to the status of king's *ollamh*, the professional hereditary exponent of some branch of native learning who was chosen to ply his craft in the king's service, was rewarded by the king with an estate of land, and was normally regarded as the leading member within his own learned family by virtue of such a royal appointment. In the first place, we are told that certain tax-free lands were set aside within a lordship for the endowment of poets, historians, and even galloglass (mercenary soldiers of Scottish origin).[70] Both the families eligible for appointment and the particular lands in question tended to remain the same. As one tract states: 'Meic Cilli Ceallaigh are the ollamhs of O Flaithbhertaigh in history and poetry; and for this they have three half-ballys which are Ceann Droma, Ath cind and Cathair na hAilighi in Cenel mBuithin'.[71] The sixteenth-century *Ceart Uí Néill* tells us that the lands allotted to the head of the poetic family of MacConmidhe in Tír Eoghain were called *Fearann an Reacaire*, 'the Reciter's Estate',[72] and it is clear that this family is regarded as having proprietary rights in them. However, in 1435, when the MacConmidhe *ollamh* of the day offended his master Ó Néill, he was banished to Connacht[73] and his lands were apparently confiscated. In a subsequent plea for reconciliation with his offended patron he referred to himself as Ó Néill's hereditary *ollamh* (*ollamh dúthach*) and asked that he might receive back his 'charter-land' (*m'fearann cairte*).[74]

It is true that the more powerful rulers, the Ó Néill chiefs in particular, could afford to withstand this insidious pressure from tradition and insist on professional competence rather than ancestral claims as the ultimate criterion for appointment. Thus the Mac an Bhaird poets and the Ó Cléirigh historians employed by the fifteenth-century Ó Domhnaill chieftains of Tír Conaill were both of Connacht origin.[75] In 1394, the Four Masters say, blood was shed between the indigenous Ó hEachaidhéin poets of Ulster and the prestigious southern family of Uí Dhálaigh over the (poetic) ollamhship of Ó Néill.[76] Yet even in those cases where an outsider was appointed to the king's service on the grounds of superior proficiency in his art, his descendants often remained remained in the area after his death and gradually established hereditary claims of their own on his office and the lands which he had been endowed. In this way the Ui Dhálaigh, who originated in Meath, were to found separate branches

69 AU 1488.

70 Morley, *Ireland under Elizabeth and James I*, p. 371.

71 O'Flaherty, *A Chorographical Description* (ed. Hardiman), p. 371.

72 Dillon, 'Ceart Uí Néill', pp. 8–9.

73 AConn, ALC, AU 1435; McC 1437.7.

74 'Ciondas do roighfinn ri Oiligh', in Killiney, Franciscan House of Studies, MS. A.25, p. 149. A similar tension between claims of *ollamh* and patron is found in 'Beith re dán dlighidh ollamh', in the Book of O Conor Don, fo 246v.

75 Walsh, *Irish Men of Learning*, pp. 151–3; O'Donovan, *The Genealogies*, pp. 72–81.

76 AFM 1394.

with hereditary claims to the post of *ollamh* in the Mac Carthaigh lands of Duhallow and Carbury, in Corcumroe and in Bréifne during the course of the middle ages.[77] In territories where one such hereditary line had achieved general recognition for its claim, the king's choice of *ollamh* in the relevant profession, whether law, history, poetry, leechcraft, or music, was in practice limited to such members of that local family as had acquired a professional qualification in their art, who were then styled *adhbhar ollamhain*, 'heir to the ollamhship',[78] by analogy with the phrase *adhbhar ríogh*, 'heir to the kingship'.[79]

A further restriction on the king's control over the learned classes who served him arose from a custom with roots in the pagan past, whereby the lands endowing such families tended to be situated in border areas between two or more independent lordships[80] and the same *ollamh* might serve two masters: for example 'Fergal Muimnech O Duibgennain, *ollam* [in history] of the Conmaicne and of the northern and southern Clann Mailruanaid', 'Gilla na Naem Mac Aedacain, judge-*ollam* of the Ui Failgi and the Cenel Fiachach', or 'Brian son of Roiberd Mac Aedacain, law-*ollam* to Conchobair Donn and O hAinlige'.[81] This arrangement could conceivably give rise to difficulties in the case of the judge, the king's *ollamh* in law, if for instance the rebellion of a group of subjects against one of his patrons was receiving support from a neighbouring power whom he also served and he was required to negotiate a settlement with punitive fines. The *breitheamh* or judge who served King Feidhlim Ó Conchobhair and died with his master at the Battle of Athenry is not styled *ollamh*[82] and it is possible that he was personally appointed rather than occupying the position of head of a local legal family.

This distinction between working judges in the royal service and hereditary masters and teachers of traditional Irish law became very marked in the later mediaeval period when some royal judges were recruited from outside the hereditary legal families and had evidently received a training in the canon law of the Church, or, less certainly, had some acquaintance with Roman civil law or English common law. Art Mac Cathmhaoil, described in 1455 as *iudex O Neill*, sprang from a dynasty of sub-chieftains and bishops of Clogher,[83] belonged to the cathedral chapter of Armagh and served on a number of occasions as a canon-law judge in that diocese.[84] In 1507 another cleric, Feidhlimidh Mac Uinseannain, was called in his obit *breitheamh Í Dhomhnaill 7*

[77] O'Donovan, *The Tribes of Ireland*, pp. 3–11.
[78] AFM 1362; AU 1440; AConn 1399.15, 16, 1400.8, 1411.22; 1414.14, 1471.16a.
[79] See above, pp. 53–4 (nn. 98–113).
[80] Ó Riain, 'Boundary association', pp. 19–21.
[81] AConn 1357.6, 1401.7, 1422.9–10 (and Freeman's notes, pp. 460–1), 1473.40.
[82] AConn 1316.5.
[83] Simms, 'The concordat', pp. 73, 78–9; AU 1185, 1238, 1251, 1346, 1358, 1368, 1432; Ó Dufaigh, 'The MacCathmhaoils', pp. 34–9.
[84] *Registrum Iohannis Mey*, edd. Quigley & Roberts, pp. 112–14, 126, 145, 150–2, 200, 203.

Oiffiscel Thiri Conaill,[85] that is, secular judge to the Ó Domhnaill chief of Tír Conaill and ecclesiastical judge to the bishop of Raphoe, whose diocese covered approximately the same area. In the sixteenth century a *breitheamh* belonging to the hereditary legal family of Mac Fhlannchaidh in Thomond is careful to style himself a qualified notary public also,[86] while the great Ó Néill of Tír Eoghain, Seaán the Proud, employed an Anglo-Irishman, William Fleming, as his *iudex*.[87]

These changes in personnel and training of the king's judges seem to reflect a simultaneous change in their role. Their former function of adjudicating on the king's own grievances against his subjects still obtained, as appears in the late tract *Ceart Uí Néill*:[88]

Whenever the Uí Chonaill should break away from their allegiance to Ó Néill, Ó Néill shall have what his own judge shall award ... The right of Ó Néill from Uí Eachach Uladh: that they come in full muster, and if they should not come, Ó Néill shall have from them what his own judge shall award...
The lordship of Ó Néill over Inis Eoghain: provision for billeting a hundred men for half the year, and a hundred marks yearly in rent, together with maintenance for himself and his army on a circuit; and if it should fail him, Ó Néill shall have what his own judge shall award.

Side by side with this traditional jurisdiction, however, there was an ever-increasing emphasis on the king's responsibility for enforcing public order between his subjects. From at least the mid-seventh century Irish churchmen, drawing on the Bible and on christian texts from the later Roman empire, built up a more interventionist ideal of kingship than the native law-tracts had allowed for. They urged their patrons 'to rule rather than to reign, to act as supreme judge, to extend royal powers and income'.[89] Specifically, they recommended capital punishment and imprisonment for crime[90] rather than a mere payment of compensation by the kin of the wrongdoer to the kin of the victim. It is indeed as a punishment for crimes against the Church that hanging figures in the twelfth-century annals, and there is little evidence to show how far it had become part of the secular system before the late fifteenth and early sixteenth centuries.[91] This kind of problem is highlighted by an ambiguous passage in the Annals of Connacht on the inauguration of Aodh son of Cathal Croibhdhearg Ó Conchobhair:[92]

No crime was committed in Connacht at the moment of his accession save one robbery on the road to Cruach, and the hands and feet of the robber were cut

[85] AU 1507. See also AFM 1390.
[86] Hardiman, 'Ancient Irish deeds', p. 50.
[87] *CSPI 1509–73*, p. 229.
[88] Dillon, 'Ceart Uí Néill', pp. 5 and 7.
[89] Ó Corráin, 'Nationality', pp. 16–18.
[90] Above, p. 25, nn. 16–18.
[91] AClon, AFM 1130; AU 1197, 1488, 1493, 1534.
[92] AConn 1224.3.

and the violation of one woman by O Mannachan's son, who was blinded forthwith for the offence.

Here the swift punishment of the criminals is cited as evidence of God's favour smiling upon the new king, and it is not made clear by whose initiative the penalties were imposed. The Four Masters, however, when re-phrasing the same entry in their seventeenth-century compilation, leave no room for doubt:[93]

> Aodh, upon his succession to the government, commanded the son of O Mannacháin should be deprived of sight as a punishment for his having violated a female, and ordered the hands and feet of another person to be cut off for having committed a robbery. This [was done] to maintain the authority of a prince (*Do choimhéd smachta flatha innsin*).

From this we may safely conclude that it was considered normal by the early seventeenth century for an Irish overlord to take direct responsibility for the punishment of rape and theft, without being as assured of the position in 1224.

Even for the late thirteenth century, however, three documents survive which indicate that the role of the kindred in prosecuting crime was giving way to the territorial jurisdiction of the lord. In one case, it was ordained that the murder-fine, if not paid by the malefactor's kindred, was to be levied from the surrounding countryside, under pain of the king's vengeance.[94] The other two texts combine to show that it was now general practice in the case of theft not only for the victim to receive two-fold compensation but for a set fine to be paid to the lord and his judge or bailiff, presumably as their incentive and reward for ensuring that justice was done. However, in contrast to the Four Masters' assumption above, the status of the lord in question might range from that of an overking to that of a landless chief or the son of a military vassal who ruled a summer-shieling of cow-herds (*ceartmac oglaig aga mbia buaile*), and the jurisdiction of the overking only became operative if such lesser nobles failed to correct the wrong.[95]

This arrangement appears to have remained in force until the mid-fifteenth century. When two parishioners of Derrynoose, in the diocese of Armagh, killed a man and fled to take up residence under the lordship of Éamonn Mac Mathghamhna in the parish of Clontibret, diocese of Clogher, the archbishop of Armagh did not appeal to the ruler of Airghialla, Feidhlim Mac Mathghamhna, but instead threatened excommunication unless[96]

[93] AFM 1224.

[94] Above, p. 76, n. 115.

[95] Above, p. 66, nn. 50 and 52. Mac Niocaill, 'Irish law and the Armagh constitutions', and 'Aspects of Irish law', pp. 30–41; Binchy, *Corpus*, II.691–2.

[96] Registrum Iohannis Prene, Lib. i, fo 186v.

Edmundus Macmaguna, temporalis Dominus dictorum Coromaci et Magonii, eosdem ad emendam pro comissis predictis compellat competentem.

As late as 1526 the covenant drawn up between MacEochagáin and 'the Fox' implies that the overlord's 'brehon' or judge did not as yet have a monopoly of cases involving his vassals since they agreed that [97]

whenever either an Englishman or an Irishman shall sue the Fox, or any person in his territory, that the decision of Muirchertach MacEgan, *or of the Brehon who shall be by them appointed*, be submitted to; and when this will not be accepted from them, then that Mageoghegan shall be bound to spend his country and the Fox's country, for obtaining justice for the Fox and his country, as well as to compel them and him to render justice.

In other words, whether the decision is issued by his own judge or another, MacEochagáin has the right and duty to enforce that decision. Later in the sixteenth century Edmund Spenser indicates that the lord's judge was acquiring mandatory jurisdiction over cases involving serious crime:[98]

The Brehon that is their judge will compound between the murderer and the friends of the party murdered ... that the malefactor shall give unto them ... a recompense which they call an Iriach [*éiric* or *éaraic*] ... And this judge, being as he is called the Lord's Brehon, adjudgeth for the most part a better share unto his Lord, that is the lord of the soil or the head of that sept, and also unto himself for his judgement a greater portion than unto the plaintiffs or parties grieved.

Irish lords were keenly aware of the financial advantages accompanying this extension of responsibility. In 1542 Maguidhir, after acknowledging himself the vassal of Maghnus Ó Domhnaill, 'granted to O Domnaill half the eric for manslaying throughout Fermanagh'.[99] A memorandum of the 'old customs of Ó Domhnaill', ostensibly dated 1626 though now surviving only in late transcripts, states that 'the *eric* for killing a man was 168 cows'.[100]

Not only are there signs in all this of an increasingly centralised concept of public justice, but the vocabulary and procedures of the law-courts in Gaelic Ireland can be shown to have been heavily influenced by Common Law from the late thirteenth century onwards.[101] Indeed, in the early seventeenth century an English observer wrote that the 'brehons' were 'assisted by Certen Sgollers whoe had learned manie and civill rules of the

97 O'Donovan, 'Covenant', pp. 193–5. My italics.
98 Spenser, *A View* (ed. Renwick), p. 5.
99 AConn 1542.19.
100 Cambridge, University Library, MS. Add. 2766 (20)(7), fo 4; Dublin, Royal Irish Academy, O.S. MS. Strongroom 14.B.7, p. 423. I am deeply indebted to Pádraig de Brún (Dublin Institute for Advanced Studies) for the first reference, and to R. J. Hunter (New University of Ulster) for the second.
101 Mac Niocaill, 'The interaction', and 'Aspects of Irish law', p. 37.

Common lawe rather by tradicion then by readinge'.[102]

Greater involvement in the dispensation of justice necessarily entailed the Irish ruler maintaining a means for enforcing its execution. Where legal fines (*cána*) fell due, the *maor* was the obvious agent to collect them and in all probability this was the officer described as a 'beadle' in the late thirteenth-century compact between the vassal chief Aonghus Mac Mathghamhna and his overlord, Ralph Pipard, baron of Ardee:[103]

> Cum 'canos' uel amerciamenta acciderint secundum consuetudinem antecessorum nostrorum per bedellum nostrum et bedellum dicti E[negus] leuantur quod si deforciantur idem E[negus] cum potestate sua et potestate dicti Domini R[adulfi] leuantur.

The *maor* was primarily a fiscal officer, and comparable instances of this arrangement for joint collection involve rent and tribute rather than punitive dues. In the fifteenth century Éinrí Ó Néill promised the archbishop of Armagh 'that Ó Néill himself will exact the lord [primate]'s rents in full, by means of his bailiff [*balliuus*] and the church's bailiff, as often as he may be requested'.[104] In 1539 the Ó Conchobhair chief of Sligo bound himself[105]

> to go with the stewards and marshals (*le maoraibh agus le maruscalaibh*) of Ó Domhnaill into every place in Lower Connacht to impose the lordship [*do thabach tigearnaiss* – 'to levy the tribute'?] of Ó Domhnaill.

In this instance the *maoir* employed by an overlord are making a circuit not through territory under his direct rule but through the land of a vassal chief. Not surprisingly, bardic poems tend to cite this sending of a king's *maoir* into neighbouring territories as the ultimate proof of his paramount authority. For instance, the fifteenth-century chief Toirdhealbhach-an-Fhíona Ó Domhnaill was praised with the words 'Do mhaoirse ar fhud Eoghanach. Tug an daoirse dheidheanach': 'Thy stewards have imposed the extreme of submission on all Tir Eoghain'.[106]

However, the *maor* by himself was not equipped to deal with a flat refusal to pay the fines or dues he requested; he needed military support. In the late thirteenth century, as we have seen, Mac Mathghamhna agreed to lead his own forces and those of Lord Ralph Pipard on hosting against recalcitrant debtors. A partially legible sentence in the register of Primate

[102] San Marino (Cal.), Huntington Library, MS. 7042 ('Lawes of Irelande'), p. [11]. I owe this reference to R. J. Hunter.

[103] Curtis, *Calendar*, I, no. 268.

[104] Simms, 'The concordat', p. 80.

[105] M. Carney, 'Agreement', pp. 288 and 290.

[106] McKenna, *Aithdioghluim Dána*, no. 20, q. 15; see also Greene, *Duanaire Mhéig Uidhir*, pp. 40–1; Fraser & O'Keeffe, 'Poems', pp. 20 (q. 31) and 46 (q. 10); Mac Airt, *Leabhar Branach*, p. 188 (lines 4926–9); and unpublished poem 'Ní leis féin a bfaghann Aodh' in Dublin, Royal Irish Academy MS. 743, p. 694.

Fleming of Armagh[107] suggests that early in the fifteenth century the archbishop's bailiffs were accompanied on their rent-collecting rounds by *turrbales* or kernes, bands of native Irish mercenary soldiers. Documents dealing with Anglo-Irish lordships during the fifteenth and sixteenth centuries frequently refer to a small permanent force of kernes in the lord's employ, the *ceithearn tighe* ('keheryntye', 'keranthy', 'kearnety', etc.), or 'household-troop'.[108] A late Irish Life of St Maighneann of Kilmainham, occurring in a mid-fifteenth-century manuscript, has a curious passage describing the *ceithearn tighe* of the Eternal King as distinguished by a gold cross on their foreheads and a silver cross on their backs,[109] and this suggests that mortal troops of the same kind may also have worn a badge or uniform. In the Desmond inquisitions of 1587 such kerne were described as 'a nomber of soldiers to aide & assist the Justices, seneshalls, receavors, stewardes of courtes, & serjeantes, in the execucion of the lawes and customes of the contries and terretories of the said late Earles, for the rule and governement of his people and landes, and the receavenge, leauienge, and gatheringe of his reve[n]ewes'.[110]

Although this detailed description of the police-role of the *ceithearn tighe* comes in an Anglo-Irish context, the earl of Desmond's neighbour, Mac Carthaigh Mór is also said to have employed a *ceithearn tighe*, 'a company of light footmen',[111] and in *Ceart Uí Néill* police-duties are ascribed to Ó Néill's *fírcheithearnn*, or 'true kerne', under the leadership of Mac Cathmhaoil, Mac Murchaidh, and Ó Doibhlín, three sub-chieftains who occupied his mensal lands or lands bordering on them:[112]

> And it is their duty to take and to guard hostages [or 'prisoners'] ... and wherever anything comes to Ó Néill in tax or as a fine for theft or bloodshed or defrauding customs, they receive a commission of two sheep on every cow ... And the *fírcheithearna* are not entitled to prey(?) upon the people of the house, save on a stranger, unless the lord say that they shall be despoiled. If kernes be billeted upon the retinue of a king's son or of a neighbour, they are not entitled to prey(?) on them. If they force entry by the king's command, they may take food. If cows are forthcoming from the guilty man, they may eat one beef, and if not, they may have a sheep.

In this passage the fact that the *fírcheithearn* were entitled to a commission out of legal fines or taxation due to Ó Néill argues that they were instrumental in levying such dues, and the allusion to billeted kernes suggests that while the leaders were hereditary vassal-chieftains, the rank and file were mercenaries, making the force closely parallel both in function and in composition to the earl of Desmond's *ceithearn tighe*.

[107] Simms, 'The archbishops', p. 50, n. 47
[108] Empey & Simms, 'The Ordinances', pp. 186–7; Hore & Graves, *The Social State*, pp. 185, 190, 199, 232, etc.
[109] O'Grady, *Silva Gadelica*, I.42, II.41.
[110] Hore & Graves, *The Social State*, p. 266.
[111] Butler, *Gleanings*, p. 20.
[112] Dillon, 'Ceart Uí Néill', p. 11.

There may well be a connexion between the appearance of the mercenary *ceithearn tighe* during the course of the fifteenth century and the eclipse of the older, more aristocratic *lucht tighe*, hitherto shown participating in warfare as the king's 'household'.[113] From the late fifteenth century the term *lucht tighe* describes not a group of people but the mensal lands lying around the chieftain's main residence, presumably the area traditionally tenanted by such people. Like the term *oireacht, lucht tighe* ('Loughtee', 'Lotie') in this territorial sense appears on sixteenth-century maps and in the names of Irish baronies.[114]

This change may reflect the increasing professionalism of the armies employed by Gaelic lords in the later middle ages,[115] but it was not the only tranformation to take place in their administration. No Irish king is recorded as having a chancellor after 1224, and the last *reachtaire* to be named in the annals died in 1301.[116] The very word *fear grádha* had by the end of the sixteenth century lost its meaning of 'court-official' and was used by the Irish *literati* themselves for 'friend' or 'boon-companion'[117] on the analogy of *fear cumainn* and *aos cumainn*.[118] Indeed, the mid-seventeenth-century antiquary Dubhaltach Óg Mac Firbhisigh may have been misled by this semantic shift when translating the fifteenth-century annals compiled by his forebears. He described the great feast held for poets and other men of learning by the lady Mairghréag daughter of Ó Cearbhaill in 1433 as having been presided over by the hostess: 'on the garretts of the greate church of Da Sinceall clad in cloath of gold, her deerest friends about her, her clergy and Judges too'.[119] The original text is lost, but in the context of this highly organised and ceremonious event, it seems quite probable that the 'deerest friends' of Mac Firbhisigh's translation were the lady's *aos grádha*, or official retinue.

Of course new functionaries and a new terminology appeared to replace the old. In the fourteenth century we first hear of a secretary (*clericus secretus*) serving the Great Ó Néill.[120] At this period also the *constábla*, the constable or commander of the king's galloglass, became a widespread phenomenon,[121] and by the fifteenth century the hereditary claims of various military families of Scottish extraction to fill this appointment in their locality and to hold the lands which endowed such an office are sufficiently demonstrated by the emergence of the phrase *adhbhar Constábla*, 'heir to the constableship', echoing the terms *adhbhar*

[113] Above, p. 82, n. 28.
[114] AU 1478; Ó Doibhlín, *Domhnach Mór*, maps facing pp. 40 and 41; baronies of Upper and Lower Loughtee, Co. Cavan.
[115] See below, chapter 8.
[116] AConn 1301.7.
[117] Knott, 'A poem', p. 244; Bergin, *Irish Bardic Poetry*, p. 133.
[118] *Ibid.*, p. 40 (q. 26), p. 41 (q. 1), p. 148 (q. 13), p. 191 (q. 2).
[119] ADF 1451.
[120] Curtis, *Richard II*, p. 136. See above, p. 86, n. 67.
[121] AConn 1365.8, 1378.2, 1398.24, 1405.15, 1465.11, 1467.9, 1474.12; AU 1444, 1447, 1460, 1485, 1486.

ollamhain and *adhbhar ríogh*.[122] Like the hereditary learned classes, one military family might supply mercenary captains to several independent Irish lordships. In 1455 Maine Mac Caba was called '*adhbur Consabla* of the two Breifni and Oirghialla and Fir Manach'.[123]

Another office of Anglo-Norman origin was that of *marusgál* or marshal. This word had earlier been applied vaguely as an honorific title indicating military command,[124] but sixteenth-century documents show marshals as professionals in charge of supplying, billeting, and discipline of kernes and galloglass.[125]

Bearing in mind, then, the tendency for Irish lords in the fifteenth and sixteenth centuries to use non-hereditary judges for the post of king's *breitheamh*, it can be said that the only administrator whose office continued unaltered from the thirteenth century to the early modern period was the *maor*, the plebeian debt-collector. In general, the ceremonial and aristocratic king's court had become the headquarters of a warlord, shorn of the trappings of royalty and utilising paid professionals to carry out key military and other functions.

122 See above, p. 88, nn. 78 and 79. In the annals the phrase *adhbhar Constábla* is first used of the MacQuillins (AU 1358), an Anglo-Norman family of hereditary mercenary commanders, for whom see Otway-Ruthven, *A History*, pp. 216–17, and McNeill, *Anglo-Norman Ulster*, pp. 120–1.

123 AU 1455.

124 Above, p. 82, n. 27; O'Donovan, *The Tribes and Customs*, p. 66; Ní Shéaghdha, 'The Rights', p. 159; Robinson, 'The Irish Lives of Guy of Warwick', p. 76; AU 1515.

125 Above, p. 92, n. 105; Brewer & Bullen, *Calendar of the Carew Manuscripts*, IV, no. 213; Gilbert, *Facsimiles*, IV.1, plate xxx; Hardiman, 'Ancient Irish deeds', pp. 65 and 74; Dillon, 'Ceart Uí Néill', p. 12.

VII

SUBMISSION AND VASSALAGE

As in the rest of mediaeval Europe, the mutual obligations of lord and vassal in early Irish society arose from a series of private agreements entered into at various social levels, and were not confined to the relationship between a king and his leading subjects. Indeed, in Ireland the economic role of the original bond of *célsine* or 'companionship' was at least as much stressed as its military or political significance. This was particularly true in the case of the base client (*céle giallnai, doerchéle*), drawn from the humbler ranks of freemen, who bound himself indefinitely to render to his lord an annual food-tribute, a winter-feast, and a fixed amount of manual labour in return for an initial grant or fief (*taurchrecc, doer-rath*) of cattle, or occasionally land, together with a payment equivalent to the amount of the client's honour-price. This payment thenceforward gave the lord the right to receive a proportion of any legal compensation awarded for injuries inflicted on his vassal freeman,[1] which implied that the lord gained the same vested interest in protecting and avenging his vassal that normally belonged to the man's kindred.

The free client (*soer-chéle*) entered a temporary alliance with his patron, terminable after three, six or seven years' duration, rendering a heavy return in cattle and produce for his 'free fief' (*soer-rath*) but maintaining his legal independence and performing the personal service of escorting his lord to feasts or public assemblies (including battles) rather than doing manual labour.[2] In early Irish society neither wealth nor landownership was the touchstone of nobility; to rise above the rank of commoner, patronage of clients was an indispensable qualification, the lowest grade of noble (*aire deso*) being credited with at least five base and five free clients, and the authority of the *rí tuaithe*, or petty king, being bolstered with many more.[3]

There was, however, a distinction between the king's patronage and that of a private lord. It appears that the king's base clients collectively yielded him a hostage in pledge for the fulfilment of their obligations (*fer gill do gíalnaib*), and that the nobles of the *tuath* gave him hostages to guarantee their allegiance. The very use of the word *gíallnae* for 'base clientship',

[1] Mac Niocaill, *Ireland*, pp. 61–5; Binchy, *Críth Gablach*, pp. 80, 96–8.
[2] Mac Niocaill, *Ireland*, pp. 60–1; Binchy, *Críth Gablach*, p. 107.
[3] *Ibid.*, pp. 70, 82 (lines 328–31, 448–50).

deriving as it does from *giall*, 'a hostage', suggests that in some earlier period even private contracts of this nature may have been guaranteed by a human pledge,[4] but by the time of the classical Old Irish law-tracts (*ca* A.D. 700) hostage-giving is confined to public transactions and has become a test of kingship. As one such tract, *Din Techtugad*, states flatly: 'He is no king who has not hostages in fetters, to whom the tribute of a lord is not given, to whom the debts of *cáin* are not paid'.[5] In the ninth century the didactic work *Tecosca Cormaic* cites 'hostages in fetters' among the things 'best for a king'.[6] Two Middle Irish poems in the Book of Leinster reinforce the point:

The king who has not hostages in keeping is as ale in a leaky vessel.[7]
Take hostages from all . so that you may be a keen prince
and be able to chastise . on every business about which you go.
Make not peace without a hostage . wherever your power extends...
Though the people be leal . let there be strife against even a shadow
until their hostages . be in your own hands...
Even the brother of a king . whose hostage has been accepted
provided he possesses a dwelling . exempt no man from giving provisions.[8]

This view in the literary sources that hostages were the most secure, if not the only, method of ensuring a vassal's obedience, that their possession constituted the reality of power, without which kingship became an empty farce, is strikingly echoed in annal-entries from the tenth to the thirteenth century. On the death of Cathal Croibhdhearg Ó Conchobhair, king of Connacht, in 1224, they explain that his son Aodh was able to succeed to his throne immediately because 'he had been king in effect (*rí ar tothacht*) by the side of his father and already held all the hostages of Connacht'.[9] In other cases the new king exacted hostages from his subjects at the time of his succession. In 1258 'Gofraid O Domnaill, king of Tir Conaill, died. Domnall O Domnaill was made king in his stead, and all the Cenel Conaill gave hostages and allegiance (*braigde & tigernus*) to him.'[10]

Since hostages were associated with the reality of power, they might be held not by the titular king of a particular territory but by the overlord who had conquered him or installed him in power in the first place. An especially elaborate version of this process is recorded for 1165, when there was[11]

[4] *Ibid.*, pp. 95–6.

[5] Binchy, *Corpus*, I.219. *Feich cána*, 'the debts of *cáin*', were apparently fines for breach of promulgated, as distinct from customary, law (see Quin, *Dictionary*, *s.v. cáin*).

[6] Meyer, *The Instructions*, p. 3.

[7] O'Donoghue, 'Advice', p. 51.

[8] O'Donoghue, 'Cert cech ríg co réil', pp. 260–1.

[9] AConn 1224.3.

[10] AConn 1258.4.

[11] AU 1165. See also AConn 1246.8, 1266.13.

a hosting by Muirchertach Ua Lochlainn ... into Ulidia, so that they harried all the country ... and they expelled Eochaidh Mac Duinnsleibhe from Ulidia. And Ua Lochlainn gave the kingship to Donnsleibhe [Mac Duinnsleibhe] and all the Ulidians gave their pledges to Ua Lochlainn, through the might of his regal power (*tria nert righe*)...

After that, Donnchadh Ua Cerbaill, arch-king of Airgialla, and Eochaidh Mac Duinnsleibhe, come into the presence of Ua Lochlainn to ask for the kingship for [Eochaidh] Mac Duinnsleibhe, so that Ua Lochlainn gave the entire [kingship] to Mac Duinnsleibhe, in return for the pledges ('hostages') of all Ulidia. So that Mac Duinnsleibhe gave the son of every chief of Ulidia and his own daughter in pledge to Ua Lochlainn.

Possession of hostages thus could signify not only control over one's own hereditary kingdom but overlordship of neighbouring territories, as we find Brian Ó Néill, who had pretensions to the high kingship of Ireland, called in 1260 'king of Cenél Eoghain, to whom the Gaedhil gave hostages',[12] or Aodh O Domhnaill more precisely described in 1333 'king of Tir Conaill and Fermanagh, who had taken hostages of both districts of Carbury and of Brefne'.[13]

In the course of the fierce competition which raged from the tenth to the twelfth century between overlords for supreme power in Ireland, the hostages of a subject territory could be snatched from hand to hand. In 1007 the Munster high king Brian Bóroimhe 'took the hostages of Ulaid from the king of Ailech by force'.[14] Earlier he had traded the hostages of Connacht to his rival, the Meath high king Maoilsheachlainn II, in exchange for the hostages of Leinster.[15] The truth was, however, that holding hostages did not automatically result in the obedience of their principals. Rebels might offer 'deceptive hostages',[16] that is, pledges for undertakings which they had no intention of fulfilling. In such cases they had either resigned themselves to the prospect of death or injury being inflicted on the people they had surrendered as a guarantee,[17] or they hoped by the violence of their uprising to intimidate an overlord into releasing their hostages in return for peace.[18] For this reason it was in the interest of the overlord to exact his vassals' nearest and dearest relatives as hostages, while the submitting chiefs hoped to yield persons less emotionally or politically indispensable. The outcome in every case was a measure of the current balance of power and of how abject was the submission involved. In 1109, for instance, Domhnall Ua Lochlainn, high king of the north of Ireland, invaded Ulaidh with his forces until 'the Ulaid gave them the three hostages they themselves chose (*na teora giallu*

[12] AI 1260.3.
[13] AConn 1333.3.
[14] AI 1007.3.
[15] AI 997.2, 998.2; and see AConn 1258.9.
[16] ALC 1291; AConn 1291.4; McC 1151.3.
[17] For example, AFM 1170, AConn 1246.8.
[18] AConn 1227.3.

rothoghsat fein doibh)',[19] and when his grandson Muircheartach repeated this attack on Ulaidh in 1149 'Ua Duinnsleibhe afterwards came into the house of Ua Lochlainn, and delivered his own son up to him as a hostage, and whatever other hostages he demanded'.[20]

In the annals hostages are normally associated with the submission of a vassal to his overlord, but they could be offered in other circumstances, for instance to guarantee fidelity to a military alliance[21] or to ensure the performance of a specific command.[22] In all cases, however, their transfer implied formal recognition of the giver's inferiority to the receiver. If this inference was to be avoided, the two parties to an agreement must exchange hostages[23] or jointly place their hostages in the hands of a neutral arbitrator.[24] So much emphasis is placed in annalistic accounts on the mere giving or withholding of hostages that one is in danger of forgetting what the compilers take for granted, that hostages are handed over to guarantee a contract; their transfer is primarily a sign that a formal treaty between leaders has been agreed upon, other such indications being a hand-clasp between the contracting parties,[25] oaths taken on relics,[26] the ceremonial bestowal of gifts,[27] even on occasion the rite of blood-brotherhood.[28] For the twelfth century we have an outside observer, Giraldus Cambrensis, to give a fuller account of Irish submissions, in which the transfer of hostages is only one component part: he also mentions, for instance, the submitting king's consultation with his own subjects,[29] and the intervention of arbitrators.[30] One such passage describes the submission of Domhnall Mac Giollaphádraig to Diarmait Mac Murchadha, king of Leinster, after his territory had been ravaged:[31]

> At last the prince of Osraige, on the advice of his own supporters, giving hostages and swearing oaths under the terms of a peace treaty which was nevertheless feigned and a pretence on both sides rather than genuine, apparently returned to his loyal obedience to Diarmait.

Later Giraldus deals with Diarmait's own submission to the high king of Ireland, Ruaidhri Ó Conchobhair:[32]

[19] AU 1109.5.
[20] AFM 1149.
[21] AI 984.2, McC 1164.1.
[22] AI 987.2.
[23] AI 984.2; Byrne, *Irish Kings*, p. 197.
[24] ALC 1102; AU 1102.8.
[25] See below, n. 33; McC 1126.11.
[26] See below, nn. 31, 32; AI 1073.2, 1093.11; AFM 1139, 1143, 1148; McC 1165.2; AConn 1277.2.
[27] See below, n. 33.
[28] AConn 1277.2; Giraldus Cambrensis, *Topographia Hibernie*, III.22.
[29] See above, p. 60, n. 12; p. 70, n. 77; p. 71, n. 80, p. 72, n. 87.
[30] See AU 1099, 1109, 1252; AFM 1144, 1165.
[31] Giraldus Cambrensis, *Expugnatio Hibernica*, I.4 (edd. Scott & Martin, p. 37).
[32] *Ibid.*, I.10 (edd. Scott & Martin, p. 51).

Ruaidrí ... kept trying, using all possible means, to reach a peaceful settlement, acting through messengers who went back and forth between the two armies. So, through the mediation of men of good will, and thanks to the inspiration of divine grace from on high, peace was eventually made on these conditions: that Diarmait would be left with Leinster, while recognizing Ruaidrí as prince and king of all Ireland and giving him due obedience. In order that this agreement should continue to be fully observed and remain unbroken, he gave Ruaidrí his son Conchobar as a hostage for its observance. Ruaidrí for his part promised to give Conchobar his daughter in wedlock when in due course of time the peace had gained stability by its terms having been translated into deeds. These conditions, then, were made public, and oaths were given on both sides to make them binding.

Not only do these accounts remind us that handing over hostages did not in itself constitute the essence of submission, but even the Irish sources themselves indicate that such a contract could and did take place on occasion without any hostage being asked or given. This was particularly true in cases where acceptance of lordship was largely ceremonial, entailing few obligations on the new vassal. Two such symbolic acknowledgements of inferiority are described in the saga *Cogadh Gaedhel re Gallaibh*, beginning with the surrender of the deposed high king, Maoilsheachlainn II, to his successful rival, Brian Bóroimhe:[33]

Maelsechlainn ... said that he came to make his submission to him, and to give him hostages.

Brian answered that, and said: "Since thou hast come unto us thus," said he, "without guarantee, without protection, without treaty, we give thee a truce for a year without asking pledge or hostage from thee" ... Twelve score steeds were then given to Maelsechlainn by Brian, and there was not one of the twelve score men who accompanied Maelsechlainn who would deign to carry a led horse with him; so that Maelsechlainn bestowed them all upon Murchad, son of Brian, who had given his hand into his hand that day. For he was the only *rigdomna* of the men of Erinn who was not in alliance [*coracus*, from *cor* = 'a contract'] with Maelsechlainn before that time.

In each of these cases the outward sign of submission is the acceptance of a ceremonial gift, and this is so clearly understood that the objective value and utility of the chattels bestowed could not, in the eyes of the former high king's followers, outweigh the humiliation of being forced to receive them. We have already seen that in the Old Irish period the private contract of clientship hinged on the client's acceptance of a 'fief' or *rath* from his patron; and, in an early tract on the reciprocal rights and obligations of the provincial overking of Cashel and his subject kings, he is shown as bestowing a *rath* upon such sub-kings every seven years, indicating that they were perceived as 'free clients' of the overking.[34] A point, however, which must be stressed, since it has too frequently been

[33] *Cogadh Gaedhel re Gallaibh*, § 75 (ed. & transl. Todd, pp. 130–3).

[34] Byrne, *Irish Kings*, pp. 196–8; Binchy, *Celtic and Anglo-Saxon Kingship*, p. 31, n. 65.

ignored by historians of the later mediaeval period,[35] is that the term *célsine* became obsolete in the Middle Irish or post-viking period, to be replaced by two different words: *biataigheacht* or *biatachas*, 'a food-providing relationship',[36] and *óglachas*, 'the service of a warrior'.[37] Correspondingly, the ceremonial gift of the overking to a sub-king in the Middle Irish Book of Rights and in eleventh- and twelfth-century annals is called not *rath* but *tuarastal* or *innarrad*, both words which were also applied to the wages of mercenary soldiers.[38]

The mere fact that these changes took place, and the appearance of *óglachas* and *tuarastal* in the vocabulary of political submissions, might reasonably lead one to suppose that the old contract of 'free clientship' (*soerchélsine*) had made way for a relationship which laid greater stress on military service than on the economic returns once owed on the initial 'loan' of the *rath*. This *prima facie* conclusion is reinforced when a detailed examination of the contexts in which the word *tuarastal* occurs at this period shows the meanings of 'ceremonial gift on submission' and 'wages for military service' to be closely connected, to the point of ambiguity on a number of occasions.

The Book of Rights, for instance, invariably uses the word *tuarastal* to describe the donations of each provincial king to his subordinate rulers – lists of weapons, garments, drinking horns, and slave-girls –, which sound not merely ceremonial but sometimes even fanciful. At the same time, in a passage dealing with the free tribes of Connacht, we find the word used in a more mercenary sense. Where the prose version states, 'They go not on an expedition or a muster save for a payment of cattle (*crod*), and they go not into battle with the king save for pay (*ara lóg*)', the verse has, 'None of them is obliged to go into battle ... unless it be for *tuarastal*'.[39] These 'free tribes' (*soerthuatha*) of Connacht were so called because they were free from the obligation to pay tribute or food-rent to the overking, and a later tract on the inauguration of Ó Conchobhair has a parallel passage to the effect that every chieftain in the province of Connacht is[40]

> bound by the law, service and maintenance (*díor 7 dligeadh, feidhm 7 fulang*) of Ó Conchubhair, save only the High King of Uí Bhriúin and Uí Fhiachrach Muaidhe and the Cinél Aodha of Echtghe. Even they owe service of raid, hosting, hostages and escort (*feacht 7 sluaigheadh 7 géillsine 7 coimhdeacht*) to the king of Connacht, and to accompany him at every need, on payment of *tuarastal*.

This undertaking to accompany the king 'at every need' (*dochum gach n-éigentais*) should be contrasted with the customary privilege claimed by various sub-kings (sometimes in texts of demonstrably earlier date) that

[35] See especially Hayes-McCoy, 'Gaelic society', p. 50.

[36] See below, n. 61; Quin, *Dictionary*, *s.v.*; Price, 'The origin'; Mac Niocaill, 'The origins'.

[37] Quin, *Dictionary*, *s.v.*.

[38] Binchy, *Celtic and Anglo-Saxon Kingship*, p. 31, nn. 65, 66; Quin, *Dictionary, s.v.*.

[39] Dillon, *Lebor na Cert*, pp. 48–9, 54–5.

[40] Dillon, 'The inauguration', pp. 190–1, 198.

they need ride on hosting with their overlord for only six weeks in the year, or even six weeks in every three years, and then not in spring or at harvest-time.[41] Apparently, if chieftains were to render military service over and beyond such limited obligations, they must receive 'wages' from their lord.

The Book of Fenagh contains a number of poems on the kings of Tír Conaill, similar in subject-matter to and not far removed in date[42] from those contained in the Book of Rights. They, too, mention *tuarastal* as part of an honourable form of vassalage owed by the king of Tír Conaill to the king of Tír Eoghain or vice versa, involving military service only, and not the payment of tribute. Here the wages seem to compensate not for the frequency of the summons but for deploying the vassal's forces away from his home-territory:

> Though the king of Conall goes afar
> In the hosting of great Tara's king,
> 'Tis not compulsion that takes him from home,
> But to earn *tuarusdal*.[43]
> When the king of Oileach is king
> O'er the battle-wounding host of Conall,
> Each man to *tuarustal* is entitled
> From the *brughaidh* to the arch-king
> When the king of Conall is king
> O'er the formidable race of Eoghan,
> He is bound to give the same to them,
> Since he is over them arch-king...
> No party of them is bound
> In consideration therefore, to the other;
> Save as to hostings, with great dispatch
> And 'rising out' (*comergi*) for hard battle.[44]

In these poems it is not made entirely clear whether *tuarastal* is paid to vassals at the time of their submission, to bind them to future service, or whether they receive it as a well earned reward after an expedition. Similarly, although most annalistic references at this time show the subordinate king receiving his 'wages' when actually submitting (expressed as 'going into the house' of his overlord) or when giving him hostages,[45] some instances could be interpreted as being directly related

[41] O'Donovan, *TheTribes and Customs*, pp. 66–7; Ní Shéaghdha, 'The Rights', pp. 159, 161, 165, 166; O Daly, 'A poem', pp. 181–2, 186.

[42] The poetry in the Book of Fenagh derives from an 'Old Book of Fenagh' which 'must have been compiled about or previous to 1300' (*The Book*, edd. Hennessy & Kelly, p. vi). One poem (*ibid.*, p. 364) is also found in *Lebor na Cert* (ed. Dillon, p. 78). Of the two quoted below, 'A liubar ta ar do lar' apparently inspired the mid-thirteenth-century poet Giolla Brighde Mac Con Midhe (ed. Williams, poem no. 1, qq. 6–9).

[43] Hennessy & Kelly, *The Book*, p. 357; Meyer, 'Mitteilungen', p. 116.

[44] Hennessy & Kelly, *The Book*, pp. 358–61.

[45] AI 1011.5, 1070.9, 1081.5, 1095.6, 1120.4. See Quin, *Dictionary, s.v. tech.*

to military service. The Annals of Ulster raise this possibility when they say that in 1080 'Donnsléibhe ua hEochada went into Mumu with the nobles of the Ulaid to seek hire (*ar cenn tuarustail*)', and that in 1083 'Domnall Ua Lochlainn assumed the kingship of Cenél-Eógain. He carried out a king's raid on the Conaille, and carried off a great prey of cattle and gave stipends from that prey to the men of Fernmag.' A similar group-payment closely linked to an expedition occurs in the Annals of the Four Masters under 1166:

> An army was led by Ruaidhri Ua Conchobhair ... to Ath-Cliath; and [he] was there inaugurated king as honourably as any king of the Gaeidhil was ever inaugurated; and he presented their *tuarastal* to the foreigners in many cows, for he levied a tax of four thousand cows upon the men of Ireland for them. On this occasion the foreigners accompanied Ruaidhri to Droicheat-atha, whither Donnchadh Ua Cearbhaill and the chieftains of Airghialla came into his house and gave him their hostages.

The parallel passage to this entry in the Annals of Tigernach adds that Ó Cearbhaill also received a donation from Ó Conchobhair amounting to 240 cows; but it may be of significance that while both accounts say that Ó Cearbhaill gave hostages to the high king, we are not told that the Ostmen of Dublin (*Áth Cliath*) had done so. Some of the sources already quoted suggest that accepting 'wages' in return for the promise or performance of military service could constitute the minimal concession to a higher power, not necessarily entailing either the surrender of hostages or the payment of tribute.

Curiously enough, the word *tuarastal* was originally a legal term meaning 'eye-witness report' or 'conclusive evidence', and was only later applied to the concept of wages.[46] *Cogadh Gaedhel re Gallaibh* tells us that under viking-rule *tuarastal* was payment received by a conscript on 'the day on which he embarked on board ship with his lord'.[47] If, like the English army's 'king's shilling', such payment was held to make future service legally binding on the recruit, this might explain the semantic development of the word. *Innarrad*, on the other hand, is consistently used of the wages of hired mercenaries.[48]

In the extract quoted earlier from *Cogadh Gaedhel re Gallaibh*, Maoilsheachlainn II had initially been prepared to offer Brian Bóroimhe a more stringent form of submission, 'to do his will' (*denum a riarsom*) and to give hostages. This word *riar* meaning 'wish', 'will', is an evocative term used of the 'will of God', of the authority wielded by a father over his son, of the demands of a patron from his client (*céle*), and the verb *riaraid* can mean either to submit to, or to subdue, depending on context.[49] *Riar, riaraid*, and *ogriar* ('complete submission') are all found

[46] *Ibid., s.v.*.
[47] *Cogadh Gaedhel re Gallaibh*, § 40 (ed. & transl. Todd, pp. 50–1).
[48] Quin, *Dictionary, s.v.*.
[49] *Ibid., s.v.*.

in the annals in connexion with the giving of hostages and the acceptance of *tuarastal*,[50] and sometimes the same concept is conveyed by the word *umla*, 'humility', 'obedience',[51] which was early used of the christian obedience owed to God[52] and may have spread into the vocabulary of secular submissions by analogy.

Compliance with the overlord's will in matters outside the yielding of hostages, tribute, or military service is demonstrated in the career of the high king Muircheartach Mac Lochlainn. In 1153, when his ally Toirdhealbhach Ó Briain fell ill and was unable to lead his followers back into Munster, Mac Lochlainn 'billeted the Munstermen upon the men of Meath, Bréifne, Airghialla, Ulidia, Tír Conaill and Tír Eoghain',[53] that is, upon all the northern Irish kingdoms which had submitted to his authority. Some years later, when granting lands to the newly founded Cistercian monastery of Newry, he added:[54]

> I will also that as the Kings and Nobles of O'neach [Uibh Eachach] or of Ergallia [Airghialla] may wish to confer certain lands upon this monastery, for the health of their souls, they may do so in my lifetime, *while they have my free will and license*, that I may know what and how much of my Earthly Kingdom the King of Heaven may possess for the use of his poor Monks.

The ultimate proof of Mac Lochlainns's overriding authority was, of course, his repeatedly exercised power to appoint or dismiss subject kings in the territories of Ulaidh, Meath, and even Munster.[55] The penalty for disobedience to his dictates was a relentless renewal of hostilities.

This brings us to the question of what a vassal hoped to gain by entering a contract of submission, whether the attached conditions were mild or stringent. Normally the first priority was 'peace' (*síth*), that is, a cessation of the prospective lord's own raids launched against him with the object of extorting his submission,[56] as when Diarmait Mac Carthaigh and his nobles invaded Kerry in 1151:[57]

> and they plundered and levelled their houses and their forts, and searched their fastnesses and woods, and they carried off hostages from Ó Conchobhair for all their requirements (*ris gac ní do iarattur*), though it was not for long that Ó Conchobhair fulfilled them.

Or again we are told that in 1235:[58]

[50] AI 907, 1011.5; AU 1156; AFM 852, 1256, 1262, 1296; AConn 1315.7.
[51] AFM 1223, 1236, 1258.
[52] Quin, *Dictionary*, *s.v.*.
[53] AFM 1153.
[54] O'Donovan, 'The charter', p. 102 (my italics).
[55] AU 1159, 1165; AFM 1153, 1155, 1157, 1159, 1160.
[56] For example, AConn 1225.13 and 16; 1235.10, 18, 19; 1236.12. See Simms, 'Warfare', pp. 99–102.
[57] McC 1151.3.
[58] ALC 1235.

The resolution O Briain adopted on the morrow was to make peace with the Foreigners, and to give them hostages and tribute; and it was too long for him until this resolution was adopted, for the greater part of his people had been plundered and burned up to that time.

The submitting chief naturally wished to procure immunity not only for his territory and subjects but for himself. Giraldus Cambrensis's account of a submission, cited earlier, spoke of 'oaths given on both sides', and the chronicles also mention oaths sworn by the overlord to his vassal at the time of submission, though usually in connexion with their subsequent violation. In 1143, for instance,[59]

Murchadh Ua Maelseachlainn, King of Meath and its For-tuatha, was taken prisoner by Toirdhealbhach Ua Conchobhair, King of Connaught, while he was under the protection of the relics and guarantees of Ireland. These were they: the altar of Ciaran, with its relics; the shrine of Ciaran, called the Oreineach; the Matha-mor; the abbot and the prior, and two out of every order in the Church; Muireadhach Ua Dubhthaigh, the archbishop, the lord of Connaught; the successor of Patrick, and the Staff of Jesus; the successor of Feichin, and the bell of Feichin; and the Boban of Caeimhghin. All these were between Toirdhealbhach and Murchadh, that there should be no treachery, no guile, no defection of the one from the other, no blinding, no imprisoning, and no circumscribing of Murchadh's territory or land, until his crime should be evident to the sureties (*las na comargibh*), and that they might proclaim him not entitled to protection; however, he was found guilty of no crime, though he was taken. He was set at liberty at the end of a month afterwards, through the interference of his sureties, and he was conveyed by his sureties into Munster; and the kingdom of Meath was given by Toirdhealbhach to his own son, Conchobhar.

However, a mere promise on the overlord's part to abstain from aggression, even if kept, would not give adequate reassurance where a territory lay on the border between two rival powers and was liable to be raided from both sides.[60] In order to obtain submissions the overlord should demonstrate convincingly not only that he was equipped to make the more devastating attacks, but also that he was able and willing to defend his vassals from the exactions and raids of neighbouring rulers. A comic tale in the Book of Leinster epitomises this point. It tells of a contentious and stubborn old woman who lived on the borders of Leinster and Munster, but paid her food-rent (*i mbiataighecht ro bái*) to the king of Leinster. The king of Munster sent his servant on billet to her house and, after eating one loaf of bread bestowed on him in common charity, he demanded a second[61]

"for it is on billet (*for buannacht*) from the King of Munster I have come". "Oh indeed!" said the woman. "This loaf has got its protection (*a commairgi*) against thee, as it is under the protection of the King of Leinster."

[59] AFM 1143; and see also AFM 1147, 1148, 1152, 1157, 1158, 1159, 1166; McC 1165.2.
[60] For example, AConn 1228.3; 1236.16.
[61] O'Nowlan, 'The Quarrel', pp. 134–5.

Though socially insignificant and physically defenceless, the old woman could defy the king of Munster because as a vassal of the king of Leinster she partook of his prestige, and his vengeance threatened anyone who deprived her of so much as a loaf.

If the effectiveness of such protection were to be maintained, it was essential that any breach of it should be instantly avenged, a principle which applied as much to ecclesiastical immunities as to the immunity guaranteed by a secular lord. In 1128 an annalist laments that[62]

> the successor of Patrick was insulted to his face, that is, his company was robbed and some of them killed ... The aftermath that came of that misdeed is that there exists in Ireland no protection (*comuirce*) that is secure for anyone henceforth until that evil is avenged by God and man.

Later in the same year the writer notes with relief that the perpetrators of this sacrilege were punished, and the honour or 'face' (*enech, oineach*) of St Patrick's community restored, by a bloody battle in which four hundred were slain. Stories like this prompted Giraldus Cambrensis to comment on the exceptionally vindictive nature of Irish saints,[63] but in the eyes of annalists and hagiographers vengeance was a holy duty, promoting stability and order in society, a fulfilment of the guarantor's oath to protect those under his safeguard (*comairce, commairghe, cumairche*).[64] When in 1166 the high king Muircheartach Mac Lochlainn treacherously blinded his vassal Eochaidh Mac Duinnshléibhe in violation of oaths guaranteed by the successor of Patrick and the chief relics of Armagh, and in breach of the *comairce* of Ó Cearbhaill, king of Airghialla, his own followers deserted the tyrant and he was 'was killed and his head cut off for the [outraged] honour (*a n-eanach*) of Jesus, Patrick, and Ó Cearbhaill'.[65]

Like the more general contracts of clientship or vassalage, undertakings by one man to protect another obtained throughout society and were not restricted to the relationship between a king and his subjects. In fact, the bond of protection could cut across territorial or political boundaries, and took precedence in the Irish code of honour over the duty owed to one's own countrymen, to one's king, even to one's father.[66] In 1212, for instance,[67]

> a depredation was committed by the Gilla-fiaclach O Baighill and a party of the Cenél Conaill, on the Cenel Eoghain, who were under guarantee (*comairce*) of O Tairchert [a sub-chieftain of Cenél Conaill]. O Tairchert overtook them and fought a battle against them. The Gilla riabhach O Tairchert, i.e. the king-chieftain of Clann Sneidhghile and Clann Finghin, was slain moreover, defending his honour (*ic cosnum a oinigh*).

62 AU 1128.5.
63 Giraldus Cambrensis, *Topographia Hibernie*, III.33.
64 Quin, *Dictionary*, *s.v.*.
65 AFM, AT, AU 1166; McC 1165.2.
66 ADF, AFM 1451.
67 AU 1212.

Similarly in 1252 Conchobhar Mac Cathmhaoil, a sub-chieftain of Tír Eoghain, was slain while defending his *comairce* against the forces of his overking, Brian Ó Néill.[68] Thus the qualities most admired in private patrons or kings were a lively sense of honour or 'face' which felt any injury inflicted on a *protégé* to be a personal affront, a blush-making insult, and sufficient courage and martial ability to vindicate this honour by avenging all breaches of their protection. The commonest eulogy bestowed by annalists on secular leaders was a commendation of their *enech 7 engnam*, 'face' and valour.[69] A king was honour-bound to protect all his territory and subjects; *Audacht Morainn* recommends him to 'remove(?) the shame of his cheeks by arms in battle against other territories',[70] but he might also extend special undertakings to individuals, whether clients or allies. Both private and public obligations are alluded to in the obituary of Feidhlimidh Ó Conchobhair, king of Connacht (*ob.* 1265):[71]

one who safeguarded and supported his own Province and his friends on every side, one who banished and plundered his foes in whatsoever place they were, a man full of honour and valour (*lan d'oinech 7 d'engnam*), of respect and importance.

The whole question as to how the ideology and practice of vassalage in Gaelic Ireland developed during the later middle ages is given an added dimension not only by the presence of Anglo-Norman colonists who had their own customs in this respect, but by the survival from this later period of many written contracts, normally recording the submission of an Irish chief to an Anglo-Irish baron or viceroy but occasionally preserving agreements between two native Irish leaders.[72] It is difficult, of course, to be confident as to how far the terms of a chief's submission to an Anglo-Irish overlord have been modelled on native custom, but most of the points covered by such documents are already familiar from twelfth-century evidence. In particular it remained normal practice for the vassal to guarantee his undertakings by yielding one or more hostages to the overlord, and the increased written evidence allows us to glimpse some of the more personal details involved: the vassal's difficulty in securing his intended hostage prior to handing him over;[73] his anxiety over the subsequent treatment of such friends and relatives, often mere children;[74] the distinctions drawn between 'valuable' and 'worthless'

[68] AU 1252.

[69] Of 158 eulogistic obits noted in AU from the twelfth century to the fifteenth, eighty-six praised the subject's *enech* and forty-eight his *engnam*. The proportions are even higher in AConn.

[70] Kelly, *Audacht Morainn*, p. 11.

[71] AConn 1265.7.

[72] See below, nn. 124, 125.

[73] Kingsford *et al.*, *Report* I.31–2.

[74] Curtis, *Richard II*, p. 134.

hostages,[75] based on their age, political importance, and degree of consanguinity to their principal. A particularly 'worthless' hostage in these respects was exacted from the Great Ó Néill in 1385: Cú Uladh Galldha Ó Néill, a fifteen-month-old baby, a younger son of his younger son, who was still to be found in official custody some sixteen years later as 'a hostage ... often forfeited' by the repeated rebellions of his grandfather.[76] As in the Middle Irish period, the transfer of hostages from the keeping of one overlord to another was associated with the transfer of immediate responsibility for, and authority over, the vassal who had yielded them. In 1305 the justiciar delivered the hostage of Giollaphádraig Mac Mathghamhna, lord of Fearnmhuighe, to Richard de Burgh, the 'Red Earl' of Ulster, with the rider: 'The Earl engages that Gilpatrik will keep the peace ... and if Gilpatrik presume to come against the premises, the Earl will restore the hostage to [Dublin] castle, that justice may be done on him, or render for him 40 marks'.[77] Similarly in 1393 King Richard II ordered his justiciar in Ireland to deliver the Ó Néills' hostages to Roger Mortimer, earl of March and Ulster, since 'the king is aware that he would keep their hostages in the more careful custody because his lands were by them and their adherents wasted, and are like to be in time to come, if the said hostages should be set free'.[78]

This command was a move to counteract a new tendency in the late fourteenth century to undermine the original purpose of hostage-giving by releasing hostages for a money-ransom as if they were prisoners of war or agreeing to exchange them for hostages of lesser political or emotional value in return for a substantial bribe.[79] Government-officials who did this may have been influenced by the current obsession with obtaining ransom-money in France during the Hundred Years' War,[80] but the Anglo-Irish colonists complained of the practice as an abuse. Even Gaelic Irish sources, however, begin to lay less emphasis on hostage-taking and more on the winning of concessions, financial or otherwise (*comhadha móra*), or the taking of great preys (*creacha móra*) as a criterion of victory during the fifteenth century.[81] Hostages were still exacted by a newly inaugurated chief from his own subjects if there was any question of a succession-dispute,[82] and they were still necessary to guarantee the authority of a paramount lord over neighbouring territories,[83] but the

[75] 'x hostages de petite eu nulle value' – P.R.O. S.C. 8/189/9434 (I owe this reference to Dr D. Johnston).

[76] *CCH*, p. 122, no. 29; *CPR 1399–1401*, p. 327.

[77] *CJRI 1305–7*, p. 13.

[78] *CCR 1392 6*, p. 157.

[79] See above, n. 75; *CCR 1392–6*, pp. 157–8; *CCR 1399–1402*, pp. 342; *CPR 1388–92*, p. 404.

[80] Hay, 'The division'.

[81] For *comhada*, see AU 1423, 1432, 1433, 1456, 1497; AConn 1368.13, 1461.25, 1468.19. For *creacha*, see AConn 1415.5, 1462.10 and 11, 1464.26 and 35, 1466.31, 1468.18, 23, 35; AU 1436, 1470, 1471, 1474, 1476, 1478, 1479 etc.

[82] AConn 1315.7, 1370.2, 1461.23.

[83] AU 1430, 1458, 1469; AConn 1537.10.

evolution of the Pale as a permanently defended frontier between the jurisdiction of the Irish lords and the English king simultaneously gave rise to a new kind of subjection, financial but not political. By repeated raids on the shrinking colony, chieftains could force the local communities to buy peace with an annual bribe of 'protection-money' (*cíos cosanta*), or 'black rent' (*duibhchíos*), and yet not extend their political jurisdiction by one yard. The rent or tribute (*cíos*) was 'black' – that is, tyrannical, unjustifiable – because it secured immunity from attack only, and did not involve the lord in any reciprocal responsibility for patronage or protection; nor did he expect any continued obedience to his will. Hostages given in pledge for the payment of black rent could therefore be released as soon as the money was forthcoming.[84]

Anglo-Irish indentures also provide more detailed information about the military service yielded by a vassal chief to his overlord. While, again, one cannot exclude foreign influence on these clauses, they are consistent with earlier native Irish sources in distinguishing two kinds of obligation: an unpaid one subject to customary limitations as to duration or geographical range; and an unlimited commitment in return for pay. For instance Eochaidh Mac Mathghamhna, *tánaiste* of Airghialla, promised Prince Thomas of Lancaster in 1401 that he would 'rise with his subjects against [any Irish enemies or rebels] whenever he shall be so required by the King or his Lieutenant and without any excuse [he] will be ready with all his Power to march with the King or his Lieutenant against the said enemies or rebels, yet at the King's charges, if he chance to go out of his own parts';[85] and the same clause occurs in the indentures between Eoghan Ó Néill and the Earl of Ormond in 1425,[86] and between Éinri Ó Néill and the Duke of York in 1449.[87]

It was the more necessary for the overlord to supply his vassal's force with wages, since the military following of any chief in the later period was increasingly composed of professional mercenary soldiers.[88] The word *tuarastal* itself was used in thirteenth-century annals and later of the pay delivered to Anglo-Norman armies who hired themselves out to Irish kings without any commitment to political vassalage,[89] and in the form 'twerestell' it occurs in a fourteenth-century patent roll with reference simply to soldiers' wages.[90] On the other hand, there are in the later mediaeval annals relatively few examples of *tuarastal* meaning a ceremonial gift presented by the overlord to his vassal at the time of submission, and when these do occur it seems to be in contexts where the symbolic assertion of superiority was of greater importance than any

[84] Graves, *A Roll*, pp. 192–3; see below, pp. 144–5, nn. 116–19.
[85] Shirley, *Some Account*, pp. 19–20.
[86] *Irish Record Commission Reports 1810–15*, p. 55.
[87] Curtis, 'The "Bonnaght" of Ulster', p. 88.
[88] See below, p. 126.
[89] ALC 1200, 1201, 1202; AConn 1225.6 and 8, 1544.3.
[90] *CCH*, p. 120, n. 30.

thought of securing future military service.[91] A dynastic succession-dispute was brought to an end by the unsuccessful candidate agreeing to accept *tuarastal* from his rival,[92] and in 1463 Éinrí Ó Néill, the overlord of Ulster, bestowed *tuarastal* on Tadhg Ó Briain, prince of Thomond, although the two leaders never joined forces on a hosting before or after that date.[93] Indeed, a curious passage in the fourteenth-century saga *Caithréim Thoirdhealbhaigh* actually undertakes to explain the meaning of *tuarastal* to the reader, as if the practice was already obsolete:[94]

Now in time of old it was the custom that whoso, being ruler whether of a cantred or of a province, accepted another chief's gift or wage did actually by such acceptance submit to the giver as to his chief paramount, and in virtue of the same take on himself to do him suit and service, to pay him rent and tribute.

It is doubtful, however, if one can lay much emphasis on this antiquarian note. Since there are no extant manuscripts for this portion of the saga antedating A.D. 1721, we may be dealing here with an eighteenth-century scribal gloss on the original text. A traditional tract on the rights of Mac Mathghamhna asserts that in the mid-fifteenth century the chief Rudhraighe Mac Mathghamhna remitted half the annual tribute due from the lands of his sub-chieftains 'in lieu of their *tuarastal*'; but in this tract it is the tribute itself which is described as 'homage (*onóir*) . . . as a token of respect, and as a sign of his authority and their obedience'.[95] This stress on the exaction of tribute rather than the payment of wages as a proof of authority is matched by the practice of sixteenth-century overlords who regularly demanded heavy bribes from newly elected sub-chiefs within their dominions as the price for ratifying their succession to office, rather than buying the allegiance of these new vassals with a donation.[96]

Another point to receive fuller documentation in the later period is the extent to which a paramount chief could impose his 'will' (*riar*) on subject territories beyond the contracted dues of tribute, hostages, and military service. In a number of the peace-treaties between such overlords and the Dublin government, the leader acknowledged responsibility for seeing that his vassal chiefs also kept the agreed terms, promising to make war on all those who breached his undertaking.[97] Similarly Niall Óg Ó Néill assured King Richard II in 1395 that he had written a letter to the Ó Conchobhair chief of Sligo 'warning him to come in to your Majesty, otherwise I would make war upon him on my part unless he would obey your lordship'.[98] Apart from thus directing the foreign policy of client

91 AU 1430, 1450, 1463, 1562; AConn 1515.3, 1525.5.
92 AU 1450.
93 See Simms, ' "The King's Friend" ', pp. 225–7.
94 Ed. & transl. O'Grady, *Caithréim Thoirdhealbhaigh*, I.3 and II.3.
95 Ó Dufaigh, 'Cíos Mhic Mhathghamhna', pp. 129, 132.
96 See above, p. 47, nn. 45, 46, 49.
97 *CJRI 1295–1303*, p. 61; Curtis, *Richard II*, p. 84; Ronan, 'Some mediaeval documents', p. 233.
98 Curtis, *Richard II*, p. 214.

chiefs, a paramount lord could issue a safe-conduct valid for their territories as well as for lands under his own direct jurisdiction, as Éinrí Ó Néill issued a pass to merchants visiting the sea-ports of Ulster on behalf of himself *et aliorum dominorum sibi subjectorum*,[99] while the same prince's request for authorisation from the archbishop of Armagh to seize the bodies and goods of all clerical concubines in the dioceses of Armagh, Clogher, Raphoe, Derry, and wherever else his power extended,[100] clearly implied that he claimed a greater jurisdiction in the lordship of Ó Domhnaill, for example, than the archbishop (as he ruefully confessed) was entitled to exercise in the corresponding diocese of Raphoe.[101]

Vassals who submitted to such domination were still thought to be entitled to their patron's protection in this later period. In 1369, for instance,[102]

> Ua Maelduin, king of Lorg, was killed in treachery by the sons of Niall Ua Domnaill. And Philip MagUidhir, king of the Seven Territories, went (with) a large fleet to avenge his vassal (*a oglaich*) on the sons of Ua Domnaill and Niall Ua Domnaill the younger was slain by him in a naval engagement on Finn-Loch.

However, the word *enech*, 'face' or 'honour', while it could still apply to a warlord who honoured his obligation to extend protection,[103] was coming to be used more frequently in its secondary sense of 'hospitality' (*enech bidh 7 dighi*),[104] in other words, the face which never has to blush for shame because hungry guests go unfed or the poet's art is unrewarded. Many notables of the fifteenth and sixteenth centuries, rather than being eulogised for 'honour and valour' (*enech 7 engnam*), were praised for 'hospitality and piety' (*enech 7 crabud*),[105] 'hospitality and humanity' (*enech 7 daennacht*),[106] or 'hospitality and charity' (*enech 7 derc*).[107] The warlord's sense of honour or dignity was now commonly expressed by the Latin loanword *onóir*, and this change in vocabulary involved a change of emphasis. *Onóir* seems to have signified primarily esteem or obedience and, as we have seen,[108] could be embodied in the annual tribute paid by vassal chieftains to their superior. *Easonóir* or dishonour was not so much the infringement of a lord's promised protection by some outsider but the defiance of his authority by a former subject, as when Hugh de Lacy the younger rebelled against King John[109] or when

[99] Registrum Iohannis Prene, Lib. i, fo 182v.
[100] *Registrum Iohannis Mey*, edd. Quigley & Roberts, no. 379.
[101] *Ibid.*, no. 322.
[102] AU 1369.
[103] AU 1420.
[104] AU 1401.
[105] AU 1421, 1427, 1431, 1432, 1480.
[106] AU 1427, 1441, 1445, 1477, 1486, 1499.
[107] AU 1427, 1428, 1472, 1476, 1477, 1480.
[108] See above, n. 95.
[109] McC 1210.2.

the chieftains of Ulster drove the Great Ó Néill into exile in 1419.[110]

In the later mediaeval annals we find the first traces[111] of a proverb which was to be repeatedly quoted in the Tudor-Stuart period, 'Spend me and defend me',[112] indicating that an Irish tenant acquiesced in being tallaged at will by his landlord, provided that he was in return guaranteed immunity from all outside interference, whether manifested in violent acts of aggression or legitimate demands for debts or taxes owed by the tenant elsewhere. The same link between the lord's profit and his protection is found in the sour comment of an Anglo-Irish observer *ca* 1515:[113]

> Every Iryshe captaine defendeyth all the subgetes, and the comyn folke, wythin his rome [realm], fro ther enymyes, asmuche as in hym is; not to thentent that they shulde escape harmeless, but to thentent to devoyre them by hymself, lyke as a gredy hounde delyveryth the shepe fro the wolffe.

An example of the more acceptable side of this practice is found in Mac Eochagáin's covenant in 1526 'to spend his country and the Fox's country, for obtaining justice for the Fox and his country, as well as to compel them and him to render justice'.[114]

The insistence here on fulfilling the requirements of justice was important because the bond of *comairce*, the express undertaking by one individual to protect another, which any lord could extend even to men from outside his own territory,[115] might be seen as an excuse for harbouring thieves, outlaws, and other refugees from well merited legal penalties.[116] The issue was a particularly sensitive one across the border between the Anglo-Irish colony and the jurisdictions of native chiefs. Eoghan Ó Néill in 1425 and Aodh Ruadh Mac Mathghamhna in 1447 promised in indentures with the King's Lieutenant in Ireland not to 'receive or aide anie rebells',[117] and in 1584 Sir Seaán Ó Raighilligh's submission included the clause: 'He shall not give "comberick" to any gent. or Lordes men, children or brethern, that shall happen to offend against the Queen's lawes'.[118]

Within the Irish lordships themselves, compacts guaranteeing protection to certain individuals could take on considerable political significance if the personal protégé of one overlord was the territorial subject of another. In the late fifteenth century Ó Ruairc of West Bréifne was a subordinate ally of Ó Domhnaill but Ó Raighilligh of East Bréifne

110 AU 1419; and see also AU 1452.

111 AFM 1395; AConn 1418.19.

112 Spenser, *A View* (ed. Renwick), p. 35; Piers, 'A Chorographical Description', p. 114.

113 *State Papers, Henry VIII, Ireland 1515–38*, p. 17.

114 See above, p. 91, n. 97.

115 For example, AFM 1319.

116 Brewer & Bullen, *Calendar of the Carew Manuscripts*, I.409.

117 *Irish Record Commission Reports 1810–15*, p. 55; Shirley, *Some Account*, p. 190.

118 Hardiman, *Irish Minstrelsy*, II.159–60.

was not, his traditional allegiance being rather with Ó Néill.[119] Yet in 1475, we are told, a dissident noble within East Bréifne, Brian son of Feidhlim Ó Raighilligh, was Ó Domhnaill's partisan and supporter (*fear rainn 7 pairte ag Ua nDomnaill*) and that[120]

a great hosting was made this year by Ua Domnaill ... to rescue Brian, son of Feidhlimidh Ua Raighilligh, from [the] Ua Raighilligh. And he went to Bel-atha-Conaill and peace was made by him with Ua Raighilligh then. And he went from that into Anghaile to aid the sons of Irial Ua Fergail, who were friends to him ... And he went from that to aid his friends in Ui-Maine.

As in the case of Brian Ó Raighilligh, it seems clear that Ó Domhnaill's 'friends' in Anghaile and Uí Mhaine did not include the respective chiefs of these districts, Ó Fearghail and Ó Ceallaigh. This fostering of a network of supporters on a non-territorial basis parallels the development of bastard feudalism in English and Anglo-Irish society at this same period.[121] As early as 1350 a somewhat similar relationship is documented between the Earl of Kildare and two chieftains of Westmeath, Mac Eochagáin and the Fox. There could be no geographical overlordship here, since both Irishmen were legally tenants of the Earl of March, but they undertook to become the Earl of Kildare's 'men' for life, saving their loyalty to the King and the Earl of March, to fight at their own expense against any neighbouring Irish hostile to the Earl, to ride to war with all their forces in any other part of Ireland at the Earl's expense, and to offer him counsel and aid. In return the Earl promised to defend them against all other Irishmen.[122]

This written contract of submission without reference to territorial overlordship, tribute, or hostages resembles the minimal allegiance in return for the payment of *tuarastal* already seen in twelfth-century sources,[123] except that here the 'wages' are clearly given to reward past service rather than forming an initial payment to secure it in future. More onerous conditions were imposed in proportion to the closeness of the tie between vassal and lord. In the case of Ó Conchobhair of Sligo, whose territory had long been forced to pay tribute to the Ó Domhnaill lords of Tír Conaill, an agreement in 1539 involved military service (*óglachas*) and submission to Ó Domhnaill's 'counsel' in all matters internal and external, secular and ecclesiastical, control of the castle and town of Sligo with its customs and burgages, and a stipulation that Ó Conchobhair should not merely allow but actively assist Ó Domhnaill's own officers to levy his tribute and to billet troops throughout Ó Conchobhair's lordship.[124] In the case of Ó Súilleabháin Béara, a powerful sub-chief

[119] AU 1429, 1449; AConn 1470.8.
[120] AU 1475; cf. AFM 1475.
[121] Examples of Anglo-Irish indentures of retinue may be found in Curtis, *Calendar*, II, nos 37, 38, 39.
[122] Mac Niocaill, *The Red Book*, no. 168.
[123] See above, nn. 39, 40, 43, 44.
[124] M. Carney, 'Agreement', pp. 282–91.

living within the territorial lordship of Mac Carthaigh Mór, he was bound to serve personally as a marshal in Mac Carthaigh's hosting, to support billeted soldiers who would 'be afore the guard of the said Earl's person', to share with his overlord the profits which he exacted from fishers and traders coming to his ports, to provide an annual feast for Mac Carthaigh and to contribute to the upkeep of his horses and hounds.[125] Families living in the vicinity of Ó Raighilligh's castle near Cavan, apparently tenants of his mensal lands, owed a heavier beef-tribute than did his other subjects, paid an additional pork-tribute, supported his guests during their visits, and supplied agricultural labourers to work his estates.[126] Failure on the vassal's part to carry out his contracted obligations was rebellion, punished with military force and punitive fines.[127] Failure on a lord's part to defend his vassal from the attacks of a rival power inevitably resulted in the victim's changing masters.[128]

Giraldus Cambrensis had poured scorn on the Irish for their *innata leuitas*, their fickle inconstancy to the most solemn oaths of allegiance, commenting severely that 'men are free to make contracts of this sort, but not to break them'.[129] The most cursory glance at Irish records, however, makes it abundantly clear that rather than being made freely, submissions and contracts of vassalage were normally extorted by military force.[130] In practice force had played a large part in building up the feudal system also, although chivalric literature and legal jargon maintained the fiction of voluntary adherence and mutual love and loyalty between the contracting parties.[131] Heroic literature of the Old and Middle Irish periods shows traces of that cult of loyalty to one's lord which is such a prominent theme of Anglo-Saxon compositions,[132] but there is little sign of the same sentiment in post-Norman Ireland. On the contrary, the lords themselves are shown advising their followers to desert to the enemy in times of adversity. In 1315, for instance, Feidhlim Ó Conchobhair[133]

> gave leave to the chieftains and sub-kings who had been with him on this ill-sped journey to repair to their own houses and to accept the lordship of Ruaidri, rather than become landless men with himself. "For if I regain power you shall be with me."

In the early stages of its development, the feudal oath of homage in Continental Europe, a mutual promise of lifelong devotion symbolised by the intermingling of hands, had elements in common with the sacrament

125 Brewer & Bullen, *Calendar of the Carew Manuscripts*, I.366.
126 O'Donovan, *Annala*, VI.1806, n. b.
127 See below, pp. 127–8, 130, 142–3.
128 See above, p. 68, n. 61; see also below, n. 133.
129 Giraldus Cambrensis, *Expugnatio Hibernica*, II.6 (edd. Scott & Martin, p. 148).
130 AConn 1315.7, 1316.2 and 4, 1334.2, 1342.11, 1349.5, 1351.3, 1405.15, 1417.18, 1464.35, 1468.22, 1474.16, 1515.3, 1526.12 and 17, 1530.4, 1536.23, etc.
131 Ganshof, *Feudalism*, pp. 30–1, 71, 74–5; Bloch, *Feudal Society*, pp. 231–8.
132 For example, Gantz, *Early Irish Myths*, p. 105.
133 AConn 1315.8; and see also 1225.13 and 19.

of marriage. Perhaps it is significant that the brutally utilitarian attitude of the late mediaeval Gaelic lords to the vassal relationship seems mirrored by their view on political marriages, shown in a touching passage from the traditional history of the Uí Raighilligh:[134]

> Ó Ruairc's daughter ... said to Seaán: "Since you did not get help from my father, leave me and take another wife with whom help will be got. And when there is peace let you have the wife you wish, or the wife who has most right to you."

In view of his celebrated disquisition on 'How princes should honour their word', one might hazard a guess that Machiavelli would not have censured the mentality revealed in the above two passages as *leuitas*.

[134] Carney, *A Genealogical History*, p. 105.

VIII

THE KING'S ARMY

In early mediaeval Ireland there was clearly no such thing as a standing army at the disposal of the local king. There are indeed obscure references, mainly in literary sources, to warrior-bands, the *fiana*, which Eoin MacNeill and others have rashly assumed to have been 'permanent military forces ... adopted no doubt in imitation of the Roman military organisation'.[1] More recent research suggests that such bands were devotees of a pagan warrior-cult, not unlike the Scandinavian berserkers, and they are often depicted as hostile not only to the christian Church but to contemporary kings.[2]

These eccentrics have no place in the defence-system of the *tuath* as envisaged by the Old Irish law-tracts, where responsibility rests on the whole community. In one interesting passage *Críth Gablach* treats of military service in the context of the delicate balance of authority between king and *tuath*. A king can issue a legally binding summons to a hosting at an *oenach*, or general assembly, provided that it is a 'just' hosting, required to repel invaders, to support him in parleying for war or peace, or, in the case of an overking, to invade another, uncooperative *tuath*. In such circumstances the king's authority derives from the fact that his measures are taken for the benefit of the *tuath* itself (*it lessa tuaithe uli insin*).[3] Those who fail to answer this summons to war become liable to distraint of their property, with a three-day stay of execution. Later glosses and commentaries on this latter ruling indicate that the call to arms could have three degrees of intensity, affecting in the first instance only landowners, at other times every shield-bearing warrior, and in extreme cases levying every 'head', every individual inhabitant. Landowners – or, in the case of female heiresses, their male proxies – were apparently expected to supply their own food and equipment on expeditions.[4] In addition, the tracts mention a similar public duty to participate in more restricted musterings for internal defence (*fuba 7 ruba*),[5] which, again according to later glosses, could include the periodic extermination of wolves.[6]

[1] O'Rahilly, *Early Irish History*, pp. 265–6.
[2] Sharpe, 'Hiberno-Latin *laicus*', p. 86; O'Rahilly, *Early Irish History*, pp. 271–81.
[3] Binchy, *Críth Gablach*, pp. 19–20 (§§ 35–37, lines 492–513).
[4] Binchy, *Corpus*, II.381, III.889, V.1687.
[5] Thurneysen, 'Aus dem irischen Recht', pt I, p. 365.
[6] Binchy, *Corpus*, II.381, V.1687.

The only permanent force attributed to the *rí tuaithe* was the hirelings (*amuis*) – four men, recruited either as freed serfs or as pardoned criminals, who surrounded the king's person as he presided over an ale-feast, while a couple of champions guarded the door of the banqueting hall and used their weapons against brawling guests.[7] These presumably corresponded to the *dóirseoir* or doorkeeper,[8] and *tréinfhear*, the strong man ('bouncer'?),[9] of later sources.

Inevitably the larger territorial units, evolving even during the period at which the law-tracts were being written,[10] would make it necessary for kings to employ greater numbers of such household-guards to impose their authority effectively in large-scale gatherings. However, evidence both from the chronicles and from more purely literary sources such as *Cogadh Gaedhel re Gallaibh* indicate that the viking-invasions of the ninth and tenth centuries played a significant part in precipitating the changes in Irish military organisation which took place at this time. A recurring theme in *Cogadh Gaedhel re Gallaibh* is the superiority of the vikings' body-armour and weapons by comparison with those of the Irish,[11] and indeed archaeology indicates that the vikings' battle-axe and longsword were eventually imitated by their opponents.[12] A new word typical of the eleventh and twelfth centuries, though later becoming obsolete, was *suartleach*, from Old Norse *svartleggja*, a mercenary soldier.[13] The author of the *Cogadh*, writing some hundred and fifty years after the event, claims that at the height of their power in Munster the invaders billeted a *suartleach* in every house and conscripted the fittest member of every family 'to take wages (*dol a tuarastal*), the day on which he embarked on board ship with his lord, [and] he must be supplied with provision, as if he was at home'.[14] Whether or not this is an accurate description of the 'Babylonian captivity' of the Irish under Scandinavian rule,[15] the mass-billeting of foreign mercenaries and the levying of native inhabitants for paid naval service were both innovatory concepts. Although the vikings are here credited with introducing them, they were soon to be parallelled by the practice of Irish overkings.

The Annals of Inisfallen record the death in 968 of Cathal son of Fogartach 'royal mercenary of Ireland (*rí-amus Herend*)', a man who is described in the *Cogadh* as commanding 'an hundred armed men fit for battle, each man of them having a large warrior's shield at his side'.[16]

[7] Binchy, *Críth Gablach*, p. 23.

[8] See above, p. 85, n. 54.

[9] AFM 448; L. Gwynn, 'De maccaib Conaire', pp. 148, 151; O'Grady, *Silva Gadelica*, I.93, 238; II.101, 270.

[10] See above, p. 79, nn. 5, 6.

[11] *Cogadh Gaedhel re Gallaibh*, §§ 40, 47, 91 (ed. & transl. Todd, pp. 52–3, 66–7, 158–9).

[12] Rynne, 'The impact' and 'An Irish sword'; Brøndsted, *The Vikings*, p. 122.

[13] Quin, *Dictionary*, *s.v.*.

[14] *Cogadh Gaedhel re Gallaibh*, § 40 (ed. & transl. Todd, pp. 48–51).

[15] AFM, AT 979.

[16] *Cogadh Gaedhel re Gallaibh*, § 51 (ed. & transl. Todd, pp. 74–5).

The same saga states that before Brian Bóroimhe's rise to power many of his kindred and subjects, the Dál gCais, had taken service as mercenaries with Uí Néill kings in the northern half of Ireland.[17] The Annals of Inisfallen mention a plundering raid in 985 on the mercenaries (*amsu*) of King Brian himself, whereby they lost three hundred cows,[18] a detail which certainly suggests a larger and more important group of men than the bodyguard of freed serfs in *Críth Gablach.*[19] The battle-hosting of the king of Aileach, as described in the Middle Irish poem *Cert cech ríg co réil*, was largely composed of his hereditary sub-chiefs and their followers, but the king is explicitly advised to surround his own person with professionals: 'Let the mercenaries (*amsaig*) of great Ailech, with the curved sword, protect you keenly; let your foreign mercenaries (*do gaill*) be at your back'.[20] In 1154, when the high king Toirdhealbhach Ó Conchobhair attacked Aileach with a navy recruited from the coastal districts of Connacht, Muircheartach Mac Lochlainn, then king of Aileach, hired Norse-Scottish fleets from the Hebrides in an unsuccessful attempt at defence before retaliating with a raid on Connacht and the Midlands as far as Dublin, where he gave 'wages' (*tuarastal*) to the Scandinavian inhabitants and was accepted by them as their king.[21]

Such large-scale expeditions, during which overkings circuited Ireland north and south and remained away from their home-territories for long periods, were typical of Irish warfare from the tenth to the twelfth century.[22] They cannot be explained in terms of the élite of fully professional soldiers, whether native or foreign, who formed only a small proportion of a king's total hosting. Rather, a key-factor in this new mobility would seem to have been the contract of military service between each king and his leading vassals, whereby the old restrictive definitions of what constituted a 'just' hosting were superseded by a promise to accompany the king 'at every need' in return for *tuarastal* or 'wages'.[23] Armies which had been led far from their own homes might be billeted on subject populations.[24]

Although this move from customary public duty to a series of private contracts, as the basis for the royal summons to war, may have increased the king's control of the political initiative as against that of his subjects, and undoubtedly gave rise to a more efficient, because more flexible, organisation, Giraldus Cambrensis describes the actual equipment and methods of Irish armies at the time of the Norman invasion as primitive in the extreme. Apart from the battle-axe, which they had adopted from the vikings, he mentions only short spears, darts, and sling-stones as their

[17] *Ibid.*.
[18] AI 985.2.
[19] See above, n. 7.
[20] O'Donoghue, 'Cert cech ríg co réil', p. 268.
[21] AFM 1154.
[22] For example, AU 941.3, 951.3, 968.3, 1005.7, 1088.2, 1101.4, 1114.3, 1166.
[23] See above, pp. 101–2, nn. 39, 40, 43, 44, 45.
[24] See below, p. 132.

weapons and asserts that they wore no armour at all.[25] Against an Irish host fighting in the open plain the archers and mounted men-at-arms of the Normans proved startlingly effective, even in small numbers,[26] and Irish kings acknowledged this military superiority by retaining Norman troops in their own service. By the end of the twelfth century not only Diarmait Mac Murchadha, king of Leinster, but Domhnall Mac Giollaphádraig of Ossory and Cathal Croibhdhearg Ó Conchobhair of Connacht had employed Norman forces to promote their own interests.[27]

The detailed Irish narrative of the Norman conquest of Connacht during the first half of the thirteenth century, versions of which occur in all the annals originating in that area,[28] is a mine of information on contemporary military matters. From this account it is clear that all the Norman forces, even those of the justiciar and other great lords whose intervention was to a large extent political or self-interested, demanded wages (*tuarastal*) from the Connacht leaders who invited their assistance,[29] although most would have indignantly repudiated the notion that they were thus assuming the role of vassals or servants to the Irish kings. On a number of occasions these Normans took prominent Irishmen prisoner or hostage as security for the eventual payment of the wages,[30] but in 1202 Cathal Croibhdhearg Ó Conchobhair allowed the soldiers of William de Burgh to levy their own wages from the people on whom they were billeted,[31] a practice which was to become only too familiar for the rest of the middle ages in Ireland under the name of *coinnmheadh* or 'coigny'.[32]

The word used in this case for the soldiers employed by William de Burgh was *sersenaigh*. Like the Norse loanword *suartleach* mentioned above, *sersenach* was to be a short-lived borrowing, appearing frequently in Irish annals from the late twelfth to the early fourteenth century but very seldom thereafter.[33] It apparently derives from the French *sergent*, a foot-soldier.[34] Troops of this description are recorded by the annalists as serving in both Norman[35] and Irish[36] armies, although where there is positive evidence they, or at any rate their leaders, appear

[25] Giraldus Cambrensis, *Topographia Hibernie*, III.10.

[26] Giraldus Cambrensis, *Expugnatio Hibernica*, I.3, 4, 24 and II.17; Hayes-McCoy, *Irish Battles*, pp. 27–8.

[27] Orpen, *Ireland under the Normans*, I.166–7, II.154–5.

[28] O'Dwyer, 'The Annals of Connacht and Loch Cé', pp. 89–101.

[29] ALC 1200, 1201, 1202; AConn 1225.6 and 18.

[30] ALC 1200, 1201, 1225.

[31] ALC 1202.

[32] Empey & Simms, 'The Ordinances', pp. 178–85; see below, p. 135, nn. 37–9.

[33] The only annalistic occurrence which I have noted after 1315 is AConn 1461.24.

[34] Quin, *Dictionary, s.v.*; Murray *et al.*, *The Oxford English Dictionary, s.v.* 'sergeant (2)'.

[35] ALC 1202; AConn 1225.18 and 20, 1230.6 and 8, 1235.8, 13 and 14, 1236.4, 1237.2, 1261.6.

[36] ALC 1195, 1196, 1199, 1208; AConn 1235.11 and 23, 1236.9, 1256.9 and 14, 1269.4.

to have been of English or Welsh extraction.[37] The contexts in which they occur indicate that they were mercenaries,[38] that they wore armour,[39] and that they were distinguished from both horse-[40] and foot-soldiers.[41] Possibly, as has been suggested, this was because they were archers,[42] but since on two occasions such men are described as wielding axes,[43] their special status may simply have been that of heavily armed foot-soldiers, forerunners of the Scots galloglass.

Another ephemeral loanword, *rúta*, was applied to a 'rout' or company of *sersenaigh* under the command of a single captain, and on one occasion this is said to have comprised two hundred soldiers.[44] *Rúta*, however, appears to have been a rather vague term. In 1252 on the occasion of a 'royal service' or hosting, proclaimed by the justiciar against the Ulster Irish, to which all feudal tenants of the Crown were obliged to contribute financially or in person, the annalists say that an internal dispute arose in the Anglo-Irish army between *in rut Midech 7 in rut Mumnech*,[45] the Meath and Munster contingents of a force which was of its nature part feudal, part mercenary. At other times we find the followers of an Irish leader from Meath, 'the Knight' Ó Maoilsheachlainn, called *an rúta Midhech*,[46] or the army brought by the king of Tír Eoghain into Connacht described as *an rut Eoganach*.[47] In these cases, and in further references to the *rúta* of the mid-thirteenth-century kings Brian Ó Néill and Aodh son of Feidhlim Ó Conchobhair,[48] it is not clear whether the annalists had any intention of implying a formal organisation or mercenary status for the troops in question. There is no room for doubt, however, that by this date there were troops of native Irishmen serving under both Irish and Anglo-Irish leaders as mercenary soldiers, known to the annalists as *ceithirne*, 'bands', and sometimes tautologically as *rautadha ceithernn*, 'routs of bands'.[49] Like the *routiers* who plagued France during the Hundred Years' War, these soldiers apparently remained organised in bands even when unemployed, indulging in brigandage with the *meic mallachtáin*, the ordinary criminals in society, so that in 1233 the new king of Connacht had to take decisive action to bring them under control.[50] By the late thirteenth century such men begin to figure in Anglo-Irish government-records as 'kerns' and 'idlemen' (*Kaernie seu*

37 AConn 1225.20, 1230.8, 1237.2, 1310.6.
38 ALC 1202, 1315; AConn 1225.18, 1310.6.
39 AConn 1235.13.
40 AConn 1230.6, 1236.9.
41 AConn 1259.9.
42 Quin, *Dictionary*, *s.v.*.
43 AConn 1311.13, 1461.24.
44 AI 1196.6; AConn 1310.6.
45 AConn, ALC 1252; Otway-Ruthven, *A History*, p. 193.
46 ALC 1200.
47 AConn 1225.10.
48 AU 1252, 1261.
49 Quin, *Dictionary*, *s.v.*; AConn 1235.8 (compare with AConn 1256.14).
50 AConn 1233.5, 1236.16.

homines ociosi)[51] and in ecclesiastical documents as 'troops' or 'troopers' (*turbe, turbales, turbiculi, turbarii*).[52]

Side by side with this evidence for a growing tendency to employ mercenary troops, the Connacht narrative has a number of passages which serve to highlight the disadvantages of the old-style levy composed of sub-chieftains and their followers. When the whole province of Connacht was being overrun by the invading Normans, each leader's primary concern was for his own area and its inhabitants, his loyalty to the would-be provincial overkings coming a poor second, as the following extracts demonstrate:[53]

The people of Mag Ai and the Tuatha fled ... into Leyney and Tirawley with their cattle, and left Ruaidri's sons without any army or territorial levy (*tinól oirechta*), accompanied by no eligible princes or chieftains of these districts, but only grooms and servants...

The son of Magnus parted from the sons of Ruaidri and went into Tirawley to look for his cattle and people...

Aed mac Cathail Chrobdeirg with his Galls came after them, and they decided that each one should return to his cattle and people and leave the sons of Ruaidri.

Preferable from almost any point of view were the Scottish *gallóglaigh*, or galloglass. Having left their original homeland, they were not diverted by local responsibilities from an exemplary loyalty to their current paymaster,[54] nor were they tempted by racial or political bias to betray their Irish employers to the English colonists, as might happen with a leader of *sersenaigh*.[55] Since the Scottish troops migrated to Ireland as clan-groups and fought under the leadership of their own nobility,[56] they never presented the disciplinary problems associated with the native kerns. The latter were denounced by a sixteenth-century writer as 'rakehels, or the devils blacke garde, by reason of the stinkyng sturre they keepe, where so ever they be'.[57]

The first Scottish leader recorded as fighting for an Irish king was 'Mac Somurli, king of Argyle', slain at the battle of Ballyshannon in 1247 while assisting Maoilsheachlainn Ó Domhnaill against the Norman lord of Sligo, Maurice Fitzgerald.[58] Then in 1259 Aodh Ó Conchobhair of Connacht married the daughter of 'Dubhghall Mac Somhairle', almost

[51] Berry, *Statutes and Ordinances*, p. 202.
[52] Nicholls, 'The Register', p. 416; Caulfield, *Rotulus*, p. 58; Register of Archbishop Fleming, fo 15r; Register of Archbishop Swayne, Lib. iii, fo 83r.
[53] AConn 1225.8, 16, 25.
[54] See AConn, AU 1366.
[55] AConn 1310.5 and 6.
[56] Hayes-McCoy, *Irish Battles*, p. 50.
[57] Holinshed, *The Historie of Irelande* (edd. Miller & Power, p. 114).
[58] AConn 1247.7.

certainly to be identified with Dubhghall mac Ruaidhri mhic Raghnaill mhic Shomhairle, then king of the Hebrides. The lady brought as her dowry a hundred and sixty fighting men under the command of 'Ailín Mac Somhairle', presumably King Dubhghall's brother of that name.[59] Two similar marriage-alliances were contracted by Domhnall Óg Ó Domhnaill (king of Tír Conaill, 1258–1281) – the first with a daughter of Mac Suibhne, a family then associated with Castle Sween in Knapdale, by whom he had a son Aodh, and the second with a daughter of Mac Domhnaill of the Isles, who bore him a son Toirdhealbhach. Once again Scottish fighting men came to Ireland in the wake of these marriages. In 1290 a succession-struggle occurred between the half-brothers, and Toirdhealbhach seized the kingship of Tír Conaill from Aodh 'through the power of his mother's kin, the Clann Domnaill, and of many other Galloglasses'.[60]

By the last decade of the thirteenth century the employment of Scottish auxiliaries was becoming general in the northern parts of Ireland. Domhnall Ó Néill of Tír Eoghain, Mac Mathghamhna of Airghialla, and MagUidhir of Fir Manach were all persuaded to accede to a series of articles drawn up by the archbishop of Armagh in 1297, promising, among other things, to restrain 'our Scots and satellites' from committing highway-robbery on ecclesiastical persons.[61] A traditional history of the Uí Néill, compiled in the late sixteenth century, claims that this Domhnall Ó Néill was the first to impose a systematic billeting of galloglass on his subjects, the troop concerned being that of Mag Buirrche, a member of the Mac Suibhne family.[62] The source of this information does not inspire confidence, but a number of considerations suggest that we may have here a fossilised truth embedded in an otherwise unreliable narrative. Mag Buirrche was indeed the name of a galloglass-leader serving in Ireland at that period, who was killed in 1305 while fighting in East Bréifne for Pilib Ó Raighilligh, side by side with the 'heir of Clann Suibhne'.[63] By 1316, letters patent issued by Domhnall Ó Néill to another archbishop of Armagh refer unambiguously to taxation and services exacted for the benefit of Ó Néill himself, his 'Scottish satellites', or any other troops.[64] It is, moreover, a curious fact that from the fourteenth century onwards the Mac Suibhne family in Ireland is found proudly and improbably linking its genealogy to that of the Uí Néill,[65] although they were in fact employed by the Uí Dhomhnaill throughout the later middle ages.

[59] AConn, ALC 1259; Anderson, *Early Sources*, II.625.

[60] AConn 1290.7; *Beatha Aodha Ruaidh*, ed. & transl. Walsh, II.158; Watson, *Scottish Verse*, pp. 257–8.

[61] Nicholls, 'The Register', p. 418.

[62] Ó Donnchadha, *Leabhar Cloinne Aodha Buidhe*, p. 31.

[63] AConn, ALC 1305.

[64] Register of Archbishop Fleming, fo 38r.

[65] Macalister, *The Book of Uí Maine*, fo lvb9; Atkinson, *The Book of Ballymote*, p. 77c16.

A hereditary association between certain families of galloglass-commanders and particular Irish lordships began to develop from the mid-fourteenth century onwards. The traditional chronicler of Clann Suibhne, writing in the early sixteenth century, assures us that 'previous to this arrangement no lord had a claim on them for a rising-out or a hosting, but they might serve whomsoever they wished. It was the Scottish habit [of military service] they had observed until that time, namely, each man according as he was employed.'[66] The prevalence of such a freelance system in earlier years is borne out by the annals' reference in 1316 to Ó Domhnaill's wife who hired a band of galloglass at that time for the narrowly defined objective of assassinating her husband's new vassal in pursuance of a family-feud, and who had earlier attacked the ecclesiastical settlement at Drumcliff 'with all the gallowglasses ... that she could obtain'.[67] The Mac Suibhne leaders played a king-making role during a prolonged succession-struggle among the Ó Domhnaill princes (*ca* 1333–1380), and were rewarded, initially with estates on the peninsula of Fanad, then with the vassal chieftainship of Fanad itself, subject to a levy of galloglass assessed in proportion to the area of land under their control.[68] As the family became established and prospered, cadet-members obtained two further sub-chieftaincies in Tír Conaill – those of Tír Boghaine and of the Trí Tuatha – to be held on similar terms, the troops thus raised having privileged billeting rights throughout the rest of Ó Domhnaill's lordship.[69] This arrangement, whereby three of the vassal chiefs of Tír Conaill were hereditary constables of foreign extraction, holding territorial lordships as endowments of their military office, their lands subject to a form of conscription, is reminiscent of the official aristocracy, the pomeshchiks,[70] which was being created for military purposes in Russia at about the same period.

Elsewhere in Ireland the assimilation of the galloglass-families was not taken to such extremes. Instead of extensive territorial jurisdictions, galloglass-leaders received scattered estates, together with billeting rights for their troops.[71] It is noteworthy, however, that one such hereditary mercenary commander was counted among the five nobles in Mayo entitled to elect MacWilliam Burke's successor in the late sixteenth century,[72] while Ó Néill's constable may have participated in the council held by magnates to discuss their lord's submission to Richard II in 1395.[73] Constables and their families continued to intermarry with the

[66] Walsh, *Leabhar Chlainne Suibhne*, p. 45.
[67] AConn 1315.20, 1316.2.
[68] AConn 1343.13, 1351.7, 1366.8, 1388.3, 1399.5; AU 1359, 1380; Walsh, *Leabhar Chlainne Suibhne*, pp. 30–3, 42–5, 50–1.
[69] AConn 1496.8, 1524.18, 1542.11, 1543.3 and 14.
[70] Pares, *A History*, pp. 148–9.
[71] Morley, *Ireland under Elizabeth and James I*, p. 364; Ó Doibhlín, *Domhnach Mór*, p. 45; Glancy, 'The Church-lands', pp. 82 and 98, n. 4.
[72] See above, p. 48, n. 50.
[73] See above, p. 71, n. 78.

most aristocratic Irish dynasties,[74] and their equality of status was recognised formally by native historians who traced most of their genealogies back to the Airghialla, while linking Clann Suibhne, as noted above, to the Uí Néill.[75]

As such genealogies themselves suggest, the galloglass were originally associated with the northern half of Ireland only. They are not recorded in Munster before the early fifteenth century, or in Leinster until a couple of generations later still.[76] Moreover, they remained at all times an expensive luxury, not easily afforded by minor chieftains.[77] The élite fighting force common to lordships of every size remained the cavalry (*marcshluagh*).

Annal-entries indicate that the cavalry in any Irish lordship was at least partially manned by the ruling classes themselves,[78] and in the sixteenth century a description of Ó Néill of Clann Aodha Buidhe who 'hath eight tall gentlemen to his sons and all they cannot make past 24 horsemen'[79] points to the same conclusion. However, there are also references to a standing force of cavalry, permanently attached to the lord's household. In 1342 it was said of Ó Dochartaigh that 'there was scarcely in Ireland a chief that had more people and a larger horse-host (*marcshluagh*)'.[80] The evidence is more conclusive for the time when Count John de Perilhos visited the court of Niall Óg Ó Néill in 1397. He was initially met and escorted by a hundred horsemen under the command of Ó Néill's constable. Later he refers to three thousand horsemen attending the king's feast at Christmastide. By contrast, he seems to have in mind a precisely defined body of men when he says of Ó Néill: 'He has indeed forty horsemen, riding without saddle on a cushion, and each wears a slashed cloak; moreover they are armed with coats of mail, and wear them girded, and they have throat-pieces of mail and round helmets of iron, with swords and sword-blades and lances very long, but very thin in the manner of ancient lances, and they are two fathoms long; the swords are like those of the Saracens which we call Genoese'.[81] Since certain families occupying Ó Néill's mensal lands in the late sixteenth and early seventeeth centuries (Uí Ágáin, Uí Chuinn, Uí Dhoibhlín) were traditionally known as his 'horsemen',[82] the retinue here described may have been recruited on the basis of hereditary obligations or contracts of vassalage, rather than consisting of mercenaries employed at random. Richard Stanihurst, however, while speaking of the cavalry soldier as a

[74] Register of Archbishop Prene, Lib. iii, fo 17v–20r; AConn 1365.8, 1400.28, 1417.11.

[75] See, for example, Pender, 'The O Clery Book of Genealogies', pp. 125–6; cf. above, n. 65.

[76] Hayes-McCoy, *Scots Mercenary Forces*, pp. 33, 36–7.

[77] See below, n. 90.

[78] AU 1366, 1367, 1493, 1496; AFM 1383, 1396, 1397; AClon 1398.

[79] *CSPI 1509–73*, p. 126.

[80] AU 1342.

[81] Mahaffy, 'Two early tours', pp. 6–8.

[82] See above, p. 86, n. 66.

man of high rank, indicated that some of them were landless, prepared to serve any employer:[83]

> to be an horseman ... is chiefest next the lord and capitaine. These horsemen when they haue no stay of their own, gad and range from house to house like arrant knights of the round table and they neuer dismount vntill they ride into the hall, and as far as the table.

Literary and artistic depictions of mediaeval Irish cavalrymen fully bear out de Perilhos's description of their lightweight armour and long spears. The galloglass who fought on foot were similarly equipped with round helmets of iron and collar-pieces or pisanes of mail worn over a mail-tunic or padded leather jack. Their most distinctive weapon was a long-handled axe, but they also used great two-handed swords, and spears. In contrast the ordinary foot-soldiers or kern who formed the bulk of any Irish army wore no armour, and ran bare-footed and bare-headed, protected only by light, round targets, wielding short swords and javelins. In the sixteenth century they might also carry guns, but Stanihurst derides their marksmanship.[84]

This equipment might seem pitifully inadequate, but it was related to the nature of the warfare being waged in mediaeval Ireland. Until the grim challenge of the Tudor reconquest, the greater Irish lords had fought primarily to build up and maintain their authority over a network of vassal chieftains, and the lesser lords fought to preserve their independence from such dominion, respectively earning eulogies in the annals as 'the man who most compelled neighbouring territories to yield him rents and tributes'[85] and 'a man that defended his territory against his neighbours'.[86] Since the country was apparently underpopulated throughout the mediaeval period, there was little inducement to take possession of additional territory by killing or displacing the original inhabitants. Rather they must be driven into subjection: this might be achieved by cattle-raiding, when the cows which constituted the victims' most valuable property might be released in exchange for hostages and submission at the close of hostilities; or the aggressor could resort to the more destructive tactic of harrying by burning homesteads, trampling down crops, and killing livestock, until terror brought the enemy to sue for terms. The lightly armed, light-footed kern were admirably suited to driving cattle or setting fire to thatched cottages, and since it was a prime object to swoop on the enemy without warning, before armed defenders could be mustered or the cattle placed in secure keeping, a confrontation between the opposing forces normally took place only when the indignant pursuers overtook the plunderers as they drove their unwieldy prey homewards. In such cases the lightly armed subordinates were sent on

[83] *Holinshed's Irish Chronicle*, edd. Miller & Power, p. 114.
[84] Simms, 'Warfare', pp. 104–7; Harbison, 'Native Irish arms', pt 1, pp. 174–80.
[85] AConn 1537.10, 1562; AU 1505; ALC 1452.
[86] AConn 1274.9, 1282.3; AU 1298, 1395, 1418, 1430, 1449, 1480, 1503, 1525, 1588.

ahead, while the aggressors' cavalry formed a protective rearguard, with or without the support of galloglass-troops. These latter could assume a valuable rôle as a moving wall of defence behind which the cavalry could retreat, rally, and emerge to make short sharp charges against their pursuers.[87]

The diminutive scale of such warfare and the small proportion of élite armoured troops involved are both suggested by the numbers given in the Annals of Ulster for two raiding parties during the fifteenth century, one comprising a hundred and forty foot and twelve horse,[88] the other sixty foot and six horse.[89] The total military establishment available to any Irish lordship could be expected to be somewhat larger, of course, and estimates were given by an anonymous Anglo-Irishman *ca* 1515:[90]

> The army of the moste region of the premysseis, besyde the comyn folke of the same, passe not 500 sperys 500 galloglasseis and 1000 kerne; and commonly the armye of every region excede not 200 sperys and 600 kernne, beside the comyn folke, and the lest region of all the premisses maye make 40 speres and two or 300 kernne, besyde the comyn folke of the same.

This constant refrain of 'beside the common folk' is a reminder of how far the chiefs had come to rely on mercenaries in their warfare. In 1607 the English government's hopes of confiscating land from the gentry of Fermanagh on the score of their participation in the Nine Years' War met a temporary hitch when it was discovered that 'M'Guire in the late wars did hire and wage the greatest part of his soldiers out of Connaught and out of the Breny O'Reilly, and made his own countrymen feed them and pay them, and therefore the jury enquiring of escheats found only two freeholders in this country, besides Hugh M'Guire himself to have been slain in the late rebellion'.[91] Even the conservative outlook of the bardic poets accepted such practice as normal. In the mid-fifteenth century the exhortation of the eminent *ollamh*, Tadhg Óg Ó hUiginn, to Neachtain Ó Domhnaill to make war on the Anglo-Irish colony was couched in these terms:[92]

> Let there be no scarcity of troops for the fight; o prince of Murbhach, think not too heavy thy burden of (paying) hired troops to meet the Goill; make all preparations before the need arises.

In addition to horsemen, kern, and hereditary galloglass, the fifteenth-century Ó Domhnaill chiefs pioneered the use of 'redshanks', seasonal armies of Scottish mercenaries imported directly from the Western Isles

[87] Simms, 'Warfare', pp. 99–107.
[88] AU 1455.
[89] AU 1457.
[90] *State Papers, Henry VIII, Ireland 1515–38*, p. 5.
[91] Morley, *Ireland under Elizabeth and James I*, p. 370.
[92] McKenna, *Aithdioghluim Dána*, I.95 and II.57 (no. 24, q. 15).

to serve in large numbers for short periods at a time.[93] This custom was to become much more widespread in the second half of the sixteenth century, with a significant effect on the nature of the warfare then waged. Since these later generations of Scots were not being asked to opt for permanent emigration, their temporary services could be secured on a larger scale, and the command of large regiments of armoured foot made pitched battles against the English feasible for those chiefs who could afford to hire them.

Even before this late development, however, the changeover to a largely mercenary army had brought alterations both tactical and political in its train. A standing army made it possible to garrison castles, for instance. From the mid-fourteenth century Irish chiefs began to occupy castles such as Ballymote, Sligo, and Lough Oughter which had originally been built by the Anglo-Norman colonists.[94] By the fifteenth century we find them building castles of their own for strategic purposes, to defend a frontier or an important line of communication.[95] The word *barda*, or 'castle-ward', begins to be commonly used by the annalists.[96] Conversely, the use of professional soldiers enabled attackers to mount prolonged sieges against such castles, and we hear that Ó Néill took six months, from the autumn of 1470 to the spring of 1471, to capture the castle of Omagh.[97] Native Irish craftsmen learnt to construct siege-machines, presumably the catapult-type,[98] while imported hand-guns and even cannon were gradually introduced into the Gaelic lordships at the end of the fifteenth and beginning of the sixteenth centuries.[99]

On the political front, an Irish lord at the end of the middle ages did not require personal military service from his subjects so much as taxation to finance his professional troops, and the system of *coinmheadh* or 'coigny' meant that taxation for military purposes was normally collected directly from the population by the soldiers themselves, making resistance on the part of individual householders difficult if not impossible. The hosting summons was therefore primarily directed at those vassal chiefs powerful enough to maintain hired troops of their own, and even these could be pressurised into compliance with the help of the forces directly employed by the overlord himself.[100] Thus Richard Stanihurst explained:[101]

> Those tyrants have chieftains of a lower rank in subjection and control, who are ready to go to war with a great number of levies whenever their prince raises the

[93] *CCH*, p. 246, no. 21; AU 1433; AFM 1461; Hayes-McCoy, *Scots Mercenary Forces*, p. 13.
[94] AConn 1369.2, 1371.5, 1375.3.
[95] AConn 1420.3; AU 1423; McKenna, *Aithdioghluim Dána*, I.84 and II.51 (no. 21, q. 21).
[96] AU 1435, 1442, 1486, 1490; AFM 1456; AConn 1467.10; ALC 1478.
[97] AU 1470, 1471.
[98] AConn 1478.22.
[99] AU 1487; AConn 1516.5.
[100] AFM, AU 1435.
[101] Stanihurst, *De Rebus in Hibernia Gestis*, pp. 31–2 (my translation).

battle-standard, and to assist him with all the power and force at their command. If this duty be omitted through negligence or treachery (for they live on his estates or in his jurisdiction bound to such military service, since no other tribute of his is imposed), the prince is accustomed to compel them to arms; or if he find them very pugnacious or stubborn, he procures a band and forces, turns his battle-standards on the defiant ones, expels them from their homes, turns them out from all their property.

Sir Nicholas Malby, president of Connacht, went one stage further in seeing mercenary soldiers as a direct instrument of political repression, a rôle which he hoped to see inherited by the English troops under his command:[102]

If any principal lord or chief of a country be ill dealt withal by his own freeholders and such as dwell under him, where the said lords were wont for suppressing such to entertain Scots and kerne and galloglas, they call to me for her Majesty's forces. At such times they give the soldiers their victuals gratis.

This is a far cry from the restrictions which the Old Irish law-tracts had placed on the king's right to issue a hosting summons, whereby the only just wars were those undertaken for the benefit of his subjects, and it is interesting to find that the anonymous observer of 1515 simultaneously stresses the absolute power of the sixteenth-century warlords of Gaelic Ireland, and denies them the title of kings:[103]

Every captayne maye be callyd a duke of his armye and retynue, and concludeyth [sic] that a kyng is moste to be dreddeid in trone, and a duke in the fylde ... for the duke and captayne of the fylde is more then any kynge: lyke as at the syge of Troye, Hector, that was no king, was duke and governour of many a kyng, and captayne of all the oste of Troye, wherin was manye a noble kyng.

[102] Brewer & Bullen, *Calendar of the Carew Manuscripts*, II.364; Hayes- McCoy, *Scots Mercenary Forces*, pp. 44–5.

[103] *State Papers, Henry VIII, Ireland 1515–38*, p. 6.

IX

THE KING'S REVENUES

Although the income of the *rí tuaithe* as depicted in the Old Irish law-tracts appears to have been modest enough, giving him little economic advantage over his own subject nobility,[1] it was drawn from a wide variety of sources; most of the exactions claimed by Irish chieftains at the end of the middle ages find their embryonic prototype in this early period. Some of these rights were held by the king in virtue of his public office, as representative and executive authority of the *tuath*, but it seems possible to argue that others may have originally belonged to the king in his private capacity, as a wealthy member of the aristocracy, and only later evolved into distinctly royal prerogatives.

Surprising as it may seem, his mensal lands come into this second category. The member of the royal dynasty who succeeded to the kingship automatically became head of his own kindred also. Like the senior member of other landowning kin-groups, he was thereby entitled not only to apportion the family-holding between himself and his relatives but to receive *cumal senorba*, 'the senior's estate', a phrase occurring in the tract *Din Techtugad*, and there glossed as meaning a seventh of the whole family-inheritance, which has been set apart from the common division of shares to pass into the possession of the kin-leader alone.[2] In the twelfth and thirteenth centuries, however, the phrases *fearann tánisteachta* and *ferann ríg*, 'the tanists' estate' 'the king's estate', occur in the Annals of Inisfallen in contexts[3] suggesting that such reserved lands were now associated primarily with the political office of the ruler, rather than with the restricted kin-group (*gelfine*) which controlled such office at any one time. At the end of the mediaeval period it was a general, though not universal,[4] custom for Gaelic chieftaincies to be endowed with crown-lands. In 1607 Sir John Davies apparently equates this royal perquisite with the private land-rights of the nobility in general. Commenting on the minute subdivisions of land brought about by a law of inheritance resembling gavelkind, he added:[5]

[1] Binchy, *Celtic and Anglo-Saxon Kingship*, p. 20.

[2] Binchy, *Corpus*, I.215–16, II.797, III.1296, IV.1548; Plummer, 'Notes', pp. 113–14; Dillon, 'The relationship', pp. 141–2; Thurneysen, 'Cóic Conara Fugill', p. 70, and 'Irisches Recht', pt II, p. 80.

[3] AI 1176.7, 1283.4; and see Byrne, *Irish Kings*, p. 196.

[4] Nicholls, *Gaelic and Gaelicised Ireland*, p. 37.

[5] Morley, *Ireland under Elizabeth and James I*, p. 372.

Notwithstanding, as M'Guire himself had a chiefry over all the country, and some demesnes that did ever pass to him only who carried that title, so was there a chief of every sept, who had certain services, duties or demesnes, that ever passed to the tanist of that sept and never were subject to division.

By this late date, however, it is not easy to draw hard and fast distinctions between private property and the rewards of political office. The 'chief of a sept' in seventeenth-century Fermanagh had in many cases succeeded to the territorial jurisdiction of a *rí tuaithe* of former times and could therefore be expected to possess regal rights.

Another source of income which the king originally had in common with other nobles was his clients, both noble and base, who supplied him with food-rents, labour-services, winter-feasts (*cóe*), and an escort to public gatherings.[6] Already in the Old Irish period, however, a distinction had been drawn between the king's base clients and those of other men, in that only the former were bound to the terms of their contract by the surrender of a human pledge, or hostage.[7]

On the other hand, profits accruing to the king from *sloiged cis 7 congbáil*, 'hosting, tribute, and maintenance', were clearly derived from his public office. Failure to respond to the hosting summons, to render tribute, or to maintain persons lawfully billeted on him made a free landowner of the *tuath* liable to distraint of his property by or on behalf of the king, and the same penalty seems to have applied to ignoring a royal ordinance or the terms of an inter-tribal pact.[8] Chattels thus seized were returnable when the owner became amenable to the due process of the law, but attempted evasion doubled the seizure[9] and outright disobedience to a king's ordinance apparently resulted in fines, – *féich cána*, or 'debts [for breach] of promulgated law'. The ability to exact such fines successfully, and to collect the royal tribute or *cís* from subjects, was regarded by the early lawyers as the acid test of a true king.[10] Glosses on the original tracts indicate that all land in the *tuath* not specifically exempted was chargeable with *sloiged cis 7 congbáil*,[11] and annals and charters from the ninth century to the twelfth show that Church-lands originally shared these obligations, until reforming ecclesiastics began the struggle to extort grants of immunity for the estates of their own monastic houses from local kings.[12]

It is interesting that, as the tract *Críth Gablach* attempts to limit the king's authority to summon freemen on hosting to three 'just' occasions,[13] so a commentary on the law of distraint confines the right to *congbáil*, 'provisioning' or 'maintenance', to three bodies of people: the king when

[6] See above, p. 96, nn. 2 and 3.
[7] See above, p. 97, n. 4.
[8] Binchy, 'Distraint', pp. 39–40.
[9] *Ibid.*, p. 36.
[10] See above, p. 97, n. 5.
[11] Dillon, 'The relationship', p. 155.
[12] Hughes, *The Church*, p. 241.
[13] See above, p. 116, n. 3.

making ordinances or treaties, or by extension the assembly of two *tuaith* when treaties or ordinances are being made between them; a synod of the Church exacting visitation-dues; and a defensive muster of the *tuath*.[14] It is clear, of course, from the annalistic record that Irish kings summoned hostings on occasions which were not 'just' in the sense intended in *Críth Gablach* (that is, for the benefit of their subjects), a discrepancy which became ever more blatant with the passing centuries; and similarly by the Middle Irish period the king's exaction of billeting bore no relation to the restrictions suggested by this commentary. Even the term used in these contexts has changed from *congbáil*, literally 'upkeep', to *coinnmheadh*, 'guesting'. Instead of the older phrase *sloiged cís 7 congbáil*, an ecclesiastical estate in the eleventh century was said to be held *cen (cis) cen chobach cen fecht cen [sh]luaged cen choinnim ríg ná toísig fuirri*, 'without rent or tribute, or expedition or hosting, or free billeting of king or chief on it'.[15] Another charter shows the king of Loeghaire exacting 'one night's *coinnmed* every quarter of a year' from the monastic site of Ardbraccan until the mid-twelfth century.[16] Both terms appear side by side in an anonymous poem in the Second Irish Life of St Maedóc of Ferns, apparently composed some time between the twelfth and fifteenth century. It depicts a dispute between king and cleric in which *congbáil* is used as a general term for billeting, while *coinnmheadh* signifies a fixed customary exaction:[17]

> 'Maintenance (*congbáil*) of a year for two hundred men
> O Concobar, it is not false,
> from thy clerks and from thy house
> And every one of them to be satisfied...
>
> Though thou wert Maedoc himself,'
> said Fergal then,
> 'I would quarter soldiers (*do cuirfinn buanna*) on thy church
> while I am king over Erin.'
>
> 'Maintenance (*congbáil*) beyond his proper refection (*coinnmedh*)
> on the family of gentle Maedoc
> for any one in the world
> I will not impose,' said Conchobar.

The word used here for a billeted soldier (*buanna*) gave rise to an abstract noun *buannacht*, meaning specifically the quartering of a king's soldiers and henchmen on his subjects.[18] On the other hand the exaction of one night's *coinnmheadh* every three months from Ardbraccan suggests a periodic feast, like the winter-feast (*cóe*) once owed to a lord

[14] Binchy, *Corpus*, I.381, V.1687.
[15] Mac Niocaill, *Notitiæ*, p. 10; and see above, n. 12.
[16] Mac Niocaill, *Notitiæ*, p. 34.
[17] Plummer, *Bethada*, II.279–80.
[18] *Dictionary*, ed. Quin, *s.v.*; and see above, p. 105, n. 61.

by his clients,[19] although here the obligation is apparently associated with the ownership of land not explicitly exempted from such duty, rather than arising from a personal contract of clientship.

The Middle Irish annals refer to *coinnmheadh* not as a customary render but as the seizure of provisions by a king and his army on campaign.[20] When the rights of Church-settlements were thus violated, the expression 'forcible guesting' (*coinnmheadh éiccne, trén coinnmheadh*) is used,[21] but secular populations were also capable of resenting unprecedented demands. In 1163 Uí Maine captured Niall, son of the High King Muircheartach Mac Lochlainn, and killed most of his two hundred and forty followers as he was making 'a royal heir's feasting visitation' (*coinnmheadh ríoghdhamhna*) through the northern half of Ireland.[22] *Coinnmheadh* as a verb is also used of Muircheartach Mac Lochlainn's decision to billet battalions of his subjects and allies on the men of Meath, in one case for as long as a month.[23] A passage of legal commentary (on the *Uraicecht Becc*) which might originate in the Middle Irish period contrasts the billeted mercenary (*amus coindmeda*) with one who shares the king's house (*amus aentighe*). This reference is consonant with what we already know of twelfth-century practice[24] but cannot become the basis for further speculation where the dating is so uncertain.[25]

The late eleventh-century Book of Rights apparently deals with the relationship between provincial overkings and their vassal-chiefs in terms of personal contracts of submission, since it lists the 'wages' or *tuarastal* which each leader receives to purchase his loyalty and military service. When it comes to the subject of tribute, however, it echoes the teaching of the Old Irish law-tracts, citing tribute as a definitive right of kingship, charged on land under the king's authority, although certain privileged occupants may be exempt:[26]

No-one is prince of Munster who does not demand the rent (*cís*).

Though the Luigne bring hither their tribute (*cáin*) for their land, it is not the Luigne who are subject to it, but the grass and the land.

No rent (*cís*) is due from an Chraeb to the gracious king of Ailech; no tax or thrall (*cáin ná cacht*) is due from Mag nÍtha for their fair lands.

It is noteworthy that the word *cáin* – which in Old Irish translated the Latin word *lex*, thus signifying promulgated as distinct from customary law – has the meaning 'tribute' in the Book of Rights, being freely

[19] Binchy, 'Aimser Chue'.
[20] ALC and AU 1063; AFM 1163.
[21] AFM 732, 1045, 1072.
[22] AFM 1163.
[23] AFM 1153, 1159.
[24] See above, p. 105, n. 61.
[25] Above, p. 80, nn. 10 and 11.
[26] Dillon, *Lebor na Cert*, pp. 29, 51, 65.

interchangeable with *cís* (or *cíos*). The amount of tribute claimed in this and related texts from the Middle Irish period[27] is normally given in round numbers of pigs, sheep, and cattle, or loaves of bread and vats of ale, a fixed quota from each population-group or territory, and at one point it is expressly stated that 'there is an equal reckoning of tax and payment without increase for wealth nor decrease for poverty'.[28]

On the other hand, ecclesiastical taxation during the eleventh and twelfth centuries was more systematically assessed. Churchmen would long have been familiar with Biblical teaching on tithes even before the late twelfth-century reformers introduced parochial tithing to bring the organisation of the Irish Church into line with that of the rest of Western Christendom. When the heads of great monastic communities brought their founders' relics on circuit through the different provinces of Ireland, they demanded tributes for the saints such as a coin from every fortified dwelling, a cow for every six persons, seven cows, seven sheep, and half an ounce of silver from every cantred (*triocha-céad*), a horse from every chieftain, a cow from every *bíatach* or from every two *bíataig*,a sheep from every hearth and so on.[29] Mediaeval saints' Lives in Irish echo these exactions and add others, for instance an animal from every herd, or a ridge from every cornfield,[30] all of them tailored to population-numbers and the presumed wealth of the contributors. As late as the beginning of the seventeenth century an inquisition taken in connexion with the Ulster plantation stated that the archbishop of Armagh's dues from his lands mensal and censual included a pork from each herd of swine, and 4d for every milch-cow on his land.[31] By that date such exactions were commonly made by secular chieftains also, and it is quite possible that twelfth-century kings shared the Church's detailed methods of taxation without this fact appearing in the heroic style of literature in which their rights are stated. The tribute, awarded to Henry II by the Treaty of Windsor, of every tenth merchantable hide from all cattle slaughtered in Ireland[32] may well have originated in Irish rather than in English custom.

If an extant poem on the rights of Mac Diarmata, chief of Magh Luirg, is correctly attributed to the twelfth-century poet Aodh Ollbharr Ó Carthaigh,[33] we have evidence from the Middle Irish period for two

[27] Dillon, 'Three texts'; Hennessy & Kelly, *The Book*, pp. 354–73.

[28] Dillon, *Lebor na Cert*, p. 101.

[29] AFM 1044, 1106, 1150, 1151.

[30] Hennessy & Kelly, *The Book*, pp. 78, 80, 92, 132, 156, 160, 170; L. Gwynn, 'The Life', p. 94.

[31] Glancy, 'The primates', p. 367.

[32] Stubbs, *Gesta Regis Henrici Secundi*, I.101–3; Stubbs, *Chronica Magistri Rogeri de Houedene*, I.83–4.

[33] Authorship by Ó Carrthaigh is claimed in the last quatrain of the poem, and other features give some support to so early a date of composition. For instance, the late surname Mac Diarmata is not used; instead, the chief is identified as head of Clann Maoilruanaidh, and by his territorial titles. Details which occur in the related prose tract, itself no earlier than the fourteenth century – lands acquired in West Connacht and Mac Diarmata's key-role in the

further royal perquisites which seem to echo English and Continental thought. One was the right to treasure-trove, the reservation to the king of precious metals found buried in the earth. As the king of Connacht's favoured vassal, the chief of Magh Luirg claimed one third of all such treasures. Secondly, the assertion that forty cows were due to the chief from any *tuath* (in Connacht) where a king had been appointed suggests that a still greater payment was owed to the provincial overking by the newly elected *rí tuaithe*, presumably to purchase consent to his taking office and a renewal of his predecessor's contract of vassalage, like the feudal payment of 'relief'. Both these demands were to become commonplace in later mediaeval tracts on chieftains' dues. This particular example is only remarkable if it really dates from the first half of the twelfth century, which would preclude the possibility of these exactions being directly attributable to the influence of the Anglo-Norman invaders,[34] although they may quite plausibly be explained as an earlier borrowing from English custom.

Once the invasion had taken place, it was inevitable that the newcomers' views on taxation and other rewards of authority would be rapidly brought home to the Irish mind. Thirteenth-century exchequer-records show the native rulers paying rent for their territories, paying fines for being readmitted to the King's peace after rebellion, and being charged with aids for the King's wars overseas.[35] At a local level there were instances of collaboration between the leaders of both sides which involved exactions acceptable to both. The first Norman troops to take service with Irish kings required cash-payments but, according to the Song of Dermot and the Earl, when Maurice de Prendergast and his followers were paid by Domhnall Mac Giollaphádraig, king of Osraighe, the inhabitants of Osraighe resented seeing their money handed over to the foreigners and conspired to murder them 'for their gold and for their silver'.[36] Cathal Croibhdhearg Ó Conchobhair and his son were also to experience difficulty in raising money from their subjects in Connacht for the wages of Norman soldiers, and in 1202 Ó Conchobhair and William de Burgh agreed 'to despatch their mercenaries (*sersenaigh*) throughout Connaught, to levy their wages'. Shortly afterwards false news of de Burgh's death spread through the province, bringing everywhere the same spontaneous reaction, 'viz.:– each man to kill his guest (*a chonme*). And thus it was done, viz.:– each *oirecht* killed all that came to them; and

---

inauguration of Ó Conchobhair – are not mentioned in the poem. The loose metre, *ógláchas* of *deibhidhe*, includes some rhymes between monosyllabic and trisyllabic words (*smacht* : *abhallghort*, *modh* : *tiodhlacadh*) more characteristic of the twelfth century than later versification. See Ní Shéaghdha, 'The Rights'.

34 Mac Niocaill, 'Jetsam', p. 109.

35 For example, Davies & Quinn, 'The Irish pipe roll', *passim*; Gilbert, *Facsimiles*, II, plate lxxiii.

36 Orpen, *The Song*, pp. 94–5.

the loss, according to the report of their own people, was nine hundred *vel amplius*'.[37]

By using the expression *conme* or 'guest' to describe a Norman mercenary in this context, the annalist is equating Ó Conchobhair's action here with the *coinnmheadh*, the billeting of armies practised by twelfth-century kings before the invasion. However, this is the first occasion on which we hear that soldiers had been ordered to levy their own *wages* from their hosts. The practice spread among both Irish and Anglo-Normans thereafter and in 1297 complaint was made to the parliament at Dublin about 'magnates and others having kernes continually living at other people's expense ... whereby the people is excessively impoverished'. It was agreed at this time that if anyone were permitted to lead an army beyond the boundaries of his own lands 'then all, as many as he shall have led, shall receive wages from their leader, that they may be reasonably supported on their expedition'.[38] Yet repeated accusations and reforming decrees over the next three hundred years show the futility of attempts to put a stop to *coinnmheadh* or 'coigny'.[39]

In the same year of 1297 the archbishop of Armagh drew up a series of reforming articles in which Ó Néill, Mac Mathghamhna, and MagUidhir undertook to abandon the customs or abuses which they had practised hitherto against the liberty of the Church, *inter alia* declaring Church-lands immune 'from all exactions of our kerns, satellites, keepers of horses and dogs or any other servants [taken] in money, food or any other mode or pretext'.[40] The fact that Ó Néill's soldiers and servants exacted money as well as food from Church-tenants suggests that they too were levying their wages directly from the subjects on whom they were billeted, as was undoubtedly the case with the 'Bonaght (*buannacht*) of Ulster', the mercenary soldiers billeted by the de Burgh earl of Ulster on Ó Néill himself and the other chieftains of the province.[41]

Another relevant document from the end of the thirteenth century is the indenture whereby Lord Ralph Pipard, Baron of Ardee, permitted Aonghus Mac Mathghamhna to reign as a vassal king in his land of Cremourne, in the modern Co. Monaghan. As well as promising to respond to Pipard's hosting summons with all his forces, Aonghus agreed that *cána* (*canos uel amerciamenta*) should be jointly levied by his own and Pipard's 'beadles' whenever the occasion arose.[42] The association of the word *cáin* with 'amercement' here indicates that the reference is not to the literary equation of *cáin* with *cíos* or royal tribute, but to the older *féich cána*, 'fines [for the breach] of promulgated law'.[43] Much later it was to be a common accusation against Anglo-Irish barons that

[37] ALC 1202. See above p. 119, nn. 30 and 31.
[38] Berry, *Statutes and Ordinances*, p. 203.
[39] Empey & Simms, 'The Ordinances'.
[40] Nicholls, 'The Register', pp. 415–16; Lawlor, 'Fragments', p. 250.
[41] Empey & Simms, 'The Ordinances', p. 180; and see below, pp. 138–9.
[42] See above, p. 92, n. 103.
[43] See above, n. 10.

they 'doo take *canes* for thefts and other offences'.[44]

From the fourteenth to the early seventeenth century evidence on the various dues claimed by Irish chieftains becomes much more detailed. Prose tracts setting forth statements of traditional claims are neither wholly factual nor indeed closely datable, both from a lack of internal evidence and because of their composite nature.[45] They may, however, be compared with the descriptions, surveys, and inquisitions of Tudor government-officials, and with letters and petitions in which the chieftains themselves listed their rights with a view to having them confirmed. Out of all this material it emerges that just as the thirteenth-century de Burghs, FitzGeralds, and Pipards had adopted the Irish exactions of *coinnmheadh, buannacht* and *cána* under the names of 'coigny', 'bonaght', and 'canes', so the later mediaeval chieftains had taken over some Anglo-Irish taxes, often borrowing even the vocabulary to describe them.

Occasional profits of lordship are referred to in the rentals of Ó Briain and Mac Conmara as *amhantuir Tiarna, amhantur* being a Romance loanword, signifying such of the lord's dues as accrued to him *par aventure*, by chance or accident.[46] Of these, treasure-trove and the payment of 'relief' when a newly elected vassal king took office have been mentioned earlier.[47] Prose tracts add to the list a right to flotsam and jetsam,[48] and the late tract on Mac Diarmata seems to hint obscurely at *ius primae noctis* or some commutation thereof by asserting that 'he has rights without doubt over the women of all Síol Conchubhair'.[49] A more straightforward instance of borrowing, or actual usurpation, was the collection by Ó Conchobhair of Sligo and his overlord Ó Domhnaill of the burgage-rents and royal cockets of the town of Sligo,[50] founded in the thirteenth century by Maurice FitzGerald but subsequently occupied by Ó Conchobhair. In the fifteenth century Ó Raighilligh of East Bréifne founded a town of his own at Cavan, and in 1585 Sir Seaán Ó Raighilligh claimed 'rents, drink and other dewties' from the town's inhabitants.[51] One of the crimes for which the officers of the Great Ó Néill collected fines was *briseadh cusduim*, 'defrauding customs',[52] and while no further details are given, the loanword indicates a borrowing from English practice. Indeed, the increased trading contacts with the outside world

[44] Hore & Graves, *The Social State*, p. 109.

[45] See above, pp. 2–3, nn. 8–10.

[46] *Dictionary*, ed. Quin, *s.v.*.

[47] See above, nn. 33 and 34.

[48] O'Donovan, *The Tribes and Customs*, p. 64; Ní Shéaghdha, 'The Rights', pp. 158, 164–5.

[49] Ní Shéaghdha, 'The Rights', p. 165. Early Irish literature demonstrates that *ius primae noctis* was a native custom (see Stokes, 'Tidings', p. 24, § 9) although an unpublished portion of the Annals of Clonmacnoise endeavours to blame the viking-invaders for setting Irishmen a bad example. For this latter piece of information I am grateful to Miss Sarah Sanderlin.

[50] M. Carney, 'Agreement', pp. 288 and 290.

[51] AFM 1585.

[52] Dillon, 'Ceart Uí Néill', p. 10.

which developed in Irish lordships from the late fourteenth century[53] could lead to the use of alien sources of revenue without deliberate imitation. In 1465 a parliament held at Trim before the Great Earl of Desmond complained that foreign fishing vessels paid the Irish enemies great tributes of money – and gave them victuals, harness, and armour – for permission to fish.[54] Similarly it was said of Ó Domhnaill in 1560: 'He is the best lord of the fish in Ireland, and he exchangeth fish always with foreign merchants for wine, by which [he] is called in other countries, the king of the fish'.[55]

A curious blend of Irish and Anglo-Irish terminology is found in the sixteenth-century phrase 'cutting upon the country',[56] that is, arbitrarily imposing a general tax on the inhabitants. The Irish equivalent is *gearradh* (cutting), but no examples of the word with this meaning have been noted before the sixteenth century, and even then its context is sometimes Anglo-Irish, as in *gearradh ó fhior ionuid an ríogh*, 'cutting [coming] from the King's Deputy'.[57] This bears out Sir John Davies's conclusion that the term was not originally Irish but derived from Anglo-French *tallier*, literally to cut, figuratively to tallage or tax without consent.[58] In Anglo-Irish lordships we hear of cuttings imposed to finance a marriage for the lord's daughter,[59] an exaction feudal in type though apparently not confined to feudal tenants. This particular pretext is not recorded for the native Irish territories, where we are told[60]

as ofte as anye of the said captaines makeith eny great coste for the comyn wealle of his rome [realm], that the costes shalbe cessyd equally on all his men and subjectes of his rome.

The allusion here to the 'common weal' as the justification for imposing taxation is in keeping with the earlier stance of *Críth Gablach*,[61] and Sir Seaán Ó Raighilligh in 1585 gave examples of the kind of expenditure which a chief might legitimately pass on to his subjects. In the first place came taxation imposed on him by an overlord, whether this were the Great Ó Néill or Queen Elizabeth. To repay himself for his trouble in levying this from the territory under his authority, Ó Raighilligh was accustomed to impose a surcharge for his own profit, a custom already enshrined in the Book of Rights, and related to the *cuit tobaig*, 'the levying share', of Old Irish law.[62] Fines imposed by the Dublin government as

[53] Carus-Wilson, *Medieval Merchant Venturers*, pp. 13–28.
[54] Berry, *Statute Rolls ... Edward the Fourth*, pp. 353–5.
[55] Brewer & Bullen, *Calendar of the Carew Manuscripts*, I.308.
[56] See below, n. 129.
[57] O'Donovan, 'Covenant', pp. 190–1; *Dictionary*, ed. Quin, *s.v.* '*gerrad*' (II).
[58] Morley, *Ireland under Elizabeth and James I*, p. 387.
[59] Hore & Graves, *The Social State*, pp. 233 and 247.
[60] *State Papers, Henry VIII, Ireland 1515–38*, p. 5.
[61] See above, p. 116, n. 3.
[62] Dillon, *Lebor na Cert*, pp. 72, 100; Binchy, *Celtic and Anglo-Saxon Kingship*, pp. 18–19.

the price of peace, any expenses incurred in connexion with giving hostages or attending parleys, and the cost of any law-suits undertaken in the common interest were all raised from the inhabitants of the territory by *ad hoc* taxation.[63] Ransoms in Irish law were normally a responsibility of the kindred, particularly the womenfolk (whose wealth largely consisted of chattels),[64] but it appears from an elegy composed on the death of Niall Garbh Ó Domhnaill in 1439 that the enormous ransom demanded by the English before the chief's death in captivity was being raised among his subjects in general:[65]

Fondly hoping to free the hero, the Gaoidhil eagerly gave up their favourite bowls of interlaced ornament(?), their bracelets and their chess-sets.

All the wealth promised by the race of Eireamhón brought no profit for its gathering...

The money promised for him – what a calamity – was a drain on the wealth of the Ulaidh.

As with the Anglo-Irish levy taken for the marriage of the lord's daughter, this contribution for the ransom of the lord's body echoes a well known feudal aid. Even more complex than the origins of 'cutting' is the later history of the 'Bonaght of Ulster'. Under the de Burgh earls the bonaght was 'a certain number of men [placed] in the county of Ulster for the defence and peace of those parts'.[66] Detachments from this troop were allotted to each of the Irish kings in Ulster, who were bound to supply the men in peace-time with wages and provisions, at a cost variously estimated as £1 or two marks *per capita* annually.[67] The MacQuillin family, which may have been of Welsh descent, supplied hereditary commanders or constables of the bonaght, the last recorded being Stephen MacQuillin appointed in 1331 by Earl William de Burgh.[68] Two years later Earl William was murdered, the earldom was taken into the King's hand, and in 1344 (it is implied) the bonaght was no longer being officially enforced.[69] Yet the Irish annalists still refer to Stephen MacQuillin as 'constable of the province of Ulster' on his death in 1368,[70] and earlier, in 1350, MacQuillin is listed in Irish exchequer-records with the Great Ó Néill and Mac Mathghamhna as one of the king's enemies and rebels threatening to destroy Co. Louth.[71] Apparently this mercenary

[63] AFM 1585.
[64] Binchy, 'The legal capacity', pp. 218–20, 222, 231.
[65] McKenna, *Aithdioghluim Dána*, no. 23, qq. 20, 21, 23.
[66] *CPR 1343–5*, p. 239.
[67] Empey & Simms, 'The Ordinances', p. 180.
[68] Otway-Ruthven, *A History*, p. 216.
[69] See above, n. 66.
[70] AFM 1368.
[71] Gerrard Papers, ed. McNeill, p. 219; P.R.O. MS. E.101/242/2. I owe the latter reference to the kindness of Dr R. F. Frame.

commander had switched loyalties and the Great Ó Néill maintained his troop by continuing to impose the 'Bonaght of Ulster' on the other Irish chiefs. This assumption is borne out by an indenture of 1390 in which Niall Mór Ó Néill was made to promise 'to yield back and not to intermeddle with the bonnaughe of Ulster'.[72] Five years later the right to make this exaction was still in dispute, but now it was spoken of as 'MacDonald's bonacht',[73] indicating that MacQuillin and his men had been replaced in Ó Néill's service by Scottish galloglass under the leadership of the Clann Alasdair Mhic Dhomhnaill. The late sixteenth-century tract *Ceart Uí Néill* alleges that Ó Néill's *buannacht* or billeting rights over the other chiefs in Ulster amounted to provisioning for a total of 1615½ soldiers annually, a considerable advance on the modest 345 claimed for the de Burgh earl in 1333.[74]

The 'Bonaght of Ulster' was a specific body of men, with detailed arrangements for its support, instituted by the de Burgh earls in imitation of Irish custom and subsequently adopted by Ó Néill. However, as a general term for the maintenance of mercenary troops, *buannacht* or 'bonaght' was universally employed in later mediaeval Ireland, distinctions being drawn between *buannacht bhuna*, basic (peacetime) billeting, and *buannacht bhairr*, billeting in excess of the customary quota,[75] a principle explained by Sir John Davies in relation to MagUidhir:[76]

> In right he had no more, and in time of pease he did exact no more; marry in time of war he made himself owner of all, cutting what he listed, and imposing as many bonaghts or hired soldiers upon them as he had occasion to use.

These exactions were known to the Anglo-Irish as 'Bonagh-bonny' and 'Bonneybur', both entailing the actual provision of meat, drink, and wages to companies of soldiers, the normal practice in Gaelic Ireland. By the late sixteenth century, however, some Anglo-Irish had commuted this obligation to a money-tax on every ploughland, called Bonaght-beg (*buannacht bheag*) or 'little bonaght'.[77]

When one comes to examine those sources of wealth already ascribed to kings in the Old Irish period, a number of developments may be noted which are not all to be explained away in terms of our more detailed knowledge of a later era. There were two kinds of land attached to the chieftain's office, that which he farmed directly, and estates held by certain hereditary vassals who yielded him a much heavier food-rent than the general tribute or *cíos* imposed on all the lands under his authority. Thus Sir John Davies wrote in 1607:[78]

[72] Brewer & Bullen, *Calendar of the Carew Manuscripts*, I.288.
[73] Curtis, *Richard II*, pp. 136, 216.
[74] Dillon, 'Ceart Uí Néill', pp. 4–13; Orpen, 'The earldom of Ulster', pt IV, p. 141.
[75] *Dictionary*, ed. Quin, *s.v.*.
[76] Morley, *Ireland under Elizabeth and James I*, p. 370.
[77] Brewer & Bullen, *Calendar of the Carew Manuscripts*, III.72 and IV.455.
[78] Morley, *Ireland under Elizabeth and James I*, pp. 368, 370.

M'Guire's mensal lands ... were free from all common charges and contributions of the country, because they yielded a large proportion of butter and meal and other provisions for M'Guire's table ... which, lying in several baronies, did not in quantity exceed four ballibetaghs, the greatest thereof being in the possession of one M'Manus and his sept ... About his castle of Enniskillen [M'Guire] had almost a ballibetagh of land [over 900 acres], which he manured with his own churls.

The same dual system appears in Sir Seaán Ó Raighilligh's statement of his rights over East Bréifne. Certain families, 'the MacBradies, the MacEnroes, the Gones and the Jordans', owed him three quarters of a fat beef from every 'pole' of land, a fat pork from every two 'poles', and provision of quarters for (visiting) strangers. These same kindreds were also obliged to maintain on billet, in numbers proportionate to the amount of land held by each family, farm-labourers who would cultivate Ó Raighilligh's own estates.[79] In the case of Ó Néill, Sir Toby Caulfield reported in 1610:[80]

For the butter and other victualling provisions they were only paid by such as they termed horsemen, called the Quynnes, Haugans, Conelands and Devlins, which were rather at the discretion of the givers, who strove who should give most to gain Tyrone's favour, than for any due claim he had to demand the same.

The traditional Irish account, *Ceart Uí Néill*, differs from the above in two particulars. Of the 'horsemen' named by Caulfield, only the Devlins or Muintir Dhoibhlín are said to owe food-rents, and the quantities are precisely defined:[81]

Twenty loaves of flour in spring from each half-quarter, and a keg of butter with each loaf, and four baskets of malt in the spring; or a barrel from each half-quarter, and a keg of butter every week; four pence of Easter money every half-year.

A further point of interest is that Muintir Dhoibhlín and other families in Caulfield's account occupied the area west of Lough Neagh which was labelled on Bartlett's map of *ca* 1600 as 'the Lotie [*lucht tighe*], which is the household or demesne lands of the O Neales'.[82] The term *lucht tighe* or 'household' had a military connotation[83] comparable to Caulfield's 'horsemen', and perhaps we should see the inhabitants of a mediaeval chief's mensal lands as perpetuating the role of the earlier king's clients, yielding food-rents and escort-duties no longer on the basis of a personal contract of submission, but as an inherited obligation. It may be significant in this context that leading members of the Mac Maghnusa family, described by Davies above as holding the greater part of

[79] AFM 1585.
[80] *CSPI 1608–10*, p. 533.
[81] Dillon, 'Ceart Uí Néill', pp. 10–11.
[82] Ó Doibhlín, *Domhnach Mór*, p. 44.
[83] See above, p. 82, nn. 25 and 28; p. 86, n. 66; p. 94, n. 114.

MagUidhir's mensal lands, sometimes styled themselves *bíatach*, 'food-providing client', as an honorific title.[84]

Another duty which had once fallen on the clients of a king or noble was the annual offering of a *cóe* or winter-feast for their lord and his retinue. Periodic feasts continued to be exacted by both Gaelic and Anglo-Irish rulers in the later middle ages, but the obligation was no longer linked to clientship. Instead we are told that certain lands or certain landowning families are liable[85] or, in Anglo-Irish areas, that all inhabitants of the lordship who can afford to give such entertainments are pressed into so doing.[86]

We have seen that in the early twelfth century the monastic settlement of Ardbraccan owed the king of Loeghaire 'one night's *coinnmed* every quarter of a year',[87] but later the terms used for one or two nights' feasting duty were *cuid-oidhche*, 'night's supper', or *cóisir*, of uncertain etymology, possibly derived from the French *causerie*. In Anglo-Irish speech these words were rendered 'cuddy' or 'cudihie', and 'cosher' or 'coshery'.[88]

A survey of Mac Carthaigh Mór's lands taken in 1597 is unusually precise about the value of this prerogative and the mode of its consumption:[89]

> Cuddy is a meales meat or a refection certaynlie knowne, and is to be spent eyther at the freeholders house if the earle of Clancarty listed, or to be sent home to his house in certayne proportions of flesh, aquavitae, ale, hony, flower or else in lieu thereof at the freeholders choyce £4 8s 8d.

Not all subjects had their liability so well defined. One variable was the size of the retinue brought by the lord – the Earl of Desmond sometimes had 'forty, sixty or a hundred together under one roof'.[90] Duration could also vary. Whereas Ó Connalaigh, the marshal of Airghialla, owed Mac Mathghamhna a day and a night's *cóisir* annually after Easter,[91] Sir Thomas Butler of Cahir charged his wealthier subjects two days' and two nights' 'coyshyr' four times a year.[92]

Interestingly, the sixteenth-century tract *Ceart Uí Néill* uses the older term *congbáil* or 'maintenance' without clearly distinguishing between a periodic feast due to an overlord and his retinue and the extended provision of billeting for the king and his followers:[93]

[84] Simms, 'Guesting', p. 72.
[85] The heavy emphasis on continuity of land-titles in customary brehon-law made these two statements almost synonymous.
[86] *Ibid.*, pp. 80–2.
[87] See above, n. 16.
[88] *Dictionary*, ed. Quin, *s.vv.*.
[89] Butler, *Gleanings*, p. 20.
[90] Brewer & Bullen, *Calendar of the Carew Manuscripts*, III.72.
[91] Pender, 'A tract', pp. 252, 256.
[92] Hore & Graves, *The Social State*, p. 233.
[93] Dillon, 'Ceart Uí Néill', pp. 7 and 9.

[Ó Catháin] is bound on account of his stipend (*a shochair*) to keep (*do chonnmháil*) Ó Néill as long as he wishes...
The lodging (*oidhcheacht*) of Ó Néill is one night from Mac Aodha and one night from Ó Ceallaigh and one night from Mac Conallaidh; and neither Ó Duibhín nor Ó Flaithbheartaigh are entitled to compensation however long Ó Néill should stay with them

In the neighbouring lordship of Ó Domhnaill an incident recorded by the traditional historian of Clann Suibhne seems to illustrate how the transition was sometimes made from an earlier to a later style of exaction:[94]

When Ruaidhri [Mac Suibhne] had been a long time in that chieftainship Nechtain O Domhnaill [king 1439–52] came on a visit to his house, and all the country thought his maintenance a great oppression (*do ba trom leiss in tir he*). Ó Domhnaill had never until then a particular claim on them, and it was at that time they decided on a king's *martaigheacht* 'contribution of beeves' for Ó Domhnaill. And this is the *martaigheacht* namely six beeves ... and even this much he should not have except three times in the year, however frequently he should come.

If this account (less than a hundred years after the event) is reliable, and there is no particular reason to doubt it, we see that the lord's prerogative was limited by individual bargaining, not by the joint-protest of all his leading subjects at a territorial council. A piecemeal approach is also suggested by the inequitable arrangements in *Ceart Uí Néill*.

The same kind of inconsistency appears in this tract's treatment of *sluaigheadh* or hosting duty (Old Irish *slóiged*). Most of the Ulster chiefs are supposed here to respond to Ó Néill's hosting summons with a 'full muster' (*líon a thionóil*) and if they fail to do so their punitive fine is assessed by Ó Néill's own judge;[95] but MagUidhir owes[96]

a hosting of two hundred men; and if those two hundred should not come, a cow for every man lacking of them; and two in-calf cows for every cow that is not delivered. And if Mag Uidhir himself should come on hosting without his people, he shall receive half the fine.

The same penalty was incurred by those ignoring the hosting summons (*gairm shluaigh*) in the lordship of Mac Carthaigh Mór:[97]

Garemsloaeg is a risinge upon a warninge given of all the able men of the countrye everye man to be furnished with sufficient weapon and three dayes victuals, and for every defalt to be fyned at a choyce cowe or xx^s old money, but such of the countrye as were his ennemies would neyther pay nor yeald to any such fyne or risinge.

Quite apart from the problem of outright defiance mentioned here, the

[94] Walsh, *Leabhar Chlainne Suibhne*, p. 59.
[95] See above, p. 89, n. 88.
[96] Dillon, 'Ceart Uí Néill', p. 9.
[97] Butler, *Gleanings*, p. 20.

exaction of one cow for every man missing from the host presupposes a fixed number being expected in the first place. In the lordship of Ó Domhnaill, Mac Suibhne Fanad, according to his own traditional historian, owed 'two gallowglasses for each quarter of land, and two cows for each gallowglass deficient, that is, one cow for the man himself and one for his equipment'.[98] A later statement of the rights of Aodh Ruadh Ó Domhnaill (*ob.* 1602) gave this as 'six score galloglass with coats of mail and a beef bullock as fine for the coat of mail missing'.[99] In the case of Mac Suibhne, the galloglass were his own natural subjects, and their attendance when summoned may be compared to the rising out of 'all the able men of the countrye' claimed for Mac Carthaigh Mór in 1597; but in 1565 the articles of submission between Ó Suilleabháin Béara and his overlord Mac Carthaigh bound the former to maintain in proportion to the area of land under his control a quota of hired galloglass and kern for service in the lord's host when summoned, and to pay a fine of '6s 8d sterling or one beef' for every man missing.[100] Certainly the more precise calculations of the hosting fine would be most appropriate in cases in which vassal chiefs employed regular standing armies of mercenaries.

These fines for failure in one's public duty to the ruler and the community had a long and venerable history behind them, but by the sixteenth century thefts and murders, which had once been considered as private cases between disputing kin-groups, were coming under the jurisdiction of the lord's brehon, with most or all of the fine from the guilty party being adjudged to the lord himself. Indeed some proportion of these profits might eventually go to an overlord, or to the chief's *tánaiste*.[101] Paying a share of the fines to one's overlord was an important step towards greater centralisation of criminal justice, because it provided the economic motivation for appeals from a lower to higher court.

The old *cíos*, or direct tribute due to the chief from land under his authority, continued to be levied in the later middle ages in a bewildering variety of forms: as fixed quantities of livestock and/or foodstuffs from named population-groups, after the fashion of the Book of Rights;[102] as fixed sums of money from named townlands, 'quarters' and 'half-quarters' of land;[103] as a tax assessed on land-area, whether expressed in livestock ('one fat beef out of every eight poles'),[104] or in money-terms ('forty-two groats for every *baile biataigh*');[105] or a tax on every beast or herd of

[98] Walsh, *Leabhar Chlainne Suibhne*, p. 45.

[99] Cambridge, University Library, MS. Add. 2766 (20) (7), fo 5; I owe this reference to Pádraig de Brún. A manuscript-translation by John O'Donovan is in Dublin, Royal Irish Academy, O.S. MS. Strongroom 14.B.7, p. 423.

[100] Brewer & Bullen, *Calendar of the Carew Manuscripts*, I.366.

[101] See above, p. 55, n. 124, and p. 91, n. 99.

[102] Dillon, 'Ceart Uí Néill', pp. 6 and 8; Cambridge, University Library, MS. Add. 2766 (20) (7), fos 4–7.

[103] Hardiman, 'Ancient Irish deeds', pp. 43–5 and 36–9.

[104] AFM 1585.

[105] Dillon, 'Ceart Uí Néill', p. 6.

beasts,[106] or on every plough.[107] Significantly, traditional statements of the chief's rights, for instance *Ceart Uí Néill* or the customs of Aodh Ruadh Ó Domhnaill, often list different modes of assessment side by side as applying to different areas under their authority, and this reinforces the impression given by variable billeting rights that limitations on a chief's demands were negotiated by individual haggling rather than by corporate protest by his leading vassals in council. The same diversity marks the rental of the FitzGerald earls of Kildare,[108] whose control over various Irish chieftains was acquired at different times and in different circumstances, each agreement no doubt being conditioned by local custom.

Interestingly, the county- or parliamentary subsidies raised by the chief governors of Ireland as a tax on every ploughland towards the defence of the colony were described in a mid-fifteenth-century poem by Tadhg Óg Ó hUiginn as '*cíos as a n-acra*', 'the *cíos* due from their acres'.[109] In a Gaelic context, however, *cíos* was not the only word used for the direct tax: it was also called *tighearnus*, 'lordship';[110] *comartha tighearnuis*, 'a sign of lordship';[111] *ceart*, 'right';[112] and *onóir*, 'honour'.[113] These expressions accord well with both the brehon law and the Book of Rights' insistence that the ability to enforce tribute was the ultimate test and proof of kingship,[114] and with the Anglo-Irish terms 'chiefry' and 'chief rent' to describe the same exaction.[115]

It was precisely this view of *cíos* as a tangible fruit of authority which earned the name *duibhchíos*, 'black' or unjustifiable tribute, for the protection-money drawn from various areas of the Anglo-Irish colony by neighbouring Irish chiefs. In order to buy immunity from attack a local community might pay an annual sum, as Co. Louth paid £40 to the Great Ó Néill,[116] and might raise this money by imposing a tax on every ploughland;[117] but the community continued to owe its allegiance to the English king and to regard Ó Néill and his like as Irish enemies. In Irish, *dubh* or 'black' in compounds has the general effect of intensifying things already disagreeable,[118] but the further implication that it can stigmatise an illegal or unjustifiable demand is contained in an account of Mac Carthaigh Mór's rents, where a customary obligation of the mountainous forest-areas

106 *CSPI 1608–10*, p. 533; Cambridge, University Library, MS. Add. 2766 (20) (7), fo 7; Hore, 'The rental book', pp. 118–24.

107 Hore & Graves, *The Social State*, p. 282.

108 Hore, 'The rental book', *passim*.

109 McKenna, *Aithdioghluim Dána*, no. 36, q. 31.

110 Hardiman, 'Ancient Irish deeds', pp. 38 and 44–5; Dillon, 'Ceart Uí Néill', p. 6; AConn 1542.14. See below, n. 122.

111 Ó Dufaigh, 'Cíos Mhic Mhathghamhna', p. 129.

112 Dillon, 'Ceart Uí Néill', pp. 6 and 8.

113 Ó Dufaigh, 'Cíos Mhic Mhathghamhna', p. 129.

114 See above, p. 97.

115 Murray *et al.*, *The Oxford English Dictionary*, *s.v.* 'Chiefery'.

116 *State Papers, Henry VIII, Ireland 1515–38*, p. 9.

117 Richardson & Sayles, *The Irish Parliament*, pp. 240, 242.

118 *Dictionary*, ed. Quin, *s.v.*.

to support the chief's huntsmen and hounds had been arbitrarily extended to his lowland-subjects as a money-tax:

This rent of Dowgollo signifieth blacke rent, and all the freeholders crye out upon yt as imposed upon them by extorcion and stronge hande.[119]

Since the legitimate exaction of *cíos* was made in right of authority rather than landownership, the same area of land could, and apparently often did, owe payments to a hierarchy of overlords. According to Sir John Davies, Fermanagh owed two hundred and forty beeves to its chief, MagUidhir;[120] but *Ceart Uí Néill* tells us that Fermanagh also owed two hundred beeves to Ó Néill.[121] MagEochagáin's claim over the lands of his vassal *an Sionnach* ('the Fox') was 'a *gníomh* of land free from every impost, and a hog cut out of every *gníomh* which pays chiefry (*tighearnus*) to the Fox'.[122] Similarly the Earl of Kildare's claim on Muintir Eolais, the territory of Mag Raghnaill within the overlordship of Ó Ruairc of Bréifne, was phrased 'on everye carton whereof O'Roryke and Magranayll racewys Rent, xii d. yerlye'.[123]

So far the different varieties of exaction have been discussed without any attempt to assess the size of income which they represented, or whether they constituted an oppressive burden on the taxpayers. Not only did customary demands vary in scale from region to region and from one generation to another, but the lack of any formal constitutional check on the lord's authority allowed dramatic changes and increases in time of war or in the reign of a warlike ruler. *Ceart Uí Néill* can be dated on the basis of the coin-names occurring in it to the second half of the sixteenth century,[124] but when in 1607 Sir Toby Caulfield came to survey the revenues of Aodh Ó Néill, the Great Earl of Tyrone, he found no trace of the varying local customs which it had listed. Instead, all the inhabitants of Tyrone's lands were charged a shilling in every quarter of a year for every milch-cow or in-calf cow which they grazed. Elsewhere Caulfield gives four shillings as the current price for a calf, indicating that Ó Néill's exaction was a heavy one indeed for a largely pastoral society. The cows were counted twice a year by Tyrone's officials, on 1 May and 1 November, and the income so collected amounted to over £2,000 Irish a year,[125] a vast sum by comparison with the total income calculated for Mac Carthaigh Mór in 1597 of £271 5s 10d and two white groats sterling,[126] even if one makes due allowance for the difference in currencies.

119 Butler, *Gleanings*, p. 20.
120 Morley, *Ireland under Elizabeth and James I*, pp. 369–70.
121 Dillon, 'Ceart Uí Néill', p. 8.
122 O'Donovan, 'Covenant', pp. 190–1.
123 Hore, 'The rental book', p. 134.
124 Dolley & Mac Niocaill, 'Some coin-names'.
125 *CSPI 1608–10*, pp. 533–4.
126 London Lambeth Palace Library, MS. 625, fo 41v.

In a subsistence economy, where most of the revenues were collected in foodstuffs and there was no market readily available for the surplus, the chief's exactions had a natural limitation in his capacity to consume, as Sir John Davies remarked of the food-rents from MagUidhir's mensal lands: 'such commodities in those parts are of little or no value, and therefore he never made any civil use of them, but spent them wastefully in a sordid and barbarous manner among his loose and idle followers'.[127] However, this protective equilibrium between supply and demand could be upset, either by the need to provision and pay large numbers of soldiers in war-time, or by the introduction of markets where surplus quantities of foodstuff collected from the taxpayers could be readily exchanged for cash or non-perishable goods. In such circumstances there was no legal protection against tyranny or rack-renting – the choice of term depending on whether the last generation of Gaelic chiefs should be viewed as rulers or landlords.[128] Captain Docwra, who commanded the English garrison at Derry in the last years of the Nine Years' War, relays a conversation of his with Niall Garbh III Ó Domhnaill, which underlines the disquieting possibilities of this situation.[129]

'The country [of Ennisowen] is mine', saith he, 'and so is all Tyrconnell, and I will use and govern it to my own pleasure...'
'Why,' (said I) 'what is your intent? Admit you shall be made Lord of all Tyrconnell, and of this country as part thereof, which I will not debate with you whether you be or no, what is the prerogative you would claim thereby?'
'I will cess my people,' saith he, 'upon the churls, I will take such things as I want, and employ the inhabitants at mine own discretion.'
'For cutting upon the country,' I answered, 'it was so poor that Her Majesty was contented for this year to forbear such rights as otherwise she might justly impose...'
He replied again, 'Let the Queen do with her rights what she will. Ennisowen is mine, and were there but one cow in the country, that cow would I take and use as mine own.'
'And how would you provide for the poor people to live?' said I.
'I care not,' saith he, 'let 1,000 die, I pass not of a pin; and for the people, they are my subjects. I will punish, exact, cut, and hang, if I see occasion, where and whensoever I list.'

[127] Morley, *Ireland under Elizabeth and James I*, p. 369.
[128] See above, pp. 39–40, nn. 108–111.
[129] *CSPI 1600–1*, p. 290.

X

CONCLUSION

The Great Ó Néill, Seaán the Proud, is said to have scorned the suggestion that Queen Elizabeth might confer the title of earl upon him with these words: 'I care not to be made an earl unless I may be better and higher than an earl, for I am in blood and power better than the best of them ... My ancestors were kings of Ulster; Ulster is mine and shall be mine.'[1] This speech was considered typical of Seaán's ranting and boastful style but, although it has often been quoted, no explanation has been offered for Ó Néill's uncharacteristically modest failure to claim the status of king held by his ancestors, since his territory and overlordship in Ulster were quite as extensive as theirs had ever been.

Bardic poets continued to address Seaán and the other Irish chiefs by their ancestral title of *rí* or 'king',[2] but it has been the main underlying argument of this book that the Gaelic lords of the sixteenth century were not seen by others, nor did they see themselves, as kings in any meaningful sense of the word. They were styled *tighearna* or *dominus*[3] and used the abstract *tighearnus*, 'lordship' or 'dominion', to signify the annual cash-payments which they collected from the inhabitants of their territories,[4] men who were rapidly becoming known as their 'tenants'.[5]

This transformation of the Gaelic ruling classes was not unconnected with developments taking place elsewhere in Europe at the end of the middle ages and the beginning of the early modern period. One such change was bastard-feudalism, the transition from a system of vassalage based on landholding to the use of money-pensions and offices by great men to build up a network of hangers-on which extended far beyond their own landed estates. Gaelic Ireland had never experienced feudalism in its classical form, but in the fifteenth century we find paramount chiefs attaching to their allegiance individual nobles who lived outside the bounds of their territorial overlordship[6] while they themselves might

[1] Froude, *History*, VIII.19.

[2] Knott, *The Bardic Poems*, no. 6 and *passim*; see also McKenna, *The Book of O'Hara*, Mac Airt, *Leabhar Branach*, Greene, *Duanaire Mhéig Uidhir*, etc..

[3] Above, p. 39, n. 104.

[4] Above, p. 144, n. 110.

[5] Above, pp. 39–40, nn. 108–111.

[6] Above, p. 113, n. 120.

enter a corresponding relationship with the king of England or the greatAnglo-Irish earls.[7]

On the Continent, and to a lesser extent in England during the Wars of the Roses, kings and great lords used the support of these factions of personal followers, together with mercenary troops, to weaken or suppress representative assemblies, for instance the Florentine councils under the Medici[8] or the Estates General of the kingdom of France.[9] In Ireland the reduction of the colonial parliament to a mouthpiece for the Great Earl of Kildare was a part of this trend. Territorial councils in the Gaelic lordships had not developed a representative rôle at any stage, but it is noticeable that whereas twelfth- to early fourteenth-century annalists chronicle decisions and actions taken by the *oireacht* as a body, often in opposition to its king,[10] their fifteenth- and sixteenth-century successors refer to the initiatives and rebellions of individual nobles only.

Elsewhere the widespread decline of 'democratic' institutions was part of a general drive towards centralisation of authority within the state, the replacement of hereditary feudal magnates in government by a middle-class bureaucracy, the abolition or reduction of private jurisdictions, the glorification of the monarch and his court as the focus for national pride and civic obedience. This was to affect Gaelic Ireland at two levels. Within each lordship the sixteenth century saw a tendency to centralise the higher levels of criminal jurisdiction,[11] and to employ paid servants rather than hereditary magnates in the administration,[12] but ultimately the nation-state within which the Gaelic lords found themselves was the Tudor kingdom of Ireland. In the eyes of its officials the chieftains' territories came to be regarded simply as further examples of the type of private jurisdiction which had been so successfully repressed in the kingdom of England in previous centuries.[13]

However, while the underlying pattern was thus shared with the rest of Europe, many surface-manifestations were peculiar to Ireland. To an unusual degree the economy of the Gaelic lordships had remained one of subsistence-agriculture, with coinage known and used by the inhabitants but not central to their system of exchange.[14] Taxation was thus largely exacted in foodstuffs and billeting rights, a method which would normally be viewed as cumbersome rather than intrinsically evil; yet it would not be too much to describe English and Anglo-Irish reactions to 'coign and livery' as hysterical. Sir John Davies quotes an earlier tract as asserting that, 'though it were first invented in hell, yet if it had been used and practised there as it hath been in Ireland, it had long since destroyed the

[7] Above, p. 113, n.122; Simms, ' "The King's Friend' ", pp. 225, 228.
[8] Rubinstein, *The Government*.
[9] Major, *Representative Institutions*.
[10] Above, p. 65, nn. 42–43, and p. 68, nn. 61–6.
[11] Above, p. 91, nn. 98–100.
[12] Above, pp. 93, n. 111, 94, nn. 113 and 120, 95, nn. 121, 124–5.
[13] Canny, *The Elizabethan Conquest*, chapter 5.
[14] Simms, 'Guesting', p. 67.

very kingdom of Beelzebub'.[15] He himself is almost as vehement in his condemnation of a taxation-system 'which made the lord an absolute tyrant, and the tenant a very slave and villain, and in one respect more miserable than bond-slaves. For commonly the bond-slave is fed by his lord, but here the lord was fed by his bond-slave.'[16]

Two considerations provide some explanation, if not justification, for these strictures. One was the growing confusion, between political lordship and landownership,[17] which not only turned subjects into tenants and tribute into rent, but allowed quite petty landowners to treat their legal tenants as subjects, to tax them at will and billet mercenary soldiers on them. The ubiquitous presence of the soldiery was the second distorting influence. So many parasitical mouths to feed involved an unusual demand for surplus-production from a subsistence-economy, and this was seen as causing poverty and lack of enterprise in the Irish peasant.[18] More relevant to the present study, however, are the political consequences. Billeting was a cheap method of maintaining soldiers and 'every lord and gentleman freeholder'[19] could afford to practise it at the expense of his own tenants. On the one hand this proliferation of private armies supplied the pressure which reduced tenants to political subjects and free landowning subjects to tenants, while on the other hand the arming of each minor lord against his neighbour encouraged constant petty warfare and this in turn justified the continued maintenance of troops. To rise above this anarchy and control it the paramount chiefs had to rely increasingly not on customary allegiance or the willing cooperation of their vassal nobility, but on possessing formidable standing armies themselves. Two major importers of mercenary forces in the later sixteenth century were Aodh Dubh Ó Domhnaill and Toirdhealbhach Luineach Ó Néill, both of whom contracted marriage-alliances with Scottish *condottieri* for this purpose.[20] The hereditary Ulster cleric Miler Magrath reported that each of these men had taken supreme power in his district 'rather by strength and policy, than by the right course according to the observations and customs of that country'.[21]

In his edition of the Old Irish poems of Blathmac mac Con Brettan, James Carney noted that the author reserved the titles of *rí* and *flaith* to describe God, the 'king of Heaven', and styled the devil merely *tigerna* or 'lord' of Hell.[22] Without drawing too sweeping a conclusion from this usage, one may safely deduce, from the mere fact that bardic poets clung

[15] Morley, *Ireland under Elizabeth and James I*, pp. 229–30.
[16] *Ibid.*, pp. 295–6.
[17] Above, pp. 39–40, nn. 106–111.
[18] *State Papers, Henry VIII, Ireland 1515–38*, pp. 10, 12, 14; Canny, 'Rowland White's "The Dysorders of the Irisshery" 1571', p. 155.
[19] Hore & Graves, *The Social State*, p. 105.
[20] Hayes-McCoy, *Scots Mercenary Forces*, pp. 98, 100, 106–9, 117, 132.
[21] *CSPI 1588–92*, pp. 497–8.
[22] Carney, *The Poems*, p. 150, n. 974. This theme is more fully explored by Lambkin, 'The Structure'.

to the term in their eulogies when it had become obsolete as a description of contemporary Gaelic rulers, that the word *rí* evoked a higher ideal than *tighearna* and consequently that both bard and patron were conscious of a decline in status by the sixteenth century. They tended to blame this decline on the Norman invasion and the Tudor reconquest,[23] but it has been the purpose of this study to demonstrate that, while these were certainly contributing factors, the process by which kingship was lost was both more gradual and more complex.

[23] Ó Cuív, 'A sixteenth-century political poem', pp. 272–3; Mac Airt, *Leabhar Branach*, nos 35, 39, etc..

ABBREVIATIONS

Chronicle-sources

AClon	Annals of Clonmacnoise (ed. D. Murphy)
AConn	Annals of Connacht (ed. & transl. A. M. Freeman)
ADF	Annals of [Ireland by] Dudley Firbisse (ed. J. O'Donovan)
AFM	Annals of [the Kingdom of Ireland by] the Four Masters (ed. & transl. J. O'Donovan)
AI	Annals of Inisfallen (ed. & transl. S. Mac Airt)
ALC	Annals of Loch Cé (ed. & transl. W. M. Hennessy)
Ann.Rawl.B.488	Annals from [Oxford, Bodleian Library, MS.] Rawlinson B.488 (ed. & transl. S. Ó hInnse, *Miscellaneous Irish Annals*, pp. 116–85
AT	Annals of Tigernach (ed. & transl. W. Stokes)
AU	Annals of Ulster (ed. & transl. W. M. Hennessy & B. Mac Carthy; new edn, to A.D. 1131, by S. Mac Airt & G. Mac Niocaill)
McC	Mac Carthaigh's Book (ed. & transl. S. Ó hInnse, *Miscellaneous Irish Annals*, pp. 2–115)

Documentary sources

CCH	*Rotulorum Patentium et Clausorum Cancellariæ Hiberniæ Calendarium*, ed. E. Tresham
CCR	Calendar of the Close Rolls preserved in the Public Record Office
CDI	Calendar of Documents relating to Ireland, preserved in Her Majesty's Public Record Office, London
CJRI	Calendar of the Justiciary Rolls on Proceedings in the Court of the Justiciar of Ireland preserved in the Public Record Office of Ireland
CPR	Calendar of the Patent Rolls preserved in the Public Record Office
CSPI	Calendar of the State Papers relating to Ireland . . . preserved in Her Majesty's Public Record Office

BIBLIOGRAPHY

ANDERSON, Alan Orr (transl.) *Early Sources of Scottish History A.D. 500 to 1286* (2 vols, Edinburgh 1922)

ANDERSON, A.O. (ed. & transl.) 'The Prophecy of Berchan', *Zeitschrift für celtische Philologie* 18 (1929/30) 1–56

ARCHDALL, Mervyn *Monasticon Hibernicum* (edd. P.F.Moran *et al.*, 2 vols, Dublin 1873/6)

ARMSTRONG, E.C.R. 'The shrine of the Cathach', *apud* Lawlor, 'The Cathach', pp. 390–6

ATKINSON, Robert (facs. ed.) *The Book of Ballymote, A collection of Pieces (Prose and Verse) in the Irish Language, Compiled about the Beginning of the Fifteenth Century: now for the First Time Published from the Original Manuscript in the Library of the Royal Irish Academy* (Dublin 1887)

AUBOYER, J. 'Le caractère royal et divin du trône dans l'Inde ancienne', in *The Sacral Kingship/La Regalità Sacra. Contributions to the Central Theme of the VIIIth International Congress for the History of Religions* (Rome, April 1955) (Leiden, 1959), pp. 181–8

BARLEY, M.W., & HANSON, R.P.C. (edd.) *Christianity in Britain, 300–700. Papers presented to the Conference on Christianity in Roman and Sub-Roman Britain held at the University of Nottingham 17–20 April 1967* (Leicester 1968)

BERGIN, Osborn (ed. & transl.) *Irish Bardic Poetry* (Dublin 1970)

BERGIN, Osborn, & MARSTRANDER, C. (edd.) *Miscellany presented to Kuno Meyer by Some of his Friends and Pupils on the Occasion of his Appointment to the Chair of Celtic Philology in the University of Berlin* (Halle a.S. 1912)

BERRY, Henry F. (ed. & transl.) *Statute Rolls of the Parliament of Ireland, First to the Twelfth Years of the Reign of King Edward the Fourth* (Dublin 1914)

BERRY, Henry F. (ed. & transl.) *Statute Rolls of the Parliament of Ireland, Reign of King Henry the Sixth* (Dublin 1910)

BERRY, Henry F. (ed. & transl.) *Statutes and Ordinances, and Acts of the Parliament of Ireland, King John to Henry V* (Dublin 1907)

BEST, R.I. (ed. & transl.) 'The Battle of Airtech', *Ériu* 8 (1916) 170–90

BEST, R.I., *et al.* (edd.) *The Book of Leinster, formerly Lebar na Núachongbála* (6 vols, Dublin 1954–83)

BEST, R.I. (ed. & transl.) 'The settling of the manor of Tara', *Ériu* 4 (1910) 121–72

BETHAM, William *Irish Antiquarian Researches*, I (Dublin 1826/7)

BIELER, Ludwig, & KELLY, F. (edd. & transl.) *The Patrician Texts in the Book of Armagh* (Dublin 1979)

BINCHY, D.A. 'Aimser chue', in *Essays and Studies presented to Professor Eoin MacNeill*, ed. J.Ryan (Dublin 1940), pp. 18–22
BINCHY, D.A. *Celtic and Anglo-Saxon Kingship* (Oxford 1970)
BINCHY, D.A. (ed.) *Corpus Iuris Hibernici* (6 vols, Dublin 1978)
BINCHY, D.A. (ed.) *Críth Gablach* (Dublin 1941)
BINCHY, D.A. 'Distraint in Irish law', *Celtica* 10 (1973) 22–71
BINCHY, D.A. 'Some Celtic legal terms', *Celtica* 3 (1956) 221–31
BINCHY, D.A. (ed.) *Studies in Early Irish Law* (Dublin 1936)
BINCHY, D.A. 'The Fair of Tailtiu and the Feast of Tara', *Ériu* 18 (1958) 113–38
BINCHY, D.A. 'The legal capacity of women in regard to contracts', in *Studies in Early Irish Law*, ed. D.A.Binchy (Dublin 1936), pp. 207–34
BINCHY, D.A. 'The linguistic and historical value of the Irish law tracts', *Proceedings of the British Academy* 29 (1943) 195–227
BINCHY, D.A. 'The passing of the old order', in *The Impact of the Scandinavian Invasions on the Celtic-speaking Peoples c.800–1100 A.D.*, ed. B.ÓCuív (Dublin 1975), pp. 119–32
BINCHY, D.A. (ed. & transl.) 'The saga of Fergus mac Léti', *Ériu* 16 (1952) 33–48
BIRD, S.R., *et al.* *Calendar of the Manuscripts of the Most Hon. The Marquis of Salisbury ... preserved at Hatfield House, Hertfordshire* (24 vols, London 1883–1976)
BLOCH, Marc *Feudal Society* (London 1961)
BOLLANDUS, J. (ed.) ' "Vita II Sanctae Brigitae" (Cogitosus)', in *Acta Sanctorum*, February, ed. J.Bollandus (3 vols, Antwerpen 1658), pp. 135–41
BREWER, J.S., & BULLEN, W. (edd.) *Calendar of the Carew Manuscripts preserved in the Archiepiscopal Library at Lambeth* (6 vols, London 1867–73)
BRØNDSTED, Johannes *The Vikings* (Harmondsworth 1965)
BROOKE, Z.N. The English Church and the Papacy from the Conquest to the Reign of John (Cambridge 1931)
*BRYAN, Donough *Gerald FitzGerald, the Great Earl of Kildare 1456–1513* (Dublin 1933)
BUTLER, Richard (ed.) *The Annals of Ireland. By Friar John Clyn of the Convent of Friars Minors, Kilkenny; and Thady Dowling, Chancellor of Leighlin. Together with the Annals of Ross* (Dublin 1849)
BUTLER, William F.T. *Gleanings from Irish History* (London 1925)
BYRNE, Francis John *Irish Kings and High-Kings* (London 1973)
BYRNE, Francis John *The Rise of the Uí Néill and the High-Kingship of Ireland* (Dublin [1970])
CANNY, N.P. 'Hugh O'Neill, earl of Tyrone, and the changing face of Gaelic Ulster', *Studia Hibernica* 10 (1970) 7–35
CANNY, N. [P.] 'Rowland White's "The Dysorders of the Irisshery", 1571', *Studia Hibernica* 19 (1979) 147–60
CANNY, Nicholas P. *The Elizabethan Conquest of Ireland: a Pattern Established 1565–76* (Hassocks 1976)

CARNEY, James (ed. & transl.) *A Genealogical History of the O'Reillys written in the Eighteenth Century by Eóghan Ó Raghallaigh and incorporating Portion of the Earlier Work of Dr. Thomas Fitzsimons, Vicar-General of the Diocese of Kilmore* ([Cavan] 1959)

CARNEY, James (ed. & transl.) *The Poems of Blathmac, son of Cú Brettan, together with the Irish Gospel of Thomas and a Poem on the Virgin Mary* (London 1964)

CARNEY, James (ed.) *Topographical Poems by Seaán Mór Ó Dubhagáin and Giolla-na-Naomh Ó hUidhrín* (Dublin 1943)

CARNEY, M. (ed. & transl.) 'Agreement between Ó Domhnaill and Tadhg Ó Conchobhair concerning Sligo Castle (23 June 1539)', *Irish Historical Studies* 3 (1942/3) 282–96

CARUS-WILSON, E.M. *Medieval Merchant Venturers. Collected Studies* (London 1954)

*CAULFIELD, Richard *Rotulus Pipae Clonensis* (Cork 1859)

CHARLES-EDWARDS, T.M. 'The heir-apparent in Irish and Welsh law', *Celtica* 9 (1971) 180–90

CHART, D.A. (ed.) *The Register of John Swayne, Archbishop of Armagh and Primate of Ireland 1418–39, with some Entries of Earlier and Later Archbishops* (Belfast 1935)

COMYN, David, & DINNEEN, P.S. (edd. & transl.) *The History of Ireland by Geoffrey Keating* (4 vols, London 1902–14)

CONE, Polly (ed.) *Treasures of Early Irish Art 1500 B.C. to 1500 A.D.* (Catalogue, Metropolitan Museum of Art) (New York 1977)

COOMARASWAMY, A.K. 'On the loathly bride', *Speculum* 20 (1945) 391–404

CROSS, F.L. *The Oxford Dictionary of the Christian Church* (London 1957)

CROSS, F.L., & LIVINGSTONE, E.A. (edd.) *The Oxford Dictionary of the Christian Church* (2nd edn, Oxford 1974)

CURTIS, Edmund *A History of Medieval Ireland* (London 1923)

CURTIS, Edmund *A History of Medieval Ireland from 1086 to 1513* (2nd edn, London 1938)

CURTIS, Edmund (ed.) *Calendar of Ormond Deeds* (6 vols, Dublin 1932–43)

CURTIS, E. 'Murchertach O Brien, high king of Ireland, and his Norman son-in-law, Arnulf de Montgomery, c. 1100', *Journal of the Royal Society of Antiquaries of Ireland* 51 (1921) 116–24

CURTIS, Edmund (ed. & transl.) *Richard II in Ireland 1394–5 and Submissions of the Irish Chiefs* (Oxford 1927)

CURTIS, E. 'The "Bonnaght" of Ulster. A Treaty between Richard, Duke of York, Earl of Ulster, Lord Lieutenant of Ireland, and Henry, son of Eoghan O'Neill, captain of his Nation [1449]', *Hermathena*, no. 46 (1931) 87–105

CURTIS, E. 'The clan system among English settlers in Ireland', *English Historical Review* 25 (1910) 116–20

DANAHER, Kevin *The Year in Ireland* (Cork 1972)

D'ARBOIS DE JUBAINVILLE, H. 'Chartes données en Irlande en faveur de l'ordre de Cîteaux', *Revue celtique* 7 (1886) 81–6
DAVIES, O., & QUINN, D.B. (edd.) 'The Irish pipe roll of 14 John, 1211–1212', *Ulster Journal of Archaeology*, 3rd S., 4 (1941), supplement
*DE BARRA, P., & Ó FIAICH, T. *Imeacht na nIarlaí* (Dublin 1972)
DE BREFFNY, Brian (ed.) *The Irish World. The History and Cultural Achievements of the Irish People* (London 1977)
DE HÓIR, É. (ed.) 'Annála as Bréifne', *Bréifne* 4 (1970) 59–86
DILLON, M. (ed. & transl.) 'Ceart Uí Néill', *Studia Celtica* 1 (1966) 1–18
DILLON, Myles (ed. & transl.) *Lebor na Cert. The Book of Rights* (London 1962)
DILLON, Myles (ed.) *Serglige Con Culainn* (Dublin 1953)
DILLON, M. (ed. & transl.) 'The inauguration of O'Conor', in *Medieval Studies presented to Aubrey Gwynn, S.J.*, edd. J.A.Watt *et al.* (Dublin 1961), pp.186–202
DILLON, M. 'The relationship of mother and son, of father and daughter, and the law of inheritance with regard to women', in *Studies in Early Irish Law*, ed. D.A.Binchy (Dublin 1936), pp.129–79
DILLON, M. (ed. & transl.) 'Three texts related to the Book of Rights', *Celtica* 6 (1963) 184–92
*DOHERTY, C. 'The Historical Value of the Medieval "Lives" of Saint Máedóc of Ferns' (unpublished M.A. thesis, National University of Ireland [University College, Dublin] 1971)
DOLLEY, M., & SEABY, W.A. ' "Le Money del Oraylly" (O'Reilly's money)', *British Numismatic Journal* 36 (1967) 114–17
DOLLEY, M., & MAC NIOCAILL, G. 'Some coin-names in "Ceart Uí Néill" ', *Studia Celtica* 2 (1967) 119–24
DRAAK, M. 'Some aspects of kingship in pagan Ireland', in *The Sacral Kingship/La Regalità Sacra. Contributions to the Central Theme of the VIIIth International Congress for the History of Religions* (Rome, April 1955) (Leiden 1959), pp.651–63
DUCKETT, Eleanor Shipley *Anglo-Saxon Saints and Scholars* (New York 1947)
DUGDALE, William (ed.) *Monasticon Anglicanum: A History of the Abbies and Other Monasteries, Hospitals, Friaries, and Cathedral and Collegiate Churches with their Dependencies* ... (new edn by J.Caley *et al.*, 6 vols in 8, London 1817–30)
ELLIS, Henry (ed.) *Original Letters, Illustrative of English History; including Numerous Royal Letters: from Autographs in the British Museum, and One or Two Other Collections* (three series, 11 vols, London 1824–46)
ELRINGTON, Charles Richard (ed.) *The Whole Works of the Most Rev. James Usher D.D., Lord Archbishop of Armagh, and Primate of All Ireland, with a Life of the Author and an Account of his Writings* (16 vols, London 1847–64)
EMPEY, C.A., & SIMMS, K. 'The Ordinances of the White Earl and the problem of coign in the later middle ages', *Proceedings of the Royal Irish Academy* 75 C (1975) 161–87

FERGUSON, S. 'On the ceremonial turn, called "Desiul" ', *Proceedings of the Royal Irish Academy*, 2nd S., 1, Polite Literature and Antiquities (1879) 355–64
*FLANAGAN, M.-T. 'Monastic Charters from Irish Kings of the Twelfth and Thirteenth Centuries' (unpublished M.A. thesis, National University of Ireland [University College, Dublin] 1972)
FRAME, R. 'Power and society in the Lordship of Ireland 1272–1377', *Past and Present* 76 (1977) 3–33
FRAME, R. 'The Bruces in Ireland, 1315–18', *Irish Historical Studies* 19 (1974/5) 3–37
FRASER, J., *et al.* (edd.) *Irish Texts* (5 vols, London 1931–4)
FRASER, J., & O'KEEFFE, J.G. (edd.) 'Poems on the O'Donnells (1200 to 1600)', in *Irish Texts*, edd. J.Fraser *et al.*, II (London 1931), pp. 1–111
FRAZER, W. 'The Clandeboy O'Neills' stone inauguration chair, now preserved in the Belfast Museum', *Journal of the Royal Society of Antiquaries of Ireland* 28 [5th S., 8] (1898) 254–7
FREEMAN, A.Martin (ed. & transl.) *Annála Connacht. The Annals of Connacht (A.D. 1224–1544)* (Dublin 1944)
FROST, James *The History and Topography of the County of Clare. From the Earliest Times to the Beginning of the Eighteenth Century* (Dublin 1893)
FROUDE, James Anthony *History of England from the Fall of Wolsey to the Defeat of the Spanish Armada* (12 vols, London 1870)
GANSHOF, F.L. *Feudalism* (3rd edn, London 1964)
GANTZ, Jeffrey (transl.) *Early Irish Myths and Sagas* (Harmondsworth 1981)
GILBERT, John T. (ed.) *Chartularies of St Mary's Abbey, Dublin with the Register of its House at Dumbrody, and Annals of Ireland* (2 vols, London 1884)
GILBERT, J[ohn] T. (ed.) *Facsimiles of the National Manuscripts of Ireland* (4 vols, Dublin 1874–84)
GLANCY, M.(ed.) 'The Church-lands of Co. Armagh. Text of the Inquisition of 1609 with introduction and notes', *Seanchas Ard Mhacha* 1 (1954/5) 67–100
GLANCY, M. The primates and the Church lands of Armagh', *Seanchas Ard Mhacha* 5 (1969/70) 370–96
GRAVES, James (ed.) *A Roll of the Proceeding of the King's Council in Ireland for a Portion of the Sixteenth Year of the Reign of Richard II A.D. 1392–3* (London 1877)
GREENE, David (ed. & transl.) *Duanaire Mhéig Uidhir. The Poem Book of Cú Chonnacht Mág Uidhir, Lord of Fermanagh 1566–89* (Dublin 1972)
GREENE, D. 'Some linguistic evidence relating to the British Church', in *Christianity in Britain, 300–700*, edd. M.W.Barley & R.P.C.Hanson (Leicester 1968), pp. 75–86
GRIFFITH, Margaret C. (ed.) *Calendar of the Justiciary Rolls or Proceedings in the Court of the Justiciar of Ireland. I to VII Years of Edward II* (Dublin [1956])

GWYNN, A. 'Brian in Armagh (1005)', *Seanchas Ard Mhacha* 9 (1978/9) 35–50

GWYNN, A. 'Nicholas Mac Maol Íosa, Archbishop of Armagh (1272–1303)', in *Essays and Studies presented to Professor Eoin MacNeill*, ed. J. Ryan (Dublin 1940), pp. 394–405

GWYNN, Aubrey *The Medieval Province of Armagh 1470–1545* (Dundalk 1946)

GWYNN, Aubrey *The Twelfth-century Reform* (Dublin 1968)

GWYNN, Edward (ed. & transl.) *The Metrical Dindsenchas* (5 vols, Dublin 1903–35)

GWYNN, L. (ed. & transl.) 'De maccaib Conaire', *Ériu* 6 (1911/12) 144–53

GWYNN, L. (ed. & transl.) 'De Ṡíl Chonairi Móir', *Ériu* 6 (1911/12) 130–43

GWYNN, L. (ed. & transl.) 'The Life of St. Lasair', *Ériu* 5 (1911) 73–109

HANCOCK, W. Neilson, *et al.* (edd. & transl.) *Ancient Laws of Ireland* (6 vols, Dublin 1865–1901)

HARBISON, P. 'Native Irish arms and armour in medieval Gaelic literature, 1170–1600', *The Irish Sword* 12, (1975/6) 173–99 *and* 270–84

HARDIMAN, J. (ed. & transl.) 'Ancient Irish deeds and writings chiefly relating to landed property from the twelfth to the seventeenth century', *Transactions of the Royal Irish Academy* 15 [Antiquities] (1825–8) 2–95

HARDIMAN, J. (ed. & transl.) 'A statute of the fortieth year of King Edward III, enacted in a parliament held in Kilkenny, A.D. 1367, before Lionel Duke of Clarence, Lord Lieutenant of Ireland', in *Tracts Relating to Ireland*, vol. II (Irish Archaeological Society, Dublin 1843), pp. iii–121

HARDIMAN, James (ed. & transl.) *Irish Minstrelsy, or Bardic Remains of Ireland; with English Poetical Translations* (2 vols, London 1831)

HAY, D. 'The division of the spoils of war in fourteenth-century England', *Transactions of the Royal Historical Society*, 5th S., 4 (1954) 91–109

HAYES-McCOY, G. A. 'Gaelic society in Ireland in the late sixteenth century', *Historical Studies* (Irish Conference of Historians) 4 (1963) 45–61

HAYES-McCOY, G[erard] A. *Irish Battles* (London 1969)

HAYES-McCOY, Gerard A. *Scots Mercenary Forces in Ireland (1565–1603). An Account of their Service during that Period, of the Reaction of their Activities on Scottish Affairs, and of the Effect of their Presence in Ireland, together with an Examination of the Galloglaigh or Galloglass* (Dublin 1937)

HAYES-McCOY, G. A. 'The making of an O'Neill: a view of the ceremony at Tullaghoge, Co. Tyrone', *Ulster Journal of Archaeology*, 3rd S., 33 (1970) 89–92

HAYES-McCOY, G[erard] A. (ed.) *Ulster and Other Irish Maps c. 1600* (Dublin 1964)

HENNESSY, William M., & MAC CARTHY, B. (edd. & transl.) *Annala Uladh. Annals of Ulster, otherwise Annala Senait, Annals of Senat; a Chronicle of Irish Affairs* ... (4 vols, Dublin 1887–1901)

HENNESSY, William M. (ed. & transl.) *The Annals of Loch Cé; a Chronicle of Irish Affairs from A.D. 1014–A.D. 1590* (2 vols, London 1871)

HENNESSY, W[illiam] M., & KELLY, D.H. (edd. & transl.) *The Book of Fenagh in Irish and English, originally compiled by St. Caillin, Archbishop, Abbot, and Founder of Fenagh, alias Dunbally of Moy-Rein, Tempore St. Patricii* (Dublin 1875)

HILL, Christopher *Puritanism and Revolution: Studies in Interpretation of the English Revolution of the Seventeenth Century* (London 1958)

HILL, [George] *An Historical Account of the Plantation in Ulster at the Commencement of the Seventeenth Century 1608–1620* (Belfast 1877)

HOGAN, J. 'The Irish law of kingship, with special reference to Ailech and Cenél Eoghain', *Proceedings of the Royal Irish Academy* 40 C (1931/2) 186–254 [+ 7 tables]

HOGAN, J. 'The Ua Briain kingship in Telach Óc', in *Essays and Studies presented to Professor Eoin MacNeill*, ed. J. Ryan (Dublin 1940), pp. 406–44

HORE, H.F. (ed.) 'Facsimiles of the signatures of some Irish chieftains, and English commanders in Ulster. Temp. Elizabeth', *Ulster Journal of Archaeology*, 1st S., 2 (1854) 1–8

HORE, H.F. (ed.) 'The rental book of Gerald FitzGerald, ninth Earl of Kildare. Begun in the year 1518', *Journal of the Kilkenny and South-east of Ireland Archaeological Society*, N.S., 4 (1862/3) 110–37; N.S., 5 (1864–6) 501–18 *and* 525–46

HORE, Herbert <F.>, & GRAVES, J. (edd.) *The Social State of the Southern and Eastern Counties of Ireland in the Sixteenth Century: being the Presentments of the Gentlemen, Commonalty, and Citizens of Carlow, Cork, Kilkenny, Tipperary, Waterford, and Wexford, made in the Reigns of Henry VIII. and Elizabeth* (Dublin 1870)

HUGHES, K. 'Introduction', *apud* A. J. Otway-Ruthven, *A History of Medieval Ireland* (London 1968), pp. 1–33

HUGHES, Kathleen *The Church in Early Irish Society* (London 1966)

JACKSON, Kenneth Hurlstone (transl.) *A Celtic Miscellany. Translations from the Celtic Literatures* (2nd edn, Harmondsworth 1971)

JONES. W.A. 'The proclamation stone of the Connacht kings', *Journal of the Galway Archaeological and Historical Society* 12 (1922/3) 46

JOYCE, P.W. *A Social History of Ancient Ireland. Treating of the Government, Military System, and Law; Religion, Learning, and Art; Trades, Industries, and Commerce; Manners, Customs, and Domestic Life of the Ancient Irish People* (2 vols, London 1903)

KELLY, Fergus (ed. & transl.) *Audacht Morainn* (Dublin 1976)

KELLY, Matthew (ed. & transl.) *Cambrensis Eversus, seu potius Historica Fides in Rebus Hibernicis Giraldo Cambrensi abrogata; in quo plerasque justi historici dotes desiderari, plerosque nævos inesse, ostendit Gratianus Lucius, Hibernus*, ... (3 vols, Dublin 1848–51)

KILLEEN, J.F. '*Fear an Énais*', *Celtica* 9 (1971) 202–4

KING, P.D. *Law and Society in the Visigothic Kingdom* (Cambridge 1972)
KINGSFORD C.L., *et al.* *Report on the Manuscripts of Lord De L'Isle and Dudley, preserved at Penshurst Place* (6 vols, London 1925–66)
KNOTT, E. 'A poem by Giolla Brighde Ó Heoghusa', in *Miscellany presented to Kuno Meyer*, edd. O. Bergin & C. Marstrander (Halle a.S. 1912), pp. 241–5
KNOTT, E. (ed. & transl.) 'Filidh Éireann go haointeach. William Ó Ceallaigh's Christmas feast to the poets of Ireland, A.D. 1351', *Ériu* 5 (1911) 50–69
KNOTT, Eleanor (ed. & transl.) *The Bardic Poems of Tadhg Dall Ó Huiginn 1550–1591* (2 vols, London 1922/6)
KNOTT, Eleanor (ed.) *Togail Bruidne Da Derga* (Dublin 1936)
KNOX, H.T. 'Occupation of Connaught by the Anglo-Normans after A.D. 1237', *Journal of the Royal Society of Antiquaries of Ireland* 32 (1902) 132–8, 393–406; 33 (1903) 58–74, 179–89, 284–94
*LAMBKIN, B.K. 'The Structure of Sacred and Secular Lordship in the Poems of Blathmac' (unpublished M.A. dissertation, Queen's University, Belfast 1985)
LAWLOR, H.J. (ed.) 'Fragments of a lost register of the diocese of Clogher', *County Louth Archaeological Journal* 4 (1916–20) 226–57
LAWLOR, H.J. [*et al.*] 'The Cathach of St. Columba', *Proceedings of the Royal Irish Academy* 33 C (1916/17) 241–443
LEGGE, M. Dominica (ed.) *Anglo-Norman Letters and Petitions from All Souls MS. 182* (Oxford 1941)
LEHMANN, Ruth (ed.) *Fled Dúin na nGéd* (Dublin 1964)
LIVINGSTONE, Peadar *The Fermanagh Story. A Documented History of the County of Fermanagh from the Earliest Times to the Present Day* (Enniskillen 1969)
LOOMIS, Roger Sherman *Celtic Myth and Arthurian Romance* (New York 1927)
LUCAS, A.T. 'The sacred trees of Ireland', *Journal of the Cork Historical and Archaeological Society* 68 (1963) 16–54
LYDON, James [F.] (ed.) *England and Ireland in the Later Middle Ages. Essays in Honour of Jocelyn Otway-Ruthven* (Blackrock 1981)
LYDON, James [F.] (ed.) *The English in Medieval Ireland. Proceedings of the First Joint Meeting of the Royal Irish Academy and the British Academy, Dublin, 1982* (Dublin 1984)
LYDON, J[ames] F. *The Lordship of Ireland in the Middle Ages* (Dublin 1972)
LYDON, J. [F.] 'The middle nation', in *The English in Medieval Ireland*, ed. J. Lydon (Dublin 1984), pp. 1–26
LYNCH, John [see KELLY, Matthew (ed. & transl.)]
MAC AIRT, Seán (ed.) *Leabhar Branach. The Book of the O'Byrnes* (Dublin 1944)
MAC AIRT, Seán (ed. & transl.) *The Annals of Inisfallen (MS. Rawlinson B.503)* (Dublin 1951)
MAC AIRT, Seán, & MAC NIOCAILL, G. (edd. & transl.) *The Annals of Ulster (to A.D. 1131)* (2 parts, Dublin 1983–)

MACALISTER, R. A. S. (facs. ed.) *The Book of Uí Maine otherwise called "The Book of the O'Kelly's"* (Dublin 1942)
MAC CANA, P. 'An archaism in Irish poetic tradition', *Celtica* 8 (1968) 174–81
MAC CANA, P. 'Aspects of the theme of king and goddess in Irish literature', *Études celtiques* 7 (1955/6) 76–114, 356–413; 8 (1958/9) 59–65
MAC CANA, P. 'The *topos* of the single sandal in Irish tradition', *Celtica* 10 (1973) 160–6
*McCONE, K. 'Fírinne agus Torthúlacht', *Leachtaí Cholm Cille* 11 (1980) 136–73
McKENNA, Lambert (ed. & transl.) *Aithdioghluim Dána. A Miscellany of Irish Bardic Poetry, Historical and Religious, including the Historical Poems of the Duanaire in the Yellow Book of Lecan* (2 vols, London 1939/40)
McKENNA, Lambert (ed. & transl.) *Philip Bocht O hUiginn* (Dublin 1931)
McKENNA, L. (ed. & transl.) 'Some Irish bardic poems', *Studies* (Dublin) 39 (1950) 437–44
McKENNA, Lambert (ed. & transl.) *The Book of Magauran. Leabhar Méig Shamhradháin* (Dublin 1947)
McKENNA, Lambert (ed. & transl.) *The Book of O'Hara. Leabhar Í Eadhra* (Dublin 1951)
McKITTERICK, Rosamond *The Frankish Church and the Carolingian Reforms, 789–895* (London 1977)
McLEOD, N. 'The concept of law in ancient Irish jurisprudence', *The Irish Jurist*, N.S., 17 (1982) 356–67
McNAMARA, L. F. 'The *Caithréim Thoirdhealbhaigh* manuscripts and O'Grady's edition', *Modern Philology* 59 (1961/2) 122–5
McNEILL, C. (ed.) 'Lord Chancellor Gerrard's notes of his report on Ireland with extracts from original Irish records exhibited by him before the Privy Council in England, 1577–8', *Analecta Hibernica* 2 (1931) 93–291
MACNEILL, Eoin *Celtic Ireland* (Dublin 1921; rev. imp. by D. Ó Corráin, 1981)
MACNEILL, Eoin *Phases of Irish History* (Dublin 1919)
McNEILL, T. E. *Anglo-Norman Ulster. The History and Archaeology of an Irish Barony, 1177–1400* (Edinburgh 1980)
MAC NIOCAILL, G. 'A propos du vocabulaire social irlandais du bas moyen âge', *Études celtiques* 12 (1968/9) 512–46
MAC NIOCAILL, G. 'Aspects of Irish law in the late thirteenth century', *Historical Studies* (Irish Conference of Historians) 10 (1976) 25–42
MAC NIOCAILL, Gearóid *Ireland before the Vikings* (Dublin 1972)
MAC NIOCAILL, G. 'Irish law and the Armagh constitutions of 1297', *The Irish Jurist*, N.S., 6 (1971) 339–44
MAC NIOCAILL, G. 'Jetsam, treasure trove and the Lord's share in medieval Ireland', *The Irish Jurist*, N.S., 6 (1971) 103–10
MAC NIOCAILL, Gearóid (ed.) *Notitiæ as Leabhar Cheanannais 1033–1161* (Dublin 1961)

MAC NIOCAILL, G. 'The "heir designate" in early medieval Ireland', *The Irish Jurist*, N.S., 3 (1968) 326–9
MAC NIOCAILL, G. 'The interaction of laws', in *The English in Medieval Ireland*, ed. J. Lydon (Dublin 1984), pp. 105–17
MAC NIOCAILL, Gearóid *The Medieval Irish Annals* (Dublin 1975)
MAC NIOCAILL, G. 'The origins of the *betagh*', *The Irish Jurist*, N.S., 1 (1966) 292–8
MAC NIOCAILL, G[earóid] (ed.) *The Red Book of the Earls of Kildare* (Dublin 1964)
MAHAFFY, J.P. (ed.) 'Two early tours in Ireland', *Hermathena*, no. 40 (1914) 1–16
MAJOR, J. Russell *Representative Institutions in Renaissance France 1421–1559* (Madison, Wisc. 1960)
MARONGIU, Antonio *Medieval Parliaments: a Comparative Study* (London 1968)
MARTIN, Martin *A Description of the Western Islands of Scotland circa 1695 by Martin Martin, Gent. Including a Voyage to St Kilda by the Same Author and a Description of the Western Isles of Scotland by Sir Donald Monro* (ed. D.J. Macleod, 4th edn, Stirling 1934)
MATHEWS, Thomas *The O'Neills of Ulster, their History and Genealogy* (3 vols, Dublin 1907)
MERRIMAN, Roger Bigelow *The Rise of the Spanish Empire in the Old World and in the New* (4 vols, New York 1918)
METTAM, Roger (ed.) *Government and Society in Louis XIV's France* (London 1977)
MEYER, Kuno (ed. & transl.) *Betha Colmáin maic Lúacháin. Life of Colmán son of Lúachan* (Dublin 1911)
MEYER, K. (ed.) 'Mitteilungen aus irischen Handschriften (Fortsetzung)', *Zeitschrift für celtische Philologie* 8 (1910–12) 102–20
MEYER, Kuno (ed. & transl.) *The Instructions of King Cormac mac Airt* (Dublin 1909)
MEYER, Kuno (ed. & transl.) *The Triads of Ireland* (Dublin 1906)
MILLER, Liam, & POWER, E. (edd.) *Holinshed's Irish Chronicle: The Historie of Irelande from the First Inhabitation thereof, vnto the yeare 1509. Collected by Raphaell Holished, & continued till the yeare 1547 by Richarde Stanyhurst* (Dublin 1979)
MOODY, T.W. (ed.) *Nationality and the Pursuit of National Independence* (Belfast 1978)
MORLEY, Henry (ed.) *Ireland under Elizabeth and James the First described by Edmund Spenser by Sir John Davies Attorney-General for Ireland under James the First, and by Fynes Moryson, Secretary to the Lord Mountjoy, Lord Deputy* (London 1890)
MORRIN, James (ed.) *Calendar of the Patent and Close Rolls of Chancery in Ireland, from the 18th to the 45th of Queen Elizabeth* (Dublin 1862)
MORYSON, Fynes *An Itinerary containing his Ten Yeeres Travell through the Twelve Dominions of Germany, Bohmerland, Sweitzerland, Netherland, Denmarke, Poland, Italy, Turkey, France, England, Scotland and Ireland* (2nd edn, 4 vols, Glasgow 1907/8)

MULCHRONE, Kathleen (facs. ed.) *The Book of Lecan. Leabhar Mór Mhic Fhir Bhisigh Leacain* (Dublin 1937)
MURPHY, Denis (ed.) *The Annals of Clonmacnoise, being Annals of Ireland from the Earliest Period to A.D. 1408, translated into English A.D. 1627 by Conell Mageoghagan* (Dublin 1896)
MURRAY, J.A.H., *et al.* (edd.) *The Oxford English Dictionary* (corrected reissue with supplement and bibliography, 13 vols, Oxford 1933)
MYERS, A.R. *Parliaments and Estates in Europe to 1789* (London 1975)
NELSON, J.L. 'National synods, kingship as office, and royal anointing: an early medieval syndrome', *Studies in Church History* 7 (1971) 41–59
NIC GHIOLLAMHAITH, A. 'Dynastic warfare and historical writing in North Munster, 1276–1350', *Cambridge Medieval Celtic Studies* 2 (1981) 73–89
NICHOLLS, Kenneth [W.] *Gaelic and Gaelicised Ireland in the Middle Ages* (Dublin 1972)
NICHOLLS, K[enneth] W. *Land, Law and Society in Sixteenth-century Ireland* (Cork 1976)
NICHOLLS, K.W. (ed. & transl.) 'The Register of Clogher', *Clogher Record* 7 (1969–72) 361–431
NÍ SHÉAGHDHA, Nessa *Catalogue of Irish Manuscripts in the National Library of Ireland* (Dublin 1961– [in progress])
NÍ SHÉAGHDHA, N. (ed. & transl.) 'The Rights of Mac Diarmada', *Celtica* 6 (1963) 156–72
O'BRIEN, M.A. (ed.) *Corpus Genealogiarum Hiberniae*, I (Dublin 1962; rev. imp., by J.V.Kelleher, 1976)
Ó CEALLAIGH, Séamus *Gleanings from Ulster History* (Cork 1951)
Ó CORRÁIN, D. '*Caithréim Chellacháin Chaisil*: history or propaganda?', *Ériu* 25 (1974) 1–69
ÓCORRÁIN, D. 'Foreign connections and domestic politics: Killaloe and the Uí Briain in twelfth-century hagiography', in *Ireland in Early Mediaeval Europe*, edd. D.Whitelock *et al.* (Cambridge 1982) pp. 213–31
Ó CORRÁIN, Donncha *Ireland before the Normans* (Dublin 1972)
Ó CORRÁIN, D. 'Irish regnal succession: a reappraisal', *Studia Hibernica* 11 (1971) 7–39
Ó CORRÁIN, D. 'Nationality and kingship in pre-Norman Ireland', in *Nationality and the Pursuit of National Independence*, ed. T.W.Moody (Belfast 1978), pp. 1–35
Ó CUÍV, B. (ed. & transl.) 'An appeal on behalf of the profession of poetry', *Éigse* 14 (1971/2) 87–106
Ó CUÍV, B. (ed. & transl.) 'A sixteenth-century political poem', *Éigse* 15 (1973/4) 261–76
Ó CUÍV, B. 'Eachtra Mhuireadhaigh Í Dhálaigh', *Studia Hibernica* 1 (1961) 56–69
Ó CUÍV, Brian (ed.) *The Impact of the Scandinavian Invasions on the Celtic-speaking Peoples c.800–1100 A.D.: Introductory Papers read at Plenary Sessions of the International Congress of Celtic Studies held in Dublin, 6–10 July, 1959* (Dublin 1975)

Ó CUÍV, Brian *The Irish Bardic Duanaire or "Poem-Book"* (Dublin [1973])
O DALY, M. (ed. & transl.) 'A poem on the Airgialla', *Ériu* 16 (1952) 179–88
Ó DOIBHLÍN, Éamonn *Domhnach Mór, an Outline of Parish History* (Omagh 1969)
Ó DONNCHADHA, Tadhg (ed.) *Leabhar Cloinne Aodha Buidhe* (Dublin 1931)
O'DONOGHUE, T. (ed. & transl.) 'Advice to a Prince', *Ériu* 9 (1921–3) 43–54
O'DONOGHUE, T. (ed. & transl.) 'Cert cech ríg'co réil', in *Miscellany presented to Kuno Meyer*, edd. O. Bergin & C. Marstrander (Halle a.S. 1912), pp. 258–77
O'DONOVAN, John (ed. & transl.) *Annala Rioghachta Eireann. Annals of the Kingdom of Ireland, by the Four Masters, from the Earliest Period to the Year 1616* (2nd edn, 7 vols, Dublin 1856)
O'DONOVAN, J. (ed. & transl.) 'Covenant between Mageoghegan and the Fox, with brief historical notes of the two families', in *The Miscellany of the Irish Archaeological Society*, vol. I (Dublin 1846) pp. 179–97
O'DONOVAN, J. (ed. & transl.) 'Fearghal Og Mac an Bhaird's poem on the Battle of Dun, in 1260', in *Miscellany of the Celtic Society*, ed. J. O'Donovan (Dublin 1849), pp. 404–15
O'DONOVAN, John (ed. & transl.) *Leabhar na gCeart or the Book of Rights* (Dublin 1847)
O'DONOVAN, John (ed.) *Miscellany of the Celtic Society* (Dublin 1849)
O'DONOVAN, J. (ed. & transl.) 'Original letters in the Irish and Latin languages by Shane O'Neill, Prince of Tyrone and proclamation of high treason against him by Queen Elizabeth', *Ulster Journal of Archaeology*, 1st S., 5 (1857) 259–73
O'DONOVAN, J. (ed.) 'The Annals of Ireland, from the year 1443 to 1468, translated from the Irish by Dudley Firbisse, or, as he is more usually called, Duald Mac Firbis, for Sir James Ware, in the year 1666', in *The Miscellany of the Irish Archaeological Society*, vol. I (Dublin 1846) pp. 198–302
O'DONOVAN, John (ed. & transl.) *The Banquet of Dun na n-Gedh and The Battle of Magh Rath, an Ancient Historical Tale* (Dublin 1842)
O'DONOVAN, J. (ed. & transl.) 'The charter of Newry', *The Dublin Penny Journal* 1 (1832) 102–4
O'DONOVAN, John (ed. & transl.) *The Genealogies, Tribes, and Customs of Hy-Fiachrach, commonly called O'Dowda's Country, now first published from the Book of Lecan, in the Library of the Royal Irish Academy, and from the Genealogical Manuscript of Duald Mac Firbis ...* (Dublin 1844)
O'DONOVAN, John (ed. & transl.) *The Tribes and Customs of Hy-Many, commonly called O'Kelly's Country, now first published from the Book of Lecan, a Manuscript in the Library of the Royal Irish Academy* (Dublin 1843)

O'DONOVAN, John (ed. & transl.) *The Tribes of Ireland: a Satire, by Aenghus O'Daly* ... (Dublin 1852)

Ó DUFAIGH, S. (ed. & transl.) 'Cíos Mhic Mhathghamhna', *Clogher Record* 4 (1960–2) 125–34

Ó DUFAIGH, S. 'The MacCathmhaoils of Clogher', *Clogher Record* 2 (1957/9) 25–49

O'DWYER, B.W. 'The Annals of Connacht and Loch Cé and the monasteries of Boyle and Holy Trinity', *Proceedings of the Royal Irish Academy* 72 C (1972) 83–101

Ó FIAICH, T. (ed.) Richard Weston agus "Beir mo bheannacht go Dundalk" ', *Seanchas Ard Mhacha* 5 (1969/70) 269–88

Ó FIAICH, T. 'The O'Neills of the Fews', *Seanchas Ard Mhacha* 7 (1973/4) 1–64

O'FLAHERTY, Roderic *A Chorographical Description of West or h-Iar Connaught* (ed. J. Hardiman, Dublin 1846)

O'GRADY, Standish Hayes, & FLOWER, R. (edd. & transl.) *Caithréim Thoirdhealbhaigh [by] Sean (mac Ruaidhrí) Mac Craith* (2 vols, London 1929)

O'GRADY, Standish Hayes, *et al.* *Catalogue of Irish Manuscripts in the British Museum* (3 vols, London 1926–53)

O'GRADY, Standish H[ayes] (ed. & transl.) *Silva Gadelica (I–XXXI). A Collection of Tales in Irish with Extracts illustrating Persons and Places* (2 vols, London 1892)

Ó HINNSE, Séamus (ed. & transl.) *Miscellaneous Irish Annals (A.D. 1114– 1437)* (Dublin 1947)

O'KEEFFE, J.G. (ed.) 'Quartering Rights of the Uí Domhnaill over Ulster. *MS. Rawl. B. 514, fo. 67b*', in *Irish Texts*, edd. J. Fraser *et al.*, IV (London 1934), pp. 29–30

O'KELLEHER, A., & SCHOEPPERLE, G. (edd. & transl.) *Betha Colaim Chille. Life of Columcille compiled by Manus O'Donnell in 1532* (Urbana, Ill. 1918)

Ó MÁILLE, T. 'Medb Chruachna', *Zeitschrift für celtische Philologie* 17 (1927/8) 129–46

O'MEARA, J.J. (ed.) 'Giraldus Cambrensis in Topographia Hibernie. Text of the first recension', *Proceedings of the Royal Irish Academy* 52 C (1948–50) 113–78

O'MEARA, John J. (transl.) *The History and Topography of Ireland [by] Gerald of Wales* (2nd edn, Harmondsworth 1982)

O'NOWLAN, T.P. (ed. & transl.) 'The Quarrel about the Loaf', *Ériu* 1 (1904) 128–37

Ó RAGHALLAIGH, T. (ed. & transl.) 'Seanchas na mBúrcach. History of the Burkes', *Journal of the Galway Archaeological and Historical Society* 13 (1924–7) 50–60, 101–38; 14 (1928/9) 30–51, 142–67

O'RAHILLY, Thomas F. *Early Irish History and Mythology* (Dublin 1946)

O'RAHILLY, T.F. 'On the origin of the names *Érainn* and *Ériu*', *Ériu* 14 (1943–6) 7–28

Ó RAITHBHEARTAIGH, Toirdhealbhach (ed. & transl.) *Genealogical Tracts*, I (Dublin 1932)
Ó RIAIN, P. 'Boundary association in early Irish society', *Studia Celtica* 7 (1972) 12–29
ORPEN, Goddard Henry *Ireland under the Normans* (4 vols, Oxford 1911–20)
ORPEN, G.H. 'Some Irish Cistercian documents', *English Historical Review* 28 (1913) 303–13
ORPEN, G.H. 'The earldom of Ulster', *Journal of the Royal Society of Antiquaries of Ireland* 43 (1913) 30–46, 133–43; 44 (1914) 51–66; 45 (1915) 123–42
ORPEN, G.H. 'The Normans in Tirowen and Tirconnell', *Journal of the Royal Society of Antiquaries of Ireland* 45 (1915) 275–88
ORPEN, Goddard Henry (ed. & transl.) *The Song of Dermot and the Earl: an Old French Poem from the Carew MS. No.596 in the Archiepiscopal Palace Library at Lambeth Palace* (Oxford 1892)
OTWAY-RUTHVEN, A.J. *A History of Medieval Ireland* (London 1968)
PARES, Bernard *A History of Russia* (London 1926)
PENDER, S. (ed. & transl.) 'A tract on MacMahon's prerogatives', *Études celtiques* 1 (1936) 248–60
PENDER, S. (ed.) 'The O Clery Book of Genealogies', *Analecta Hibernica* 18 (1951) 1–194
PERROTT, James *The Chronicle of Ireland 1584–1608* (ed. H.Wood, Dublin 1933)
PIERS, Henry 'A Chorographical Description of the Co. Westmeath written A.D. 1682', in *Collectanea de Rebus Hibernicis*, ed. C.Vallancey (2nd edn, Dublin 1786–1804), I.1–126
PLUMMER, Charles (ed. & transl.) *Bethada Náem nÉrenn. Lives of Irish Saints* (2 vols, Oxford 1922; rev. imp., 1968)
PLUMMER, C. 'Notes on some passages in the Brehon laws' *Ériu* 8 (1916) 127–32; 9 (1921–3) 31–42, 109–17; 10 (1926–8) 113–29
PLUMMER, C. (ed. & transl.) 'The Miracles of Senan', *Zeitschrift für celtische Philologie* 10 (1915) 1–35
PLUMMER, Charles (ed.) *Vitae Sanctorum Hiberniae partim hactenus ineditae* (2 vols, Oxford 1910; rev. imp., 1968)
*PONSONBY, F., & PONSONBY, E. 'Diary of a tour through Donegal 1837', *Donegal Annual* 10 (1971/3) 281–91
POWER, N. 'Classes of women described in the Senchas Már', in *Studies in Early Irish Law*, ed. D.A.Binchy (Dublin 1936), pp.81–108
POWICKE, F.M. 'The *dispensator* of King David I', *Scottish Historical Review* 23 (1925/6) 34–40
POWICKE, F.M. (ed. & transl.) *The Life of Ailred of Rievaulx by Walter Daniel* (Edinburgh 1950)
PRICE, L. 'The origin of the word *betagius*', *Ériu* 20 (1966) 185–90
PUHVEL, J. 'Aspects of equine functionality', in *Myth and Law among the Indo-Europeans*, ed. J.Puhvel (Berkeley, Cal. 1970), pp.159–72
PUHVEL, Jaan (ed.) *Myth and Law among the Indo-Europeans. Studies in Indo-European Comparative Mythology* (Berkeley, Cal. 1970)

QUIGGIN, E.C. (ed. & transl.) 'A poem by Gilbride Macnamee in praise of Cathal O'Conor', in *Miscellany presented to Kuno Meyer*, edd. O.Bergin & C.Marstrander (Halle a.S. 1912), pp. 167–77

QUIGGIN, E.C. (ed.) *Essays and Studies presented to William Ridgeway*... (Cambridge 1913)

QUIGGIN, E.C. (ed. & transl.) 'O'Conor's house at Cloonfree', in *Essays and Studies presented to William Ridgeway*, ed. E.C.Quiggin (Cambridge 1913), pp. 333–52

QUIGLEY, W.G.H., & ROBERTS, E.F.D. (edd.) *Registrum Iohannis Mey. The Register of John Mey, Archbishop of Armagh, 1443–56* (Belfast 1972)

QUIN, E.G. (gen. ed.) *Dictionary of the Irish Language based mainly on Old and Middle Irish Materials* (Dublin 1913–76)

QUINN, David Beers *The Elizabethans and the Irish* (Ithaca, N.Y. 1966)

RASHDALL, Hastings *The Universities of Europe in the Middle Ages* (2nd edn, 3 vols, by F.M.Powicke & A.B.Emden, Oxford 1936)

REEVES, W. 'The seal of Hugh O'Neill', *Ulster Journal of Archaeology*, 1st S., 1 (1853) 255–8

RICHARDSON, H.G., & SAYLES, G.O. *The Irish Parliament in the Middle Ages* (Philadelphia, Pa. 1952)

RICHARDSON, H.G. 'The origins of parliament', *Transactions of the Royal Historical Society*, 4th S., 11 (1928) 137–83

ROBINSON, F.N. (ed. & transl.) 'The Irish Lives of Guy of Warwick and Bevis of Hampton', *Zeitschrift für celtische Philologie* 6 (1907/8) 9–180, 273–338, 556

RONAN, M.V. (ed.) 'Some mediaeval documents', *Journal of the Royal Society of Antiquaries of Ireland* 67 [7th S., 7] (1937) 229–41

RUBINSTEIN, Nicolai *The Government of Florence under the Medici (1434 to 1494)* (Oxford 1966)

RYAN, John (ed.) *Essays and Studies presented to Professor Eoin MacNeill D.Litt. on the Occasion of his Seventieth Birthday, May 15th, 1938* (Dublin 1940)

RYMER, Thomas (ed.) *Foedera, Conventiones, Litterae, et cujuscunque Generis Acta Publica, inter Reges Angliae et alios quosvis Imperatores, Reges, Pontifices, Principes, vel Communitates; ab Ingressu Guliemi I in Angliam, A.D. 1066, ad Nostra usque Tempora* ... (4 vols, rev. A.Clarke *et al.*, London 1816–20)

RYNNE, E. 'An Irish sword of the eleventh century?', *Journal of the Royal Society of Antiquaries of Ireland* 92 (1962) 208–10

*RYNNE, E. 'The impact of the vikings on Irish weapons', in *Atti del VI Congresso Internazionale delle Scienze Preistoriche & Protostoriche, Roma 1962* (Roma 1966), pp. 181–5

SCHRÖDER, F.R. 'Ein altirischer Krönungsritus und das indogermanische Rossopfer', *Zeitschrift für celtische Philologie* 16 (1926/7) 310–12

SCOTT, A.B., & MARTIN, F.X. (edd. & transl.) *Expugnatio Hibernica. The Conquest of Ireland, by Giraldus Cambrensis* (Dublin 1978)

SHARPE, R. 'Hiberno-Latin *laicus*, Irish *láech* and the devil's men', *Ériu* 30 (1979) 75–92

SHEEHY, Maurice P. (ed.) *Pontificia Hibernica. Medieval Papal Chancery Documents concerning Ireland 640–1261* (2 vols, Dublin 1962–5)

SHIRLEY, Evelyn Philip *Some Account of the Territory or Dominion of Farney, in the Province and Earldom of Ulster* (London 1845)

SIMMS, K. ' "Gabh umad a Fheidhlimidh" – a fifteenth-century inauguration ode?', *Ériu* 31 (1980) 132–45

SIMMS, K. 'Guesting and feasting in Gaelic Ireland', *Journal of the Royal Society of Antiquaries of Ireland* 108 (1978) 67–100

SIMMS, K. 'Niall Garbh II O Donnell, king of Tír Conaill 1422–39', *Donegal Annual* 12 (1977/9) 7–21

SIMMS, K. 'The archbishops of Armagh and the O'Neills 1347–1471', *Irish Historical Studies* 19 (1974/5) 38–55

SIMMS, K. 'The concordat between Primate John Mey and Henry O'Neill (1455)', *Archivium Hibernicum* 34 (1976/7) 71–82

SIMMS, K. ' "The King's Friend": O Neill, the Crown and the earldom of Ulster', in *England and Ireland in the Later Middle Ages*, ed. J. Lydon (Blackrock 1981), pp. 214–36

SIMMS, K. 'The legal position of Irishwomen in the later middle ages', *The Irish Jurist*, N.S., 10 (1975) 96–111

SIMMS, K. 'The medieval kingdom of Lough Erne', *Clogher Record* 9 (1976/8) 126–41

SIMMS, K. 'The O Hanlons, the O Neills and the Anglo-Normans in thirteenth-century Armagh', *Seanchas Ard Mhacha* 9 (1978/9) 70–94

SIMMS, K. 'The O'Reillys and the kingdom of East Bréifne', *Bréifne* 6 (1978–81) 305–19

SIMMS, K. 'Warfare in the medieval Gaelic lordships', *The Irish Sword* 12 (1975/6) 98–108

SPENSER, Edmund *A View of the Present State of Ireland* (ed. W. L. Renwick, Oxford 1970)

STALLEY, R. 'The long middle ages', in *The Irish World*, ed. B. de Breffny (London 1977), pp. 71–98

STANIHURST, Richard *De Rebus in Hibernia Gestis* (Antwerpen 1584)

STOKES, W. (ed. & transl.) 'The Annals of Tigernach', *Revue celtique* 16 (1895) 374–419; 17 (1896) 6–33, 119–263, 337–420; *and* 18 (1897) 9–59, 150–97, 267–303, 374–91

STOKES, W. (ed. & transl.) 'The Death of Crimthann son of Fidach, and the Adventures of the Sons of Éochaid Muigmedón', *Revue celtique* 24 (1903) 172–207

STOKES, W. (ed. & transl.) 'The Gaelic Maundeville', *Zeitschrift für celtische Philologie* 2 (1898/9) 1–63 *and* 226–312

STOKES, W. (ed. & transl.) 'Tidings of Conchobar mac Nessa', *Ériu* 4 (1910) 18–38

STUBBS, William (ed.) *Chronica Magistri Rogeri de Houedene* (4 vols, London 1868–71)

STUBBS, William (ed.) *Gesta Regis Henrici Secundi Benedicti Abbatis. The Chronicle of the Reigns of Henry II. and Richard I. A.D. 1169–1192; known commonly under the name of Benedict of Peterborough* (2 vols, London 1867)

SWEETMAN, H.S. (ed.) *Calendar of Documents relating to Ireland, 1171–1307, preserved in H.M. Public Record Office, London* (5 vols, London 1875–86)

THORNLEY, Isobel D. *England under the Yorkists 1460–1485, illustrated from Contemporary Sources* (London 1920)

THURNEYSEN, R. 'Aus dem irischen Recht', *Zeitschrift für celtische Philologie* 14 (1923) 335–94; 15 (1924/5) 238–76, 302–76; 16 (1926/7) 167–230; *and* 18 (1929/30) 353–408

THURNEYSEN, R (ed. & transl.) 'Cóic Conara Fugill: Die fünf Wege zum Urteil. Ein altirischer Rechtstext', *Abhandlungen der Preussischen Akademie der Wissenschaften* (1925), Philosophisch-historische Klasse, Nr 7

THURNEYSEN, R. 'Irisches recht', *Abhandlungen der Preussischen Akademie der Wissenschaften* (1931), Philosophisch-historische Klasse, Nr 2

THURNEYSEN, R. (ed. & transl.) 'Morands Fürstenspiegel', *Zeitschrift für celtische Philologie* 11 (1916/17) 56–106

THURNEYSEN, R. 'Zur Göttin *Medb*', *Zeitschrift für celtische Philologie* 18 (1929/30) 108–10 *and* 19 (1931–3) 352–3

TITOW, J. 'Evidence of weather in the account rolls of the bishopric of Winchester 1209–1350', *Economic History Review*, 2nd S., 12 (1959/60) 360–407

TODD, James Henthorn (ed. & transl.) *Cogadh Gaedhel re Gallaibh. The War of the Gaedhil with the Gaill*... (London 1867)

[TRESHAM, E. (ed.)] *Rotulorum Patentium et Clausorum Cancellariæ Hiberniæ Calendarium: Henry II – Henry VII* (Dublin 1828)

UA CADHLA, C. (ed.) 'Geinealaighe Fearmanach', *Annalecta Hibernica* 3 (1931) 62–150

UA MUIRGHEASA, E. (ed.) 'An Irish account of Bruce's invasion, entitled: "The Battle of Fochart of St Bridget" ', *County Louth Archaeological Journal* 1 (1904–7), no. 2, pp. 77–91

USSHER, J. 'Veterum Epistolarum Hibernicarum Sylloge', in *The Whole Works of the Most Rev. James Ussher*, ed. C.R. Elrington (16 vols, London 1847–64), IV.383–572

VALLANCEY, Charles (ed.) *Collectanea de Rebus Hibernicis* (6 vols, Dublin 1781–1804)

WALSH, Paul *Irish Men of Learning* (Dublin 1947)

WALSH, Paul (ed. & transl.) *Leabhar Chlainne Suibhne. An Account of the Mac Sweeney Families in Ireland, with Pedigrees* (Dublin 1920)

WALSH, Paul, [& O LOCHLAINN, C.] (edd. & transl.) *The Life of Aodh Ruadh O Domhnaill transcribed from the Book of Lughaidh Ó Cléirigh* (2 vols, London 1948/57)

WATSON, William J. (ed. & transl.) *Scottish Verse from the Book of the Dean of Lismore* (Edinburgh 1937)

WATT, J[ohn] A., *et al.* (edd.) *Medieval Studies presented to Aubrey Gwynn, S.J.* (Dublin 1961)

WATT, John [A.] *The Church in Medieval Ireland* (Dublin 1972)

WHITE, Newport B. (ed.) *Irish Monastic and Episcopal Deeds A.D. 1200–1600 transcribed from the Originals preserved at Kilkenny Castle* (Dublin 1936)
WHITELOCK, Dorothy (transl.) *English Historical Documents c.500–1042* (2nd edn, London 1979)
WHITELOCK, Dorothy, *et al.* (edd.) *Ireland in Early Mediaeval Europe. Studies in Memory of Kathleen Hughes* (Cambridge 1982)
WILLIAMS, N.J.A. (ed. & transl.) *The Poems of Giolla Brighde Mac Con Midhe* (London 1980)

GLOSSARIAL INDEX

Anglo-Irish terms are marked with an asterisk. Where an institution continued beyond the Old Irish period, Irish terms are given in Classical Early Modern spelling, with cross-references from other versions. I am indebted throughout to the Royal Irish Academy's *Dictionary of the Irish Language*, gen. ed. E. G. Quin.

Term	Definition	Pages
adbar ríg	see *adhbhar ríogh*.	
adhbhar ríogh	'the material of a king': one eligible for kingship	41, 53–4, 88, 95
aenach	see *aonach*.	
aes	see *aos*.	
airchinneach	'headman': leader, superior, especially of a church-community, or church-tenants; in the later middle ages, an official, normally hereditary, under the authority of the local bishop, with responsibility for maintaining the fabric of a church and providing for the celebration of divine service when not himself ordained	28, 30
aire	(Old Irish) in law tracts a technical term for any freeman having independent legal status, but in general Old Irish literature the sense is already confined to 'noble' or 'chief'.	60
airecht	see *oireacht*.	
airechtas	see *oireachtas*.	
amhantur	'accident', 'chance' (English or Romance loanword): casual perquisites of the lord such as flotsam and jetsam	136
amhas	'a hireling': servant, mercenary soldier	80, 82, 117–18, 132
amus	see *amhas*.	
aonach	in early mediaeval Ireland a periodic assembly of the inhabitants of a given territory, whether *tuath* or province, for sporting contests and other public business; in Modern Irish 'a fair'. For nuances in mediaeval period see the present work.	27, 60–3, 73–45, 116
aos cumainn	'friends'; singular, *fear cumainn*, 'friend'	94
aos grádha	(singular, *fear grádha*): literally 'men	viii, 65, 71,

	of love', with some evidence for confusion with 'men of rank' (*aos gráidh*); in practice servitors or confidential retainers of an ecclesiastical or secular lord	84–6, 94
aos gráidh	see *aos grádha*.	
baile biataigh	'the steading of a *biatach*' a variable land-measurement described as 900 English acres in Co. Monaghan in 1607	140, 143
*ballibetagh, *ballybetagh	see *baile biataigh*.	
balliuus	see *maor*.	
banais ríghe	wedding of kingship': inauguration-rite	39
barda	'ward' (English loanword?): garrison of a castle	128
bedellus	see *maor*.	
biatach	'food-provider': a vassal or tenant who rendered in food his dues to his lord. Where the lord in question was a king, *biatach* could signify high social rank, frequently equated with *brughaidh*; but a *daor-bhiatach*, a bond-*biatach*, was a serf.	73, 87, 133, 141
biatachas, biataigheacht	'food-providing': a clientship based on rendering food to the lord.	101, 105
*bonaght, *bonagh-bonny, *bonney-bur, *bonaghtbeg	see *buannacht*. For 'Bonaght of Ulster' see General Index.	
*booley	see *buaile*.	
*brehon	see *breitheamh* and also General Index s.w. 'brehons', 'judges of native Irish law'.	
breitheamh	'judge'	79, 88–9
brethem	see *breitheamh*.	
briugu	see *brughaidh*.	
brughaidh	'hospitaller': a wealthy landholder, the highest non-noble social grade, with a traditional obligation to provide public hospitality. The *brughaidh céadach* was said to reckon his stock in hundreds (for example, 100 cows, 100 pigs, 100 horses etc.).	73, 85, 87, 102
buaile	'cattle-pen': more especially the summer steading for cow-herds, associated with transhumance	90
buanna	a billeted mercenary	131
buannacht	the billeting of mercenaries, or servants.	105, 131, 135–6, 139
buannacht bhairr	'excess billeting': beyond normal requirements, *bonneybur	139
buannacht bheag	'little bonaght': a commutation of the obligation to a money-payment, *bonaghtbeg	139

buannacht bhuna	'basic billeting': the normal or peacetime quota, *bonagh-bonny	139
cáin	Latin *lex*, 'promulgated law' as distinct from custom; fines for the breach thereof; tribute in a more general sense	54, 92, 130, 132, 135–6
caithréim	'battle-career': list or narrative of a hero's victories	5
*cane	see *cáin*.	
*canfinny	see *ceann-fine*.	
*carton	see *ceathramha*.	
capitaneus (Latin), *cheueteyn* (French), *captayne	the head of an aristocratic lineage, whether Irish or Anglo-Irish, a chieftain	34, 37–8, 52 55
ceann-fine	'kin-head': head of a landowning kindred, usually a fairly small, close-knit group	58
ceatharnaigh	Latin *turbales, turbarii*: native Irish mercenary foot-soldiers, members of a *ceithearn*, 'a band', Latin *turba*, or 'retained band' (*ceithearn congbhála*). The Anglo-Irish term *kern, *kernes, could apply to bands or to individual soldiers.	18, 20, 74, 93, 95, 120, 125–8, 135, 143
ceathramha	'a quarter': a measure of land, sometimes described as a quarter of a *baile biataigh*, a *carton	143, 145
ceithearn tighe	'household-band': a lord's permanent retinue of mercenaries, often employed on police-duties	93–4
célsine	(Old Irish), the institution of clientship in early mediaeval Ireland. *Dóerchéle* signified a base, though not personally unfree, client, *sóerchéle* a 'free' or 'noble' one.	96, 101, 103, 130, 132, 141
*chiefry	see *tighearnus*.	
cíos	'tribute': a payment, usually annual, to a king from his subject-territory, often misleadingly called 'rent' in the later mediaeval period	109, 130–3, 135, 139, 143–5
cíos cosanta	'tribute of defence': protection-money or *blackrent (*duibhchíos*)	109, 144
cís	see *cíos*	
*coarb	see *comharba*	
cóe, cáe, coí	(Old Irish) a feast owed to a patron in early mediaeval Ireland by each of his base clients (*dóerchéli*) whom he visited with a train of guests during the 'feasting season' (*ráithe cue, aimser chue*) between New Year's Day and Shrovetide	130–1, 141
*coigny	see *coinnmheadh*.	
coimhéirghe	hosting-duty, *rising-out, the	102, 109,

	obligation of a subject to join his lord's or king's hosting to war when summoned	135
coinnem	see *coinnmhe*.	
coinnmhe	'guesting band': troops on billet	134–5
coinnmheadh	'guesting', *coigny, *coyne: the exaction of free billeting for soldiers and servants, sometimes also horses and dogs	119, 128, 131–2, 135–6, 141
cóisir	*cosher, *coshery: an obligatory banquet provided once, twice, or even four times a year by certain Irish vassals to their lord in the later middle ages, or in Anglo-Irish areas by all the wealthier tenants to the great landlords	141
comairce, commairghe	protection, sanctuary, the act of protecting, guarantee, safe-conduct, protector, guarantor. The formal undertaking to protect another was called by the Anglo-Irish *comberick or *comerryke.	viii, 105–7, 112
*comberick, *comerryke	see *comairce*.	
comhadha	'gifts', 'bribes', 'considerations': conditions for peace, to end or avoid war	108
comharba	'heir': especially abbot, or layman in that office, who succeeded to the authority and revenues of the founder of an early monastery or group of monasteries, a *coarb	23, 33
comhdháil	see *dáil*.	
congbáil	see *congbháil*.	
congbháil	'keeping', 'maintaining', 'entertaining': especially mercenary troops, or groups otherwise legally entitled to support	130–1, 141–2
constábla	'constable' (Anglo-Norman loan-word): military commander in the service of some Irish or Anglo-Irish lord	70, 94–5, 123–4, 138
*cosher, *coshery	see *cóisir*.	
creach	'plunder', 'booty': especially with reference to livestock; 'raid'; 'a plundering band', 'a raiding party'	108
*cuddy, *cudihie	see *cuid oidhche*.	
cuid oidhche	'a night's portion': a periodic feast exacted by an Irish or Anglo-Irish lord from his vassals, identical with *cóisir*, but this expression lays greater emphasis on the food and drink supplied, than on the festive occasion. The obligation could be	141

	commuted to a money-payment.	
cuid tabhaigh	'levying share': the proportion of a payment legally due which was retained by the power or authority who assisted the principal creditor to levy the whole	137
cuit tobaig	see *cuid tabhaigh*.	
cumal senorba	(Old Irish) 'the senior heir's *cumal* [of land]'. *Cumal* originally signified a female slave or unit of equivalent value, but evolved into a rather loose description of a measure of land.	129
cusdum, custam	'custom(s)', 'toll(s)' (English loan-word)	136
*cutting	see *gearradh*.	
dáil	an encounter; a meeting, assembly, convention; a law-case; a judgment; a contract; a circumstance. *Comhdháil*, 'an assembling together'; *mórdháil*, 'a great assembly'	60–2, 72
dál	see *dáil*.	
daoi	'unskilled': boorish churl – opposite of *saoi*, 'learned'	50
deibhidhe	name of a common bardic metre	134 n. 33
deiseal	'sunwise' or 'right-handed' (turn, circuit)	31
dispensator regis	see *ronnadóir*.	
dóerchéle	see *célsine*.	
dóerrath	see *rath*.	
doirseoir	'doorkeeper'	82, 85 n. 54, 117
*dowgollo	phonetic rendering of some Irish phrase containing the element *dubh*, 'black', translated as 'blackrent': a tax, held to be unjustified, for the support of MacCarthaigh Mór's hunt	145
duibhchíos	see *cíos cosanta*.	
dúthchasach	'hereditary proprietor'; 'native inhabitant'	86
eanach	see *eineach*.	
éaraic	see *éiric*.	
écen	see *éigean*.	
éigean	compulsion, force, violence, emergency	43, 101, 132
eineach	'face': honour; status; protection; hospitality	viii, 106–7, 111
éiric	'payment': compensation; legal fine, especially for violation of honour (*eineach*) or manslaughter	76, 91
*erenagh	see *airchinneach*.	
*eric	see *éiric*.	
exactator	see *maor*.	
feadhmannach	'functionary', 'agent' (of king or lord)	84

fearann	piece of land, estate. *Fearann táinisteachta, fearann ríogh*, land endowing the positions of *tánaiste* and king respectively	54–5, 87 129
fear cumainn	see *aos cumainn*.	
fear grádha	see *aos grádha*.	
fénechas	(Old Irish) 'the customs of the *Féni*' (seen as the dominant stock among the early Irish peoples): the body of customary law	60
fer	see *fear*.	
fiana	(Old Irish) roving bands of hunter-warriors, adherents of a warrior-cult, sometimes employed as professional soldiers	116
fírcheithearn	'true [mercenary] band': see *ceithearn tighe*.	
flaith	'lordship', 'sovereignty'; a prince or lord	48, 59, 149
fuba ocus ruba	(Old Irish) 'attack and defence': compulsory military service within a territory in the event of various emergencies, as opposed to hostings beyond the borders	116
gairm anma	'calling of the name': proclamation of a chief as head of his surname	32
gairm shluaigh	'hosting summons': or fine imposed by a lord for ignoring such a summons to war	142
gairm ríogh	'proclamation of the king'	32(–3) n. 64
gallóglaigh	'foreign warriors': *galloglass, Scottish mercenarie who fought as heavy-armed foot	18, 20, 70, 87, 94–5, 120–8, 139, 143
*galloglas, *galloglass, *gallowglasses	see *gallóglaigh*.	
gearradh	'cutting': tallaging, arbitrary taxation	137–8, 200
gelfine	(Old Irish) 'clear family': the inner group of a landowning kindred, sons and grandsons of a common paternal ancestor	129
giolla grádha	see *aos grádha*.	
gníomh	a measurement of land, comparable in scale to the *tate or *táite* (the latter was defined as 60 English acres in seventeenth-century Monaghan)	145
imirce	migrating; a migrating band; the chattels of such a migrating band	68
immirge	see *imirce*.	
innarrad	see *tuarastal*.	
ius primae noctis	(Latin) a lord's right to deflower subject brides on their wedding night	136
*karrentee, *kernety	see *ceithearn tighe*.	
*kernes, *kerns, *kaernii, kernarii*, *ketheryng	see *ceatharnaigh*.	

*Loughtee, *Lotie	see *lucht tighe*.	
lucht grádha	see *aos grádha*.	
lucht tighe	'household': a lord's military retinue (12th–13th cent.); mensal lands about the lord's chief residence (15th–16th cent.)	82, 86, 94, 140
mac ríogh	'king's son': a prince of the ruling dynasty	57–8, 72
maer	see *maor*.	
maor	collector of dues; custodian (of horses, relics, etc.); official; may translate Latin *balliuus, bedellus, exactator*	67, 75, 82–3, 90, 92–3, 95, 135
marasgál	'marshal' (Romance loanword)	67, 92, 95, 114, 141
marasgál tighe	'commander of the household [troop]'	82
marcshluagh	'horse-host': cavalry	124–6
martaigheacht	a supply of beef (form of taxation), from *mart*, a slaughtered beef-carcase or living head of cattle destined for consumption	142
mogh	slave or servant	84
oenach	see *aonach*.	
oes	see *aos*.	
óglach, óglaoch	'(young) warrior': military vassal, servitor	85, 90, 111
óglachas	(1) 'military vassalage' (2) 'warrior's (*or* layman's) style' a simple form of bardic verse	101, 113, 134 n. 33
oineach	see *eineach*.	
oirchinneach	see *airchinneach*.	
oirdneadh	'ordination' (of priests, etc.); 'inauguration' (of kings)	32–3
oireacht	originally a public assembly of free-men? (see *aire*); a court of law; a territorial council; the body of nobles who attended such a council; a territory or lordship	viii, 24, 44, 57, 60–2, 64–5, 67–70, 73, 82, 94, 121, 134, 148
oireachtas	an assembly; sovereignty, authority	64–5, 73–4, 77–8
ollamh	master of poetry, or other learned or skilled profession in the native tradition, as law, history, medicine, music, smithcraft, etc	23–4, 30–1, 46, 73, 81, 87–8, 126
ollamhnacht	'ollamship': the office of *ollamh*, endowed with land and obtained only by appointment or approval of the local king	34, 88
onóir	'honour' (Latin loanword): respect, dignity; tribute in acknowledgment of a lord's authority	110–11, 144

ord an anma	'ritual of the name': ceremony for inaugurating a chief	32
primogenitus	(Latin) 'first-born son' (of chief); used as a title of authority in the Ó Néill family, 14th–15th cent.	49 n. 62
rannaire	see *ronnadóir*.	
rath	(Old Irish) 'goods', 'property': in legal contexts the loan of cattle or land which secured the contract of clientship. *Sóerrath* was the 'noble loan' given to free clients (*sóerchéli*), *dóerrath* the 'base loan' or *taurchrecc*, 'fore-purchase' which bought the allegiance of the humbler base clients (*dóerchéli*).	96, 100–1
reachtaire	'director', 'overseer': a royal official equated with Latin *seneschallus*	16, 32, 65, 71, 79–82, 84, 94
rechtaire	see *reachtaire*.	
rí	'king': Latin *rex, regulus*	11, 17, 34, 36–9, 43, 52, 58, 147, 149
rí tuaithe	'king of a *tuath*', (petty king)	11, 15, 60, 96, 117, 129–30, 134
riar	'will'; 'rule'; 'demand' (noun)	103
riaraidh	'obeys'; 'ministers to'; 'subdues'	103, 110
rígdomna	see *ríoghdhamhna*.	
ríoghadh	'enkinging': the inauguration of a chief	32–3
ríoghdhamhna	'the material of a king': one eligible for kingship	41, 53–4, 58, 100, 132
*rising-out	see *coimhéirghe*.	
ronnadóir	'carver', 'divider', Latin *dispensator*: a royal officer in charge of distributing food at the king's banquet	81
rúta	'rout' (Anglo-Norman loanword): company of soldiers	120
secnap	(Old Irish) 'deputy-abbot', 'prior': Latin *secundus abbas*	54, 80
seirseanach	(French loanword?), mercenary soldier	119–21, 134
sersenach.	see *seirseanach*.	
síodh	'peace': a truce; peace-terms	104
síth	see *síodh*.	
slat	'a rod'. The inauguration-rod was variously termed *slat na ríghe*, 'the rod of kingship', *slat tighearnuis*, 'rod of lordship', and *slat sheilbhe*, 'rod of possession'	30–1
slógad, slóiged	see *sluaigheadh*.	
sluaigheadh	'hosting': *rising-out, military service; a military expedition; an army	101, 130–1, 142

sochar	in Old Irish law-tracts, 'a contract'; later, dues; privileges; profit, benefit	142
sóerchéle	see *célsine*.	
suartleach	(Old Norse *svartleggja*), a mercenary soldier	117, 119
taisech	see *taoiseach*.	
tánaiste, tánaise	'second': one second in rank to the chief, the heir apparent	53–9, 72, 109, 129–30, 143
*tanist	see *tánaiste*.	
taoiseach	'first': leader, chief; Latin *dux*	11, 34, 37, 44, 55, 57, 82
taoisigheacht	leadership, chieftainship	82
terchomrac	(Old Irish) 'assembly', 'convocation', 'muster'	*60*
tiarna	see *tighearna*.	
tigerna	see *tighearna*.	
tighearna	'lord': Latin *dominus*	34, 39–40, 57, 111, 136, 147, 149
tighearnus, tighiornus	lordship, dominion; dues or territory of a chief; power, dominance. In the sense of dues or tribute, it was equivalent to *chiefry.	viii, 31, 92, 97, 144–5, 147
tír	'ground'; 'portion of land'; 'territory'	11
tréinfhear	'strong man': champion	117
triocha-céad	'thirty hundreds': a force of fighting men; a territorial division, cantred	133
tuarastal, tuarasdal	in Old Irish law-tracts, 'evidence of an eye-witness'; later, ceremonial gift to seal a vassal's submission; stipend, wages; as 'wages of fighting men', can be used interchangeably with *innarrad*, 'wages', 'reward'	12, 24, 67, 101–4, 109–110, 113, 117–19, 132
tuath	'a people'; a territory (petty kingdom); the state as opposed to the Church – laity, lay property	10–11, 39, 60, 76, 79, 96, 101, 116, 129–31, 134
uirrí	'satrap', 'viceroy'; tributary king, chieftain	69
umhla	'humility'; submission, obedience	104
*urraght	see *oireacht*.	

INDEX TO FIRST LINES OF POEMS CITED

INDEX OF MANUSCRIPTS CITED

(See also General Index *s.nn.* [Books of] Ballymote, Fenagh, Lecan, Leinster, Uí Mhaine.)

DUBLIN, Trinity College Library:

1291 (H.1.17) 24 n. 12
Miscellany on parchment, transcribed by Hugh O'Daly, 1755; fos 109–23 contain material also found in T.C.D. MS. no. 1381
1337 (H.3.18) 80
Miscellany, written on vellum and parchment, largely dating from the 16th century and containing legal material from the MacAodhagáin school.
1381 (H.5.9) 24 n. 12
Miscellaneous collection of verse, written on parchment by Turlough O'Reilly and at least two other scribes c. 1684.

KILLINEY, Co. Dublin, Library of the Franciscan House of Studies:

A.25 87 n. 74
Paper-manuscript of the early 17th century, containing heroic tales and bardic poetry.

LONDON, British Library:

Egerton 88 fos 2–93 24 n. 12
Vellum miscellany of legal, grammatical and saga material, written c. 1564 by Domhnall Ó Duibhdábhoirenn
Additional 40766 24 n. 12
Verse miscellany, written on paper in Fermanagh during the late seventeenth century.

LONDON, Lambeth Palace Library:

625, fos 28–41 86 n. 65, 145 n. 126
Survey of the lands of Domhnall MacCarthaigh Mór, 1st Earl of Clancarty (ob. *1597).*

LONDON, Public Record Office:

E.101/242/2 138 n. 71
Issue-rolls of the Irish Exchequer, 23–28 Edward III.
S.C. 8/189/9434 108 n. 75
Ancient petitions: petition from Roger Mortimer, Earl of March and Ulster, then a minor, to Richard II, ca *1393.*

OXFORD, Bodleian Library:

Rawlinson B.502 (*S.C.* 11849) 6
Vellum miscellany, eleventh to twelfth centuries, containing legal, genealogical, chronological, hagiographical and saga material.

SAN MARINO, California, Huntington Library:

7042 92 n. 102
Early 17th-century paper-manuscript containing tract on the 'Lawes of Irelande' signed H. B.

GENERAL INDEX

STUDIES IN CELTIC HISTORY

Already published

I · THE SAINTS OF GWYNEDD
Molly Miller

II · CELTIC BRITAIN IN THE EARLY MIDDLE AGES
Kathleen Hughes

III · THE INSULAR LATIN GRAMMARIANS
Vivien Law

IV · CHRONICLES AND ANNALS OF MEDIAEVAL IRELAND AND WALES
Kathryn Grabowski and David Dumville

V · GILDAS: NEW APPROACHES
M. Lapidge and D. Dumville (edd.)

VI · SAINT GERMANUS OF AUXERRE AND THE END OF ROMAN BRITAIN
E. A. Thompson

VII · FROM KINGS TO WARLORDS
Katherine Simms

VIII · THE CHURCH AND THE WELSH BORDER IN THE CENTRAL MIDDLE AGES
C. N. L. Brooke

IX · THE LITURGY AND RITUAL OF THE CELTIC CHURCH
F. E. Warren (2nd edn by Jane Stevenson)

X · THE MONKS OF REDON
Caroline Brett (ed. and trans.)

XI · EARLY MONASTERIES IN CORNWALL
Lynette Olson

XII · IRELAND, WALES AND ENGLAND IN THE ELEVENTH CENTURY
K. L. Maund

XIII · SAINT PATRICK, AD 493–1993
D. N. Dumville and others

XIV · MILITARY INSTITUTIONS ON THE WELSH MARCHES: SHROPSHIRE, AD 1066–1300
Frederick C. Suppe

XV · UNDERSTANDING THE UNIVERSE IN SEVENTH-CENTURY IRELAND
Marina Smythe

XVI · GRUFFUDD AP CYNAN: A COLLABORATIVE BIOGRAPHY
K. L. Maund (ed.)

XVII · COLUMBANUS: STUDIES ON THE LATIN WRITINGS
Michael Lapidge (ed.)

XVIII · THE IRISH IDENTITY OF THE KINGDOM OF THE SCOTS IN THE TWELFTH AND THIRTEENTH CENTURIES
Dauvit Broun

Printed and bound by CPI Group (UK) Ltd, Croydon, CR0 4YY

29/09/2024

14565351-0001